RIVERS
OF CHANGE
Trailing the
Waterways of Lewis
and Clark

Tom Mullen

Roundwood Press
Malibu, California

Rivers of Change
Trailing the Waterways of Lewis and Clark

Copyright © 2004 by Tom Mullen

Published by:
Roundwood Press
P. O. Box 6533
Malibu, California 90264
roundwoodpress@riversofchange.com
www.riversofchange.com

Printed in the United States of America
10 9 8 7 6 5 4 3 2 1

Library of Congress Control Number: 2003096237
ISBN: 0-9743416-0-6

For my parents

Acknowledgments

There are many to thank for aiding this project.

Profound thanks to Chana Hauben for painting a splendid cover image; to siblings who assisted during this venture — especially brother Rick (and family — Jenny, Marshall, Tatiana) who let me stay in a wonderful beach pad in Malibu while putting this book together.

Other thanks go to:

Editorial Assistance:
Huge thanks to the following authors and individuals for reviewing text:

Dayton Duncan (author of *Out West*)
Michael Gillespie (author of *Wild River, Wooden Boats*)
Robert Kelley Schneiders (author of *Unruly River*)
Greg Hawley (author of *Treasure in a Cornfield*)
Garry Anderson (author of *Canadian Pacific Trans-Canada Limited*)
Bill Dietrich (author of *Northwest Passage*)
Chad Smith (Director, Missouri River Field Office – American Rivers)
Carolyn Porter (*One on One Book Production*, West Hills, CA)
Sharon Goldinger (*Peoplespeak*)
Richard Chilton, Nebraska
Patricia Rempen
Peter Mullen
Rick Mullen
Chana Hauben

Graphics:
Special thanks to Creative Force Inc., of Tampa, Florida, for supplying base maps used in this book; Susannah Iltis of Columbia Basin Research, University of Washington — graphic of dams on

Snake and Columbia rivers; Kim McLean, Museum Curator DeSoto National Wildlife Refuge, Iowa — images of Bertrand steamboat; One on One Book Production for layout; Todd Meisler of PC Bureau for maps.

Accommodation and Pre-Trip Support:
Dyna Rios Ruiz (and family) for support; Dave Grove, Karen Schwartz & Julie Liveris for daring me to take this trip while we drank beers on Saint Patrick's Day in Cuzco, Peru; Family — sister Trish for accommodation in New Mexico, brother Pete and wife Ann for a place to sleep in Denver, brother Steve for putting me up in Monterrey, California; Lisa Theodore, Monica and Wolfgang Rempen for the unwavering confidence, farewell lunch and forwarded mail; Terrence, Teresa and Tiana Ward for weekend in Denver; Carl and Tracey Tappert and family in Ashland, Oregon; Andrew, Sage and Carolyn Deenik in Hood River, Oregon; Sunshine Van Bael and Allen Herre of the Smithsonian Tropical Research Institute in Panama.

Ireland:
Aidan Egan for sending me *Travels with Charley* while on the trail and for putting me up for three weeks of relaxing and editing at his home before magnificent Ballyness Bay in County Donegal, Ireland.

England:
Jim and Caroline Grundy for hospitality in Devon.

Information on the Trail:
In addition to those interviewed and mentioned in the book, the following provided information along the road.

Help with contacts from Sue Schwartz; Curtis Steffler of Cavin Wrecker Service, Inc., in El Reno, Oklahoma for taking hours on a Sunday morning to repair a damaged tire and refusing payment; Mimi Jackson of the Lewis and Clark Center and James King of St. Charles; Glenn Covington of the U.S. Army Corps of Engineers in Kansas City; Marilyn Fontenot in Atchison, Kansas; Jake Geiger of Robinson, Kansas; John Remus and Roy McAllister of the U.S. Corps of Engineers, Omaha, Nebraska; Pat and Lowell Jenny in Norfolk, Nebraska; Robert Kuzelka of the University of Nebraska, Lincoln; Carlyle Ducheneaux and Daryl Garter of the Standing Rock Indian Reservation, South Dakota; Nick Stas of Billings, Montana; Robyn Niver and Scott Larsen of the Fish and Wildlife Service in Pierre, South Dakota; Denis Wright for his CD showing art along the trail; John LaRandeau for sharing a paper by the Iowa Geological Society on how the Missouri River changed over time; Mike Olson and Allyn Sapa of the Fish and Wildlife Service is Bismarck, North Dakota. And to many, many others who provided support along the trail.

Again, many thanks.

Table of Contents

Section One: MISSOURI

Section Two: KANSAS

Section Three: IOWA and NEBRASKA

Section Four: DAKOTAS

Section Five: MONTANA

Section Six: BRITISH COLUMBIA, WASHINGTON, OREGON

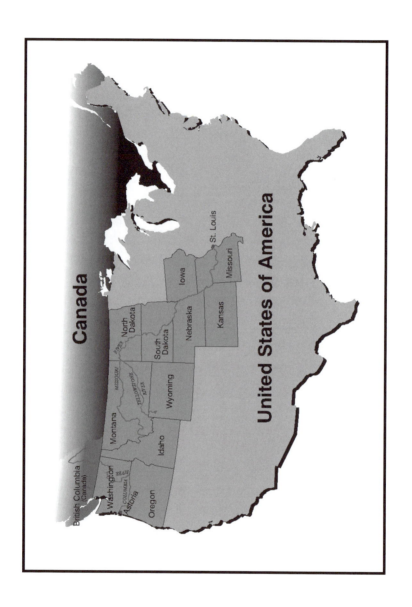

SECTION ONE:

MISSOURI

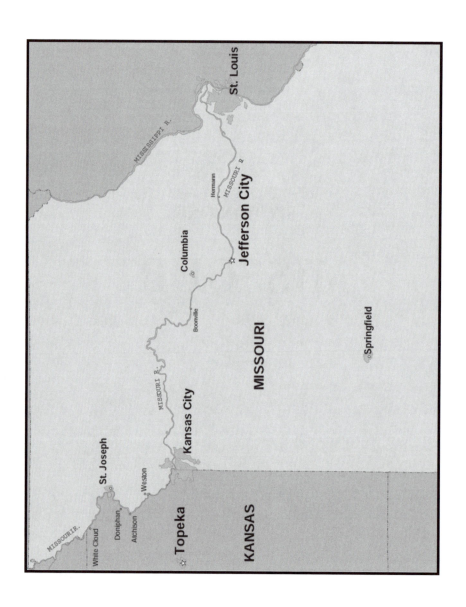

Chapter 1

FLOOD

In July and August of 1993 the Great Flood of the Midwest destroyed more than ten thousand homes, killed fifty people, inundated fifteen million acres of farmland, halted barges for two months, suspended the region's rail traffic and wreaked $15 billion worth of damage. This most significant flood ever to hit the United States was also one of the country's greatest ever natural disasters.

This flood that twitched through the Midwest that summer originated from the two largest river systems in the United States: the Missouri and Mississippi. From June through August precipitation on the northern plains and throughout the central U.S. leaped to three times its normal volume. Regions used to nine days of rain each July felt the sudden hammer of twenty wet afternoons. By mid summer soils were saturated, leaving rainwater with no other avenue than to shoot over land.

The Missouri and Mississippi river confluence sits fifteen miles upstream of St. Louis. When floodwaters crashed past this point, sandbags failed, residents fled, and levees burst like buttons popping off a snug shirt. Passengers evacuated the Spirit of St. Louis airport; jailers unlocked cells to whisk inmates to safety. The deluge closed down a water treatment plant and swamped a sewage facility serving seventy-five thousand homes. The surge blocked four major bridges spanning into the metro area. Rising waters swept fifty propane tanks from their moorings and police, fearing an explosion, evacuated hundreds of nearby residents. Engineers drilled holes in the Gravois Bridge to prevent its uprooting by the River Des Peres.

Every second more than a million cubic feet of water roared past the Gateway Arch of St. Louis, flooding over five hundred businesses and swamping Highway 40 under six feet of water. A concert to raise funds for victims from an earlier flood had to be cancelled. Meanwhile, con artists swooped in to reap a profit from calamity. When the waters subsided in St. Louis, police spotted an industrious pair pacing near Jefferson and Gravois avenues. They toted cans and collected cash from drivers. Their cans read: *Flood Releif 93 / Salvation Army.* Recalling that 'i' comes before 'e,' officers arrested the sloppy imposters.

Panicked residents outside St. Louis bought water bottles by the dozen, homeowners prayed, and farmers cursed busted levees when river water dumped sand on their crops. As though to emphasize catastrophe, three tornados twirled above St. Charles during an afternoon of the deluge. In Hardin, Missouri, floodwaters plucked coffins and burial vaults from a cemetery, shoving hundreds like hockey pucks across corn and bean fields.

"They'd take off in all different directions," one resident recalled. "Then you'd just watch them glide off into the sunset."

At its peak, the '93 floodwaters covered sixteen thousand square miles, more than the surface areas of lakes Ontario and Erie combined. Throughout the state of Missouri the disaster obliterated all previous flood records for stage, volume, peak discharge, duration and frequency. In Kansas City in July, the Missouri River rose more than two feet higher than its unprecedented crest of 1951.

In the flood's aftermath the Salvation Army raised $6.5 million in aid, billionaire Ross Perot flew out to the Midwest to pledge another million dollars and the Anheuser Busch brewery shut down its St. Louis beer taps to fill six packs with fresh water for the city of St. Joseph. Already that year in the state of Missouri wet weather halted crop planting on three-quarters of a million acres. The floodwaters confiscated two million acres more. Astonished farmers sighed when they saw hundreds of their acres coated with sediment. By piling sand from inches to feet thick on sixty percent of its lower floodplain, the Missouri River ruined dozens of farms. For many, the cost to remove this petrified pollution was more than the value of land it covered, creating so significant an impact that the Soil Conservation Service labeled the flood a "geologic event."

Close to a decade later I drove across the state of Missouri, hunting for anecdotes about how this flood stirred havoc along its sinuous trail. Rumors told how the event delivered not only devastation but elicited creative resilience from those affected. Surprisingly, I found a vast difference between my expectations and reality.

Chapter 2

DECISION

This book tells the story of a journey taken along three rivers in the western United States — the Missouri, Yellowstone and Columbia. In making this journey I tried to answer three questions: How does changing a river's course affect the lives and attitudes of those who live and work along its banks? How do these changes impact wildlife? Finally, what stories best portray how rivers and attitudes shape each other?

After twelve years spent living and working outside the United States, I decided to travel along these rivers to get reacquainted with the country. I had worked in the mountains of Malawi and the Namib Desert of Africa, had prepared technical proposals in Dubai hotels and tromped around sweltering Panamanian rainforests gathering data and designing water systems. One day on a street corner in rural Guatemala, the next step grew clear — it was time to return to the U.S.

Weeks later I left my job and flew into Albuquerque, New Mexico, with a shopping list, a reasonable bank balance and a map of the United States stabbed with red dots and question marks. I wanted to ease my transition back into the country by traveling along three great rivers in the Western U.S. and talking with Americans who lived along their banks. Curiosity was a motive: how had Americans shaped the paths of rivers that helped build their country?

Partially inspired by early explorers, I decided to follow portions of the route taken by Captains Meriwether Lewis and William Clark when they crossed the United States with three boatloads of hardened woodsmen. Their expedition, launched in 1804 and lasting until 1806, was the first to cross the emerging country. The voyage was a spry adventure of paddling across half a continent, fighting dysentery, bartering handkerchiefs for mules and smoking tobacco with Indian leaders that included Black Cat, Chief of the Mandan. Men on the expedition butchered horses to stave off hunger, sketched quill and ink drawings of vultures and maple leaves, ingested mercury to treat their own syphilis, plodded famished across the chilled Bitterroot mountains and doled out 'peace medals,' like election flyers, to riverside tribes.

When President Jefferson sent Lewis and Clark across the United States, their crew's submission to stern discipline and respect for their leaders won a huge part of the expedition's success. Much of the balance of the men's providence pivoted on two key behaviors. First, they solicited local knowledge along the trail. Second, rather than fight against the environment they traveled through, they worked in concert with its elements.

The route I planned to take differed slightly from that of the expedition (they named themselves the 'Corps of Discovery') by sacrificing movement along the Snake River to follow the Missouri and Columbia rivers in their entirety. I would also move along a portion of the Yellowstone River. This path would wind through nine U.S. states and one Canadian province. The purpose of the trip was not to relive history but to learn how changing a river's flow impacts those who live on its banks. The flow of rivers might mirror how national attitudes changed over time.

I flew from Guatemala to Albuquerque and bought a truck and camper. Both were bright, light and solid and mated together like a horse and chariot ready to drive off to battle. I paid cash, linked them together and drove off to my sister's house. I then filled the camper shelves with linguini, couscous, thyme, oranges, vinegar, chopping knives, apple-cinnamon tea, cheap cigars and a bottle of vodka, stashed a pair of crooked boots and a cheap rain slicker inside a cabinet, wrapped sheets over the small mattress like cellophane over cheese and flushed chlorine through the 12 gallon water tank. The camper was small, one of the simplest 'Six Pac' units from a company in California. Though the camper had no shower or toilet, its ice box was sizable, the sink had running water, the mattress was clean and comfortable and there was ample shelf space.

During the final days in Albuquerque, I raced around securing registration and insurance, renting a P.O. box, filing taxes, joining American Automobile Association, downloading newspaper articles and raiding Borders bookstore for titles appropriate for the trail: *Unruly River, Empty Nets, Northwest Passage*. Before departure, Albuquerque friends delivered a shoebox filled with gifts — pencils, a weathered collection of poetry, a bean bag dog sprawled on all fours and a tub of powdered lemonade. They served up slices of walnut carrot cake, a mug of amaretto coffee, and finally waved me off.

Decision

To begin the journey west, I first had to drive east to St. Louis — toward the confluence of the Missouri and Mississippi rivers. Along Albuquerque's 4th and Alameda streets wind gusts slapped the truck and camper all over the road. If weather at a journey's onset foretells how an excursion will unfold, this trip was to blow life in directions beyond control.

Chapter 3

GATEWAY

In its 2,315 mile journey, the Missouri River snakes across the high plains and heartland of the United States. It cascades 3,630 vertical feet between Montana's Rocky Mountains and its confluence with the Mississippi River near St. Louis. The Missouri is the longest river in the United States and falls at a gentle, spellbinding slope of just 11 inches per mile.

This river once curved a path along an edge of a continental glacier that covered portions of the northern U.S. This route defined its present course. To visualize the shape of the river today, imagine viewing, from the side, two staircase steps running downward from left to right. The Missouri runs through Montana (along the top step), drops through the Dakotas, Iowa, Nebraska and Kansas (between steps), then levels off and crosses Missouri state (the bottom tier).

The drop between these steps gashes across the heartland at an angle from northwest to southeast. Sioux City, Iowa, lies two thirds of the way along this slant, marking the dividing point between the 'Upper' and 'Lower' Missouri River. Today the upper river is stacked with six huge and several smaller dams, while most of the lower river slides through the confines of a narrow, engineered channel.

Early settlers from the east coast complained that the 'Big Muddy' Missouri River was 'too thin to plow and too thick to drink.' Today its water suspends ten times as much sediment as the same quantity of flow in the Lower Mississippi. The river flushes so much debris from adjacent land — cracked branches, festering carcasses, brittle ice cakes — that the first Europeans who watched the Missouri pour into the Mississippi River (French explorers Marquette and Joliet in June, 1673) called it a frightful mass of trees and floating islands.

The river technically ends at its confluence with the Mississippi River near St. Louis, miles upstream from the Gateway Arch.

When Finnish-born architect Eero Saarinen was contracted to design a monument for the city of St. Louis, he wanted a shape that embodied simplicity. He chose the arch, reminiscent of triumphal structures ancient warriors once hauled their spoils of victory beneath. When his work was underway Saarinen realized that the shape was also a portal, so named it *Gateway to the West*.

Today, the Gateway Arch yawns sixty-three stories high in an inverted silver parabola, suspending the weight of an aircraft carrier above its riverside plot. Quarter-inch thick plates of stainless steel, each as big as a freight car side, sheath the concrete core and wink in sunlight.

Constructing the arch created rousing challenges. A measurement error of just one sixty-fourth of an inch would have jeopardized both curves meeting flush at the apex. Risk analysts predicted that thirteen workers would die during construction — yet all lived, shattering probability.

Days after leaving Albuquerque, Six Pac reached the outskirts of St. Louis and pulled into a wooded campsite. The next day I parked in the city and walked beneath the arch on a May afternoon. The temperature was 82 degrees. Synchronized sprinklers and

American flags coated the landscape. I walked into a subway tunnel below the arch and entered the Museum of Westward Expansion. A ceiling plaque on a wall read: "Dedicated to the People of the United States — May 25, 1968." The dedication was refreshing — made to people, not politicians. It was a remembrance to families who aimed west hauling hatchets, bedrolls and mason jars in rattling covered wagons or on cramped, sooty steamers. From the early 1800s onward, the city of St. Louis formed a nexus for immigrants moving to the continent's interior, a launching point for trappers, miners and settlers wanting to forge into the obscure interior of a vast, bison-laced land. When steamboats chuffed into action in the 1820s, groups started moving inland along the Missouri River — the biggest highway running west.

Today, adventurers use the Gateway Arch as a reference point for river journeys. In October of 1980 an exercise physiologist jumped seventy-five feet off a Kansas City bridge to start his week-long swim toward St. Louis. Sponsored by a beer manufacturer that donated a thousand dollars and three cases of brew, he floated 375 miles to the Gateway Arch, hauled his soggy torso ashore and raised one fist in triumph.

A year later five men and two women hammered and lashed oil drums, telephone poles, mosquito nets and planks together to build a twenty-eight-foot-long raft. They packed it with canned food, sleeping bags, two copies of *The Unabridged Mark Twain* and floated southeast from Kansas City toward New Orleans. They named their craft *Eulenspiegel,* after a German folklore character renowned for prodding people toward unconventional thinking. The name turned prophetic: when the crew bobbed past the Arch, puzzled tourists stared at them in awe.

In 1984 a man suited up in helmet, goggles, gloves and vest, then strapped on water skis and wove hundreds of miles from

Kansas City to the Gateway Arch. He donated all funds he raised to the Muscular Dystrophy Association. The reason, he told a reporter, was that after years of skiing for boat companies and himself: "I thought it was time to ski for someone else."

The Missouri and Mississippi rivers meld together fifteen miles upstream of St. Louis before chugging south toward the Gulf of Mexico. The waters then join the Atlantic Ocean and disperse. A sixteen-year old Nebraskan teen-ager penned his name and address on a piece of paper, stuffed it into a Coca-Cola bottle and screwed the cap on. He tossed this into the Missouri River south of Nebraska City. A year later he ripped open a mysterious envelope from Northern Ireland and read a four page letter sent by a sixteen-year old lass. She told how she had found his bottle near her home in Downpatrick, Northern Ireland.

I thought it curious that littering — chucking a soda bottle into a river — denies that everything is connected, while throwing a corked bottle with a message inside embodies hope that all things are intertwined.

Hungry for thin roads and sweet country air, I left the Arch, and zipped out of St. Louis to the city of St. Charles. Blue road signs hinted about nature and exploration: Pike and Forest roads intersected near Boone and Powell streets. St. Charles calls itself the 'oldest town on the Missouri River' because French Canadians settled the area in 1769 (though Mandan, Arikara and other Native American tribes might disagree).

West of St. Louis and St. Charles lay classic Heartland, U.S.A. Grass was cut, fences stood aligned, and tilled fields ran in neat rows. This landscape affirmed how humans had wrestled with nature, and prevailed. I drove through a hundred miles of these tended vistas and gentle hills to the town of Hermann, along the Missouri River's southern bank. The town's 2,700 residents derive from German settlers who cherish their festivals: Hermann's entrance sign reads "Home of Maifest" while more than ten thousand visitors pour into town to sample local wines during each Oktoberfest. Broad streets and trimmed gardens gave Hermann a clockwork appearance, reflecting a tight knit and self-reliant community. For decades town residents have piled sandbags to protect themselves when the Missouri floods. I wanted to know more of how the town weathered its biggest flood ever, in 1993.

"Talk to Dallas," a plump woman with fleshy elbows told me at the bakery. "He'll tell you 'bout it. He worked the river, hauling people across."

I moved to the waterfront and saw the KS Fish Bait Shop, a red and white shack perched on a steep bank.

To the right of the door a sign read:

Welcome Friends
If-I-got-any

Cellophane flags fluttered beside the shack, bulky antlers hung over its door and eight lanky wind chimes dangled from an elm tree. In the shade below branches sat spectacled Dallas Krupp mending a fish net. His eyes looked small but deep. He gave me a quick, wry smile.

I told Dallas about my interest in how the flood of '93 impacted the town. He listened quietly and sized up my intentions. His gaze was bold, his demeanor respectful. His small frame was packed with energy — like a mousetrap ready to spring. He kept his fingers weaving as he told me of his efforts in an eighteen-foot Lowell boat with a forty-horsepower motor during the flood of '93.

Dallas Krupp of Hermann, Missouri

"We knew the flood was comin'," he said. "Got predictions, government reports. We knew what that mother was going to do. Built land levees, tried to hold everything out by sandbaggin' around buildings. Floods upset everybody here. But Hermann's a good town. German settlement. People get along. Everybody pitches in, helps each other."

When customers dribbled in to his bait shop, Dallas dodged back inside this cramped shed. I followed. A man in a yellow boiler suit clutched a lanky fishing pole, and three squirming boys asked the price of night crawlers. Dallas sold bait and shared a joke. I looked at a photograph on a wall that showed his shack during the flood, a solitary isle of blue trimmed windows half immersed in water. A black flagpole vaunted from the rooftop, stars and stripes fluttering above.

After these customers filed away, we moved outside.

"Road was closed," Dallas added. "Railroads were shut down. We were just blocked off. I made between twenty and thirty-six trips across the river a day, hauling passengers — workers from the nuclear plant, nursing home employees. They pitched in and paid for gas. I hauled a lot of blood and medical supplies back and forth for the hospital. I even brought a three-tiered wedding cake across that river. Whatever you'd haul on a truck, that's what I took on the boat."

Wind gusted off the nearby Missouri River. Dallas described how the Coast Guard, concerned for his safety, insisted that he stop boating back and forth across the flooding waters. He ignored them, winning support from most Hermann residents.

"I rescued a few people who ran the road block on Highway 19," he continued. "I went out at two in the morning. A couple were stuck on top of their pickup cab. I was equipped with a generator and could run lights, but didn't want to go out at night unless it was an emergency. There was too much debris in the river. I couldn't see. There were thirty-, forty-, fifty-foot long trees, railroad ties, deep freezes, 'frigerators, barrels in the water.

"Water was up to the middle of my shop window and across the railroad tracks. It lasted thirty-some days. It went down, came back again, washed out the road a second time. The flood of '93 was the biggest. That was the granddaddy."

Was he worried on the water?

"Nope. I wore a life jacket and watched where I was going. I had everything under control ninety-eight percent of the time.

"Been on the river all my life. My dad was a farmer and went broke during the floods of '41, '42, and '43. He went to work on the river for the government — the Corps of Engineers."

16

Dallas gazed toward the bubbling brown water. He sniffed the spring humidity and bent his hip.

"The river changed some," he said. "They built levees higher and closer together. The water moves faster now; they try to maintain that nine-foot deep channel. A half-inch of rain and it goes up a few feet. I've seen it rise fifteen feet overnight."

He looked beyond the shore and mused aloud.

"Got no control over that water," he said.

Heading north on the Lewis and Clark trail through Missouri

After leaving Dallas, I leaned back in the truck and considered the stories he recalled. Before arriving in the Midwest, I expected to hear nasty complaints about the flood of '93. Instead, voices recalled tales of quiet heroism and unified strength. In this unexpected way the Missouri River began to reveal her own story.

Chapter 4

THE GROOMED MISSOURI

The Lower Missouri River stretches between Sioux City, Iowa, in the north to St. Louis, Missouri, in the south. I wanted to know how its flow changed after being confined to a channel. But who to talk to? The answer came in Hermann. I sat beside the Missouri River and watched its hundreds of foot wide sludge- brown flow. The water moved rapidly. From the riverside I saw a blue and white tug named *Omaha* push a barge downriver. The sight sent me to a payphone. I pumped quarters in the slot, phoned a barge company in St. Louis, then asked the owner if I could ride one of his boats and chat with its pilot.

"Out of the question," he stammered. "Insurance problems. Send me a description of what you're writing and, eh, copy of your qualifications. I'll see what we can do."

Copy of my qualifications? I hung up, disgusted. It was obvious that not a drop of the Missouri River's spirit careened through his bloodstream. Determined to speak to a river pilot I chased down more phone numbers, then dialed a barge directly. A pilot named Alex answered. He spoke to me with laid back candor while maneuvering his barge downstream. I asked him to describe working on the river.

"Pretty wild up here," he began. "Fast currents. Get good and bad places. Bad ones always give you a headache. But we don't get new pilots up here no more — they have better rivers to run. The speed of the current is why they don't like it. It gets up to eight, nine miles an hour when its really runnin'. Shore 'nuff bad if you're not used to it.

"I started as a pilot on this river thirty-nine years ago," he continued. "The current used to change in a few hours, 'till they diked it in. Got it controlled. This barge? It's two hundred by thirty five feet, fourteen hundred tons. Carries fertilizer, corn, soybeans, wheat, molasses. There are nine people on board. Two in the pilot house, two in the engine room, four on deck and one crew."

I pictured Alex at the wheel — maneuvering bends and tooting at motorboats.

"I'm from Dayton, Mississippi. Came up here because of work. I don't like the area much, 'cept the river. It works on you pretty good over the years though.

"Corps of Engineers put dikes in," Alex continued. "Controlled the river some. Did a magnificent job, you know. Now we run from St. Louis to Kansas City, round trip every seven, eight days. Takes a while to come up, but we boogie back down pretty good."

Had he seen the river change?

"I've seen boat traffic diminish. River doesn't have the commercial traffic it used to. There are about six commercial boats up here now. Sometimes seven. Used to be twenty-five. The Coast Guard has taken over the bouyin' now, too. Those are the biggest changes. And there are the environmental people. They trying to get 'em to cut the water off!"

His voice trailed off, but I understood his message: barges, replaced by trucks and railroads, were fast turning to relics along the Missouri River.

How long did it take him to learn to navigate?

"It takes two or three years to learn the river. With a good instructor you can break in in six months to a year."

He paused.

"You asked if there are frustrations? When I can't get relief, can't get another pilot. And there's the weather. We don't run when it's foggy, or nights. Got radar, but that's just an aid. It don't get you there."

His voice lightened up.

"It's beautiful scenery though. I'm just below some bluff banks now; I can see the Katy Trail, old railroad grade. At this time of year, summer's comin,' you see a lot of bikers out on the old Katy line."

His spirits soared when he mentioned bicyclists.

Old Katy line—a bicycle trail by the riverside? I had to see this.

"Thanks for your memories," I told Alex.

"Anytime."

Barge gliding downriver near Hermann, Missouri

From Hermann I drove west past the town of Rhineland. Shoreline cedars cloaked river banks, making it difficult to see the Missouri River. When I did get a glance, it looked like a prim alley confined between fixed banks. I stopped at a gas station to thumb through the Yellow Pages, then phoned a store that rented bicycles near the Katy line.

The MKT, or 'Katy Line,' stands for the Missouri — Kansas — Texas railroad, which stopped running in 1986. Missouri state's Department of Natural Resources then bought over two hundred miles of the route between St. Charles and Clinton and created a state park and bicycle path. Segments of the trail and river meander close to each other, almost touching in places.

A week had passed since I left St. Louis. Between Jefferson City and Columbia, I drove past spacious homes with swinging porch chairs and entered the town of Hartsburg (*Population 118: "Home of Pumpkin Fest"*). Rental bicycles lay stacked on the deck of a stately mansion. I rented a lime-green mountain bike with sturdy shocks and wobbly handlebars. I began pedaling from Mile Number 153.6 of the Katy Trail. A notice displayed such trail rules as: *Be courteous to all other users.*

Another sign warned of washouts, fallen trees, rough surfaces and large rocks. This hyperbole was legal nonsense: the gravel path was groomed like a bowling lawn. I cycled past a crumbling shack and glimpsed at the nearby Missouri's sheen. Two miles ahead I swerved past corn stalks, then dismounted to look at the water. The Missouri River did not meander in any lazy way here but raced through a pair of fixed banks.

I pedaled on, feeling a stream of warm air on my forehead. I peered at covered barns, birch smoke, and chubby rabbits. The only traffic in view on the river were two speedboats filled with tan couples swilling beer. Belts of thin poplars stood on both riversides, obstructing much of the view.

Bicycling the Katy Trail along the Missouri River

I stopped at Coopers Landing Lodge & Store (*"Live Bait, Laundry, Welding"*) and bought a chocolate bar. Just before River Mile Marker 173 I saw a red, white, and blue sign poking out from brambles on the left. An image showed two crossed logs smoldering over a painted campfire. The words read:

Lewis & Clark Campsite, 6 June 1804.

The sign made me curious. I later read the expedition's journals, which explained how the men met two French trappers the day before camping there. These trappers were returning east after wintering upriver. William Clark wrote that these men "cought a great quantity of beaver," but lost most of these valuables in a prairie fire. The story highlighted the unpredictability of life on the frontier.

About this time, Clark was delighted when, "my Servent York Swam to the Sand bar to geather greens for our dinner." Though portions of their trip were testing, having a crew member sidestroke to an island and pluck fresh salad greens was an odd service no captains know today.

After twenty-two miles of pedaling, I wheeled around to head back. I then returned the bicycle and sat beside the rickety deck of the Hartsburg Globe Hotel. While licking ice cream lacquered in chocolate sauce I considered the day's carefree zip past turf and water and considered the Missouri River's history.

A century earlier, the unconfined river often spilled into waterside towns. Those days were gone. Except for the odd massive flood, the Missouri River was now pegged inside a fixed course, a barge path. Confining the river had advantages: it freed up land for farms and tamed floods. Most floods, that is. Not all. To find out more I drove north to where a flood had clawed away a railway bridge.

Chapter 5

GLASGOW

Curious how a flood could incapacitate a railway line, I drove to the town of Glasgow, located 240 river miles west of St. Louis.

There the flood of '93 barreled into the Gateway Western Railroad — gouging two gaps in the railroad bed, knocking out a bridge support pier, slicing through tracks and wiping out a year's profits in days.

View of Missouri River near Glasgow, Missouri

Glasgow

Glasgow has twelve hundred residents and is dominated by a row of monstrous grain silos squeezed between a steep hill and the river's impatient flow. In 1863 the town was laid out on bluffs near where the Chariton River meets the Missouri. It thrived as a shipping point until a new rail line was laid twenty-seven miles north. This reduced local business. The economy was rescued fifteen years later when a new railroad bridge was built at Glasgow.

I parked at the train depot at 3rd and Jackson Streets beside a sign pointing west toward Kansas City — 108 miles away. The building was locked and empty. A notice on a door said to phone Sue Ann Crigler for assistance. I scribbled her number down, then drove to the town's hushed and sloping main street. An orange spaniel spread beside a wooden door of the Glasgow Missourian weekly newspaper (*"A Live Paper in a Good Town"*). I stepped in, where warm light bathed a room the size of a country chapel burnished in timber. Within seconds two women and a man gathered around, ready to help a traveling stranger research the flood of '93. A photographer named Mike Heying pulled a slender blue volume from a shelf and showed me articles from the past. He ran his thick fingers through newspaper articles, then spoke with fresh bewilderment about this pivotal past event.

"I stood on a hill at Arrow Rock," he said, "and watched houses float downriver."

One of the newspaper's publishers, Barbara, stood before me and shook her head.

"We went down to look at the river during the flood," she said. "The water was so high I just held my children's hands. Didn't let go."

A copy of the *Glasgow Missourian* from May of 1993 reported that nine thousand acres of land lay beneath flood waters. Photographs showed Army Company C 158th Aviation Unit helicopters ferrying D-9 tractors in to repair damaged levees and dropping tons of stone onto land ripped out by the river. The July 22 *Missourian* included a front page plea for assistance, listing addresses of senators and congressmen to write to. It added:

"Let's cover them with some letters and phone calls pushing for some help for our small railroad."

Mike Heying, Editor of Glasgow Missourian Newspaper

A blonde woman named Sally moved past the counter edge and said she was going to get photos of the flood from her home. Ten minutes later she showed pictures of the severed railway line.

The character of small-town America glowed inside this office. When the Missouri River changed its mood and delivered trouble, these residents banded together to fix the damage. They knew the river that heralded catastrophe had also helped deliver Glasgow's prosperity in the past.

Just as flood waters elicited quiet heroism in Hermann, its receding flow shook Glasgow's community spirit awake. Three years before the flood of '93, Gateway Western brought the nearby railway line out of bankruptcy. They reopened the railroad — after sinking $30 million into improving its tracks — and ran three daily round trips between St. Louis and Kansas City. The flood then smashed the line.

I thanked the staff, closed my notebook and stepped outside the newspaper office. On the sidewalk, I pulled out Sue Ann Crigler's phone number. The newspaper office staff hinted that Sue Ann was a bit of a town icon, the woman who seized fixing a ruined railroad as her personal mission.

I phoned her. Sue Ann was eager to talk about the flood.

"It tore through a section that was 2,200 feet wide and in places eighty feet deep," she recalled. "It

Sue Ann Crigler, Glasgow, Missouri

pretty well devastated that railroad. They were a company that had just purchased the line and did extensive upgrading. They had it in tip-top shape. Then the flood hit in July. The high river stage and current ate away pilings under the railroad. Two spans of the bridge collapsed in the river. It left only the rails hanging." Sally had laid photographs out in the newspaper office. They showed the failed bridge span and illustrated what Sue Ann described — rusty rails curving like viper fangs toward the river.

"They couldn't run the trains," Sun Ann continued. "Business had come to a halt in July. It's an important line. It runs from Kansas City to St. Louis. Any damage has a domino effect on shippers, communities and employment in the whole state."

Sue Ann decided to get involved. She met and organized local leaders and encouraged them to write letters to Congress to support rebuilding the railroad.

"I was just a concerned citizen willing to help," she recalled. "It worked. They got federal funding. By January of '94 the bridge was repaired."

The flood that gripped Glasgow propelled Sue Ann to fight for her community. The tragedy gave her incentive to work harder than ever before. Hearing her story gave me an appreciation not only for the power of the Missouri River, but for the values and work ethic it took to survive and thrive next to the river. These were assets most Midwesterners took for granted.

"It's emotional when you think back to the '93 flood," she added. "It kind of proves that when tragedy happens, you know, it makes you proud to live in America. People band together, work together. People you've never met — they're your best friends. You help each other through a tragedy. It really gives you a sense of, well, it's patriotism."

The Missouri River flows across fine sediments of an alluvial plain. This means that the river's sandy base once moved, letting the current paint oxbows, loops, and bends with the whim of a fickle artist. To try to stop the river from wandering and to extricate snags and sandbars that blocked barges, projects were created to confine the lower river to a narrow chute. Seeing photographs of how the flood damaged Glasgow helped me understand why people wanted to control the river's flow. Two other reasons for controlling the river became clear later that week. First, the river was dangerous to navigate. Second, the river moved and flooded land.

Both reasons became clear when I inspected buried treasure hauled out of the floodplain.

Chapter 6

SNAGS AND STEAMBOATS

In Kansas City I stepped inside an unusual museum that illuminated perils of navigating the Missouri River.

On September 5, 1856, passengers aboard the Steamboat *Arabia* sat down to dinner. Waiters topped their glasses of champagne and dished out chunks of beef, steaming carrots and an ice cream dessert topped with walnuts. None suspected how soon this meal above the river would end.

Running between St. Louis and Sioux City, Iowa, the *Arabia* was a 'packet' boat that hauled both cargo and passengers. Fifty-two feet wide and more than three times that long, its triple decks moved upstream past the thousand residents of Kansas Town (now Kansas City) and headed west. The *Arabia* was designed to navigate through shallow water: fueled by roaring timbers in a flaming firebox, all four hundred tons floated in just four and a half feet of river.

For cabin class passengers, meals and bedrooms were close to regal — similar to those found at an expensive hotel. On the level below, passengers paying cheaper 'deck' fares crammed in with rank goats and packing crates and had to shout to each other above the din of the roaring engine. Toughening up before they even arrived at the frontier, these passengers slept on strips of white pine and had to fan boiler heat from their faces.

The river water below the *Arabia* was dotted with 'snags.' Heavier tree bases swept into the river lay anchored in river bottom silt while their lighter trunks angled upward and downstream. Each snag formed a powerful battering ram, able to puncture the belly of a boat like a sharpened pencil jabbed through tissue paper.

While the *Arabia* moved toward Parkville, cabin passengers — wearing suits and long dresses — sat at tables. Suddenly cutlery slipped. Plates smashed to the floor. In the murky water below, a walnut snag (a submerged tree trunk jammed in the river bed) had punctured the *Arabia*'s oak hull. The perforated steamer shook and leaned to one side, sending panicked passengers fleeing to its decks. The tragedy was rapid — the boat sank in a dozen feet of water in minutes. Yet all 130 passengers were shuttled to shore by rowboat while the *Arabia* vanished behind them in a cauldron of mucky bubbles. Although passengers survived, most cargo disappeared.

More than one hundred and forty years later, between 1988 and 1989, a group of Missourians excavated the *Arabia's* cargo and a portion of its hull. Exhuming this merchandise started almost as a lark.

"At the age of twenty-seven, I found myself firmly entrenched as a husband, father of two children, and blue-collar worker attempting to make ends meet," Greg Hawley wrote in the book *Treasure in a Cornfield*. Greg had worked in his family's refrigeration business in Independence, Missouri. His fortune changed during 1985 when his father Bob, brother Dave and business associate Jerry Mackey phoned and asked him to join them at the local Hi-Boy for lunch. When the four gathered, Bob mentioned a recent service call where the client talked of steamboats buried beneath the Missouri River floodplain.

This conversation inspired a notion of treasure hunting that soon blossomed into reality: the men decided to find and excavate a steamboat. They spent weeks combing library archives before tromping through fields and along river banks eliminating potential wrecks: scraps of the *George Washington* were scattered along miles of the Missouri River, while the site of the *Mars* lay too close to an oil refinery pipeline. The stern of the *William Baird* was buried under a levee owned by the Corps of Engineers — who wanted $100,000 to move (and later replace) their sod wall. Sample cores drilled in the *Twilight* unearthed nothing but a brass label from a sardine can. In comparison, the *Arabia* appeared to be a sound target — except that others who had tried unearthing its cargo spent loads of cash, then failed.

Once the Hawley/Mackey group decided to excavate the *Arabia*, they lugged a magnetometer across an empty cornfield to locate its metal boilers. Because the river had moved, the boat lay underground rather than under water. They next drilled holes thirty-five feet down to the wooden boat and flagged the outline of its hull with survey tape on the field above. Seen from the air, these markings on black soil looked like a surgical incision line awaiting a scalpel.

In November, 1988, temperatures dropped and sleet drove across these bottomlands. During this brutal weather the group laced dewatering pumps around the site, fired up heavy machinery and dug down through moist soil to find a lattice of imploded timbers. They added dewatering wells on a day when the temperature dropped to seventeen degrees below zero. The excavators' families joined the toil, working eighteen-hour days in the pit. These families and subcontractors coped with 100-hour work weeks for almost five months, anxious to complete their task before the next year's planting season began in the cornfield.

On December 1st, 1988, a wet hand hauled out their first find — a rubber shoe. The act of rubbing away mud from its 1849 marking galvanized the group, inspiring them to continue downward. They wasted no time: their investment of a quarter million dollars would be swallowed up within weeks. They would then have to take out a bank loan to continue.

The group waded through freezing water and hip-high muck to hoist out butter kegs, cognac bottles and handfuls of corroded thimbles — glittering heirlooms of disaster.

This treasure-hunting escapade offered those involved the chance to sell antiques. But once the shivering excavators began pulling out their haul — Davenport Ironstone dishes, gold plated earrings, cast iron ladles, ornate key chains, ceramic door knobs and braided leather whips — they realized that this tomb of nineteenth century lore was a treasure for all to see. The group decided to open their own *Arabia* Steamboat Museum in Kansas City.

Today these salvaged artifacts rest under bright lights behind glass walls, providing a vignette of life along the Missouri River in the mid-Nineteenth century. Excavators discovered dishes from France and England, guns from Belgium, Chinese silk and Bohemian glass blown beads. The tons of cargo include seven hundred window panes, a million nails, two prefabricated homes, seven thousand cigars, five million beads (for trading with Indians) and just twenty-six cents winnowed from two hundred tons of cargo.

A visit to the museum is no passive ramble through static hallways but starts off with a guided tour about the *Arabia*'s foundering and recovery. Under the glow of powerful lights, I inspected the cargo. This included spiced pig's feet, tobacco chews and curry combs for horses. Our guide was a history graduate named Susanna who told how the only creature killed on the boat was a tethered mule — now nicknamed Lawrence (of *Arabia*, no less).

Susanna told of the deal on which the excavators and landowner agreed.

"They needed permission from the land owner, retired Judge Sortor. In 1864 his family bought land from the Indians. The judge thought it wasn't possible for them to find the boat, but added that they could try if they wanted. The deal was that landowners would get fifteen percent and excavators eighty-five percent of the cargo's value."

Changing the project's goal altered this agreement.

"The excavators decided not to sell what they found but put it in a museum. So the judge told them he didn't need his fifteen percent. Instead, he chose twenty-five objects for his children."

Inside the museum a group of us watched a movie about the excavation. Scenes showed hands extricating buried treasure. Bob Hawley stood before the camera and told how their venture's success renewed his faith in the American way; it illustrated how desire and persistence can pave a road toward accomplishment. When the movie ended, the real Bob stepped inside the small theater. He was a smiling patriarch full of easygoing energy. He told the audience about their days of working in the dewatered cornfield, of teasing mud away from perfume bottles that retained their scent and of sampling still edible pickles and drinking champagne after its century-plus interment.

"There's something about huntin' old steamboats that's really exciting," Bob told children seated in the front row.

When this group decided to open their own museum without government funding, critics initially scoffed. In his book, *Treasure In A Cornfield*, Greg Hawley lauded such skepticism: "Since nothing is more inspirational than a challenge," he wrote, "These negative remarks gave us ample motivation to succeed on our own merit."

The museum they created excelled beyond anyone's expectations.

Missouri River at dusk

The attitude of these Missourians embodied a warrior spirit. It reminded me of how Dallas Krupp in Hermann churned his boat over toothed waves to deliver both nurses and antihistamines to a hospital during a flood, or of how Sue Ann Crigler orchestrated telephone calls to resurrect a gutted railway line in Glasgow. These people were admirable. They shoved pessimism aside, embraced massive financial risk and dedicated themselves to specific challenges. Dallas, Sue Ann, and the Hawley / Mackey team did their work not for selfish gain, but for what they believed was right for the communities they belonged to.

Years before this triumph of excavation, and more than two hundred river miles north of where the *Arabia* was buried, two men shoveled cargo from another steamboat mired in soil. This 'mountain steamer' named the *Bertrand* was built to haul men and supplies north to Montana's gold fields. One hundred and sixty-one feet long, its 250 tons sank in minutes after a snag gutted it like a ripsaw at DeSoto Bend in April, 1865. Like the *Arabia*, no lives were lost.

Bertrand Steamboat on Missouri River
(Courtesy, U.S. Fish and Wildlife Service)

In 1967, Jesse Pursell and Sam Corbino began a search and recovery effort of the *Bertrand*. They worked from old maps and newspaper accounts, then tromped around the floodplain hauling a 'fluxgate magnetometer' to pinpoint the sternwheeler's metal boiler. Once located, they hammered out a contract with the federal government, lowered themselves into a pit of dirt and took two years to complete their recovery. Today their haul sits in an exhibit at the DeSoto Wildlife Refuge, east of the Missouri River in Iowa.

I walked into DeSoto's sleek visitor's center. Tons of artifacts hoisted from the dig lay on polished museum tables. In contrast to the *Arabia* museum, the rooms were low lit and the atmosphere quieter.

The *Bertrand*'s trove provided a glimpse of life during the Civil War. Table tops were covered with shingling hatchets, powder kegs, bottles of 'aromatic schnapps,' and Kelly's Old Cabin Bitters. There were cans of strawberries, clay pipes, green ink, white clover honey, bottles of "Wm. Brown's Highly Concentrated Essence of Ginger," London Club Sauce (in translucent pea green bottles) and Drake's Plantation Bitters. Some jumbled pieces — including Tally-Ho buttons, brandied cherries, men's felt hats (*'el sombrero mejicano'*) and hobnailed boots — were both gaudy and practical. Spread out on glimmering tables behind polished glass, these wares represented the sunken Bertrand.

Both the *Bertrand* and the *Arabia* represent reasons why the Missouri River no longer runs free, wild and vagrant as a happy tramp.

In the nineteenth century, shallow water, a wandering river course, snags, sandbars and crumbling river banks were constant hazards to navigation. Driving a steamboat up the river was like using an outdated map to navigate a busload of paying passengers through a minefield. The chances of meeting catastrophe were enormous. Seven out of every ten steamboats that ran the river sank. Their average lifespan was estimated at five years. Cargo insurance cost up to ten percent of the value of shipped products. The *Arabia* and *Bertrand* owners *expected* these boats to sink; their goal was to turn a profit before their vessels' inevitable demise.

A nineteenth century writer described navigating the Missouri at low tide as "putting a steamer on dry land and sending a boy ahead with a sprinkling pot." When author Mark Twain rode upriver as a passenger he called it 'a confused jumble of savage looking snags,' and said his boat could have headed to St. Joseph by land, because she walked most of the trip anyway. The result was that wrecks lay all over the river bed. In 1867, Major C.W. Howell counted 1,798 snags in the Missouri, each eager to punish a distracted boat pilot. In 1897, Captain Chittenden of the U.S. Army Corps of Engineers drafted a map of all sunken steamers between St. Louis and Pierre, South Dakota. His count of 289 wrecks was conservative. Later tallies pushed the number up to over four hundred.

Another reason the Missouri River was so dangerous was because it moved. Neither the *Arabia* or *Bertrand* were found in water. The *Arabia* was interred forty feet below a Kansas cornfield, hundreds of yards away from any riverbank. The *Bertrand* was exhumed from land away from the river. The reason? The Missouri River changed course so often that it wagged over the floodplain like the tail of an excited dog. Sometimes its main channel moved miles during a flood.

The problem with this wandering river is that when it changed mood, it flooded farmhouses and fields with little advance warning. In 1907, George Fitch described the Missouri as the hungriest of all rivers — eating "eighty acres at a mouthful" and "picking its teeth with the timbers of a great red barn."

These navigation hazards and constant floods incited the U.S. Corps of Engineers to try to strap a collar on this waterway, forcing it to shoot through one swift and narrow channel. Although the effort took decades, the Corps' determination to mellow this wet bully succeeded. Yet today the achievement is as controversial as the mindset that fostered it.

Chapter 7

ENGINEERING A WATERWAY

In the Joslyn art gallery in Omaha, Nebraska, a painting shows a group of men huddled on a dock in blue light. Behind them the Missouri River is wrapped in deep fog. One man carves his hand through the night while telling a story; another gnaws a corn cob pipe. The others listen. The moon above them wears a scarf of clouds. The river below looks dark and dangerous.

George Caleb Bingham painted this image *Raftsmen by Night**. Until he passed away in 1879, this temperamental painter spent years living along the Missouri River. There he wielded both his words and paintings to criticize the government's neglect of western waterways. His romantic compositions of gliding skiffs, foggy waters and dank islands harbored the potent message that obstacles along the river menaced even the grizzliest boat pilots.

If he were alive today, Bingham might smile at how the U.S. Army Corps of Engineers 'fixed' the Missouri River by confining 734 miles of its lower course to a narrow channel. Channelization of the Lower Missouri evolved through decades of legal disputes, technical experiments and changing national priorities.

*Also known as *Watching the Cargo by Night*.

On arriving in Kansas City, I entered the Richard Bolling Federal Center at 12th and Cherry Streets, and rode the elevator to the eighth floor — location of the Planning and Natural Resources Department of the U.S. Army Corps of Engineers. A Corps of Engineers employee named Mary Lucido led the way past a labyrinth of drafting tables and opened a wide set of thin wooden drawers.

"I'm a cultural resources specialist," she said, then smiled to explain. "That means protector of maps."

Mary pulled out a book titled *Comparison of Conditions — Missouri River — Rulo, Nebraska to Mouth — 1879 to 1954.*

I moved to a vacant drafting table and opened the bound sheaf. The maps outlined the Missouri River before and during 'channelization.' This process of channeling the river was the Corps' long-term feat of transforming it into a nine-foot deep barge channel.

The maps were printed in red and blue — red showing the 'old' river of 1879 and blue the 'new' river as of 1954. Red was a fat artery that defined the past floodway. Blue was a narrow ribbon within this artery, like a lone strand inside a sheathed rope, or one ragged light pulse ricocheting within a fiber optic cable. The red ink ran wide and messy; blue ink glided in a thin and disciplined line. The river channel of 1879 flowed ten times wider than the river of 1954 (or today's Missouri River). Before the Corps set out with gum boots and pile drivers and hunkered in to resculpt the river channel — making it barge and farmer friendly — the water was far from being a smooth sine wave that pushed northwest. It was instead an erratic collection of acute meanders and channels — a broth of roots, stumps and floating dead mammals inside a corridor of possible flow streams.

Before either roads or rails bisected the prairie heartland, the Missouri River formed an upcountry highway. During that time, in addition to the government's desire to increase private commercial gain and settlement along the river, efforts to 'improve' its course were partially born from the nation's zeal to defend itself.

Major Stephen Long of the U.S. Army Corps of Engineers was a mathematics instructor at West Point, a surveyor, and later a consulting railroad engineer. Major Long proposed building an arc of military forts along the Missouri River. Knowing that a keelboat's round trip from St. Louis to the Yellowstone River took an exhausting 150 days, he supported using steamboats to whittle down transport time. In 1818, the U.S. Army awarded contracts to a Kentucky entrepreneur to move supplies and soldiers by steamer. A year later the *Independence* thrust up the Missouri River loaded with whiskey and iron, the first ever steamer to make the trip. Impressed by the boat's potential, Long decided to inspect the route himself. The next year he stood on the deck of another steamer, the *Western Engineer,* surrounded by an inquisitive support crew of military men and civilian naturalists.

More than six hundred miles upriver, the *Western Engineer* was forced to turn around. Silt had clogged boilers and a cylinder burst. But for Long, the trip proved the benefits of steamboats for long journeys, which he listed to secure government funding to improve the river's course.

When Secretary of War John Calhoun recalled how soldiers, field rations and munitions moved up and down the Missouri River during the War of 1812, he mentioned this in a report to Congress on needed national defense works. Calhoun thought the river was more than just a corridor for commerce — it was also a pipeline for servicemen and armaments.

Input from Calhoun and Long incited the War Department's Superintendent of Western Rivers to construct 'Heliopolis,' the first ever *snagboat*. Cranes and winches on its foredeck plucked snags out of log-crammed waters. In 1838, two of these sidewheelers, nicknamed "Uncle Sam's Toothpullers," started yanking more than thirty snags a day from the Missouri River. Although winching dead trees out of river muck cut down on wrecks, the process stopped no floods. To halt flooding, the Corps needed to control the river's erratic flow.

At a convention in St. Joseph, Missouri, in 1881, several men urged Congress to open its wallet to pay for controlling the rambunctious 'Big Muddy' river. They told how improving navigation would aid commerce. Delegates also boasted how controlling the river would free up cropland. Remember, they insisted, new farmland increases tax revenues!

That same year, a huge flood added urgency to these delegates' agenda. It changed the Missouri's course and redrew geography — wiping out ports and obliterating local economies. This event helped push Congress to alter the Missouri River. The next year Congress doled out $850,000 to the Corps of Engineers. Major Charles Suter and his crews then worked on creating a barge channel, with the hope of harnessing the Missouri's own silt-laden power to gouge out a single water channel. Suter had no doubt: he wanted the 'complete rectification of the river.' Once begun, his 'Suter Plan' reduced the river's width and eased its flow at bends. Yawls, skiffs, graders, quarter boats, pile drivers, and sweating men in rubber pants were cranked into action. By the early 1900s, this platoon churned out a six-foot deep channel along forty-five miles of the Lower Missouri.

While this work proceeded, attitudes fluctuated within the Corps toward modifying the river. After Suter started his work, the Corps' Captain Hiram Chittenden suggested taking a bolder stance toward the future: "Turn this river out upon the lands," he wrote. "Unlock its imprisoned power. Where the rains do not flow, let it supply the need...Utility will take the place of romance. The buffalo, the Indian, the steamboat, the gold-seeker, the soldier will be seen in its valley no more, but in their stead the culture and comfort, and the thousand blessings that come with civilization."

Chittenden's words turned prophetic. Five years later the Missouri River Navigation Congress announced that the river should be improved "on a grand scale," and the work "made permanent."

Ironically, the job of implementing this work was eventually passed to a Corps engineer named Lt. Col. Deakyne. During those days most engineers revered the challenge of controlling the Missouri River. But Deakyne took a broader perspective than his peers. In 1915, he submitted a scathing condemnation against any proposal to reshape the Missouri. He declared that the amount of barge traffic that ran the river would never justify the effort and supported abandoning the channelization project. He suggested that the Corps continue pulling snags from the river instead.

Because rail had then triumphed as king of cargo transportation, Deakyne was right from the perspective of commerce and navigation. There was also less need to have a river so easily navigable because fewer barges ran its water. By 1932, more than sixty-million dollars had been pumped into taming the water's course while, paradoxically, shipping tonnage had sunk to a third of what it was in the 1860s.

Speaking in hindsight about channelization (or stabilization) efforts along the Missouri River, a Corps publication today admits that "from the point of view of commercial tonnage, the engineering accomplishment has been wasted effort." It also states that since the Corps adopted a policy of experimenting with channel work, "no more boats have been put into the river than if the work had not been done."

The project still had advantages. Confining the river stopped it from meandering, freeing up acres that tractors then transformed to corn fields. When Deakyne alleged that stabilization wasted money, farmers greeted his opinion with frog-eyed hysteria, then banded together to voice their refute. For these men, increasing farmland improved their security. In 1916, this group's rebuttal of Deakyne helped push the Board of Engineers to reject his recommendations.

The Missouri River soon turned into an engineering project. The Corps laid a dedicated siege to scour out a deep riverbed and ease the water's flow at bends. They charged at their objective with such zeal that by the time World War II erupted, waterway crews had gouged out nine-foot deep segments along parts of the Missouri's path. Every day for months pile drivers hammered poles of pine and cypress into the silt. Men wearing reed hats and stiff suspenders anchored woven willow mats to the river bottom with hefty rocks to halt erosion. Where the river's flow arced wide, the Corps decapitated meanders, pruning away miles of channel.

Shaping the river also generated money. The Missouri River Navigation Association gloated when marshes turned into taxable cropland — an amount of land they predicted was to be "more than the entire cost of the Missouri River Improvement."

In March, 1946, another effort began to tame the wild Missouri. Governors from Missouri, Kansas and the Dakotas shook hands to celebrate the beginning of this one-and-a-half-billion dollar Pick-Sloan Flood Protection Project — a 'basin wide project to curb river' one newspaper blared. The legislation unified and increased control work on the river.

"While several hundred persons looked on, General Pick and Governor Sharpe led the ground-breaking ceremony... each turning over a spadeful of earth — symbolic of the start of the Government's effort to conquer the Missouri and confine it between giant flood levees along its winding course."

Before World War II, attempts to bridle the river's course were born from different programs with disparate goals. Arguments for and against these civil works then flopped back and forth between state and federal agencies. After years of bickering over water rights and control of the upper and lower Missouri basins, the Pick-Sloan Plan was considered a legal panacea to treat several economic and political ills. It was supposed to quell "internecine congressional battles on the whole subject of taming the Missouri River."

Among its other achievements, the Pick-Sloan Plan eventually stacked five massive dams on the Missouri's upper reaches (a sixth dam, the massive Fort Peck in Montana, had already been built as part of President Roosevelt's fight against the Depression).

The legislation also delivered jobs. Four months before D-Day during World War II, South Dakota's Governor Merrill Q. Sharpe praised this new flood control effort as a benefit to returning soldiers. He considered victory in the war imminent and flood control as a job opportunity for soldiers returning home from battle.

Pick-Sloan was grandiose. It was not just a plan but a vision of economic plentitude and environmental control extending from Montana's badlands to bovine studded farms near St. Charles, Missouri.

While Pick-Sloan was being implemented, the Rivers and Harbor Act of 1945 bestowed the Missouri River with a nine-foot deep, three hundred-foot wide barge route as far as Sioux City. Those who embraced this project ignored the truth that the amount of barge traffic was decreasing. But the act gave engineers the authority they needed to clip the Missouri River onto a thick leash.

One government pamphlet described river control as "five fingers on the guiding hand of man." Shackling streams and erecting dams, it concluded, "will guide its water into many beneficial, constructive uses, and away from its wasteful, destructive ways." This quote embodied attitudes that were part of the national consciousness of the day — that unharnessed rivers wasted water and wild rivers were inherently destructive, foes to be attacked with the same steel resolve that pushed enemy, or 'Axis,' leaders to sit and sign documents of surrender.

More than a century after the Corps began redirecting the Missouri River's flow, they announced in the early 1980s that the lower river was stabilized. Quarried limestone lay dumped along hundreds of its riverbank miles and thousands of wing dams filled the water below Sioux City. This shotgun matrimony between landscape and engineering trimmed the lower river, let her run faster, and reduced the original acreage it covered by sixty percent. This streamlined new creature no longer thrashed across the floodplain like a scruffy dog but raced its thin course like a sleek greyhound. More than a century of invasive surgery between its banks had pruned the river of logs that rammed boats; it freed up enough land to convert damp prairies into fertile cornfields.

This process that trimmed away wetlands turned the lower river into a canal shaved of biological intricacy. Channelization lopped off 127 river miles beneath Sioux City and eliminated over 180,000 acres of area over which the river flowed, nine-tenths of all islands and ninety-seven percent of all sandbar surface.

Unfortunately, the process of freeing up farmland by channeling the river also decimated woodland. Forests that had loomed over three quarters of the nineteenth century floodplain coated just ten percent of the same land by the 1970s. This helped to eradicate one-third of a million acres of wildlife habitat. Confining the river away from the lands it once flooded separated water from many meadows, woodlands and wetlands it had coursed through.

Few who rant against the Corps' stabilization program ever lived next to the river when it flooded and destroyed homes. Building dams and reshaping shorelines were considered necessary acts to control this force of nature. Yet the shape of today's Missouri River offers a distorted mirror on the society that molded it. After all, the purpose of the channelization project was to help farmers, boaters and riverside dwellers, not to squeeze the life out of ecosystems.

Times have changed. Priorities have shifted. Engineers, biologists, Indian leaders and politicians are now charged with forging a new vision for the Missouri River's future. These groups have been forced to grapple with finding a common syntax for how to manage its gushing flow.

Before starting this trip, I spent years managing water resource development projects in different countries, and was used to hearing about institutional and bureaucratic resistance to change. But moving along the Missouri River exposed another attitude. During months of roving along water banks I listened to dozens of voices speak about the consequences of channelizing and damming a river's course. Some whispered with reason; others ranted in sour disgust. Yet each time a stranger spoke about the future of the Missouri River, his or her attitude showed an unexpected degree of optimism, so strong that it often bordered on the bizarre. Together, these voices formed a collective attitude that a river's richness derives from variety — both of life it nourishes as well as the viewpoints of those who manage it.

The first voices came from wary scientists.

Chapter 8

VARIETY

A watershed is an area of land that drains water to a common destination—usually an ocean. Viewed from above, the Missouri River watershed looks like a bulky amoeba. Its spread of rivers and rivulets forms an organic draining board, one that funnels one-sixth of all U.S. surface water along its base. This 'base' is the river itself, the route that drains 580,000 square miles where ten million people now live. This swelling population constantly creates fresh problems for the river.

Each decade the Missouri River faces some new signature crisis, often more of perception than reality. Prophecies ballooned in the 1970s that constructing new power plants along the river would threaten drinking water and irrigation supplies. The Missouri River Basin Commission prepared a gloomy report that predicted that by the turn of the millennium six hundred million gallons would vanish from the river each year, spewed into the atmosphere via evaporation ponds and cooling towers. This, they complained, could lower flow levels, constrict navigation seasons and concentrate chemical pollution already pouring into water treatment plants.

This feared scenario never came to pass.

In the 1980s, diversion and pollution turned to twin threats along the Missouri River. Fears that irrigation water would vanish from the High Plains region of the U.S. prompted the Corps of Engineers to study a massive water transfer out of the river. One imagined scenario envisioned a canal more than 600 miles long channeling over six million acre-feet* of water each year from South Dakota to a reservoir in eastern Colorado (enough to coat the state of Vermont or the country of Wales a foot deep in water). From this pool, water would irrigate crops throughout Colorado, Nebraska and Kansas, thereby replacing supplies lost from the depleted Ogallala Aquifer.

This plan was eventually shelved.

More fears about lowering the river level erupted when Secretary of the Interior James Watt authorized a water transfer from South Dakota's Lake Oahe Reservoir (part of the Missouri River) into Wyoming. This grandiose plan would extract sixteen billion gallons of river water each year, mix it with Wyoming coal and shoot this slurry through a pipeline to Louisiana. Fearing Watt's action might set a precedent for future diversions, states in the Missouri River Basin grumbled, then sued. A court ruled that Watt lacked authority to pursue the deal and the plan was scrapped.

During the decade of the '80s, pollution ran rampant along the Missouri River. Studies showed that deadly chemicals in the water included chlordane, DDT, aldrin, dieldrin and heptachlor. This originated from leaks and spills all along the waterway. In November, 1980, more than two dozen train cars derailed on a bridge and dumped forty-thousand gallons of methylene chloride and chloroform into the Rock Creek tributary in the state of Missouri. On Christmas Eve in 1989, a ruptured Shell Oil pipeline in the state of Missouri sent more than three quarters of a million gallons of crude oil into the Gasconade River near Vienna. Days later, this marble tinted sheen poured into the Missouri River and flowed 150 miles downstream to the St. Louis Chain of Rocks Water Treatment Plant. Small boats scurried around the slick, herding its flow with high pressure hoses. Both cleanup costs and criticism soared. A St. Louis beer manufacturer was so concerned with how this would impact the taste of water that they shut down their brewery and sent thousands of staff home without pay.

In the decade of the 1990s and into the twenty-first century, three species of animal gained fame and notoriety as the Missouri River's flagship problem. Two species of bird — the piping plover and least tern — and a slow, suave fish known as the pallid sturgeon were marked as endangered by the federal government. Curiously, what impacted these species was not diverted water, spilt oil or chemical leaks, but changes to the way the Missouri flowed, modifications wrought by humans over the course of a century. To learn more of how channeling the river threatened these animals' existence, I drove back to St. Louis for a day.

"The flood of '93 put the fear of God in a lot of people," geomorphologist Steve Gough told me at a café on the outskirts of St. Louis.

"People backed away from big rivers after the flood," he said. "Whole farms were covered with five, six feet of sand. Levies broke between St. Louis and Kansas City — unbelievable. People said this is a force bigger than us."

I met Steve at his white stucco home near the Big Bend highway exit. Books on watersheds and riparian systems lay on his dining room table. A Corps of Engineers award hung next to his kitchen door. Steve was a heavy set and easygoing man who took his consulting work seriously. Armed with two degrees in forestry, he decided to delve into geomorphology — varied disciplines that relate landforms to subsurface geology.

Beneath a slate gray sky we walked from his home to Aesop's café. There we sat on slatted benches. Speakers pumped out Buffalo Springfield tunes before a blackboard that listed gourmet coffee, Mexican omelets and exotic bean salads.

"Look at a river system," Steve said. "Watershed and landscape. What's coming out of the river's mouth integrates everything going on in the watershed. You can take it to an absurd degree — the guy asphalting the parking lot over here," he said and pointed his thick finger past a window frame, "influences this local watershed."

While I bit into a banana walnut muffin, he continued.

"What I study is basically formal process in the river. Why a river behaves the way it does, how it moves sediment, how the flowing water interacts with the shape of the channel, vegetation that's moving on it, things like that. Geomorphology is one of the few disciplines that encompass all others. It's not a science that says you've got to bring everything down to two or three little variables."

The condition of the wiry Lower Missouri River both baffled and irritated Steve. He turned over his paper placemat, uncapped a felt tipped pen and sketched two aerial views of the river. The top line represented the natural river, before it was confined to a channel. This meandering flow was wide and sloppy and included braided currents, backwaters, eddies, sloughs and wetlands. These locations provided diverse wildlife habitat. The second line Steve drew was a thin corridor with shapely curves — almost as geometrical as those of the Gateway Arch. This represented the channeled Missouri River, fixed in its course.

After inspecting these lines, I understood Steve's irritation. The first showed a river that flowed through a messy, lush floodplain where red foxes, white tailed deer, hairy woodpeckers and double-crested cormorants once thrived. The second was a canal, the mathematical solution to a hydraulics problem that channeled flow from position A to B with minimum cost and maximum navigation benefits. I stared at these drawings next to Steve's iced coffee. The discrepancy between the natural and channeled rivers was huge.

"Look at the river two hundred years ago," Steve said as he jogged the pen nib over to a void near his butter knife.

"Throughout here you've got sloughs and swamps and trees."

Steve leaned closer. His voice turned low and reverential, clueing me into the truth that geomorphology was not his job, but his vocation. Rivers and riparian terrain were a symphony to this man. He tapped the blue pen on the drawing of the channeled river.

"This area here," he pointed to the region that used to be floodplain beside the water, "is now completely disconnected. Ecologically dead. This is really screwed up because today the banks are all armored with rock and the river's much deeper and swifter."

In other words, what were once moist regions beside the river stood dry.

I asked how this affected wildlife.

"It'd be like having a family of birds living in a leafless tree in a hurricane, as compared to a forest. All this stuff is gone."

That 'stuff' included the natural wetlands, sandbars and side channels that once thrived beside and within the Missouri River's main path. When the Corps of Engineers narrowed and confined the river between raised levee banks, the action severed the flow from much of its watershed.

Smoothing the river also increased its speed. Confined to a channel, the restless river water needed to dissipate energy. Because it could no longer writhe sideways like a snake, it squirmed downwards, chewing and deepening its unlined bed. The result was that water tables plummeted and oxbow lakes dried up.

The Flood of '93 reminded people that a river lives. It kicks and squirms and adjusts its position like an agitated passenger on a transatlantic flight. The Lower Missouri River evolved along an alluvial floodplain that sprawled between two and ten miles wide across prairies. The decision to clamp the river down and confine it to a barge channel between fifteen hundred and eighteen hundred feet wide severed it from much of the surrounding land it once nourished. When it flooded, the river displayed its natural need to spread and writhe and shed energy — behaviors that ran counter to the Corps' goal of restraining it to a nine foot deep alley.

One architect of legislation that changed the course of the Missouri River foresaw this problem of confining water. Colonel Lewis Pick of the U.S. Army proposed maintaining a wide floodway between Sioux City and St. Louis in order to give the Missouri River wriggling room. Unfortunately, his proposal was ignored.

"Whenever we take people familiar with the Missouri River up in a Cessna plane, they get quiet for ten or fifteen minutes," Steve continued. "You want to cry. The river is a ghost of what it used to be. Imagine this two mile wide ecosystem brimming with fish, birds, everything, then suddenly seeing remnants of all that from the air."

Caffeine quickened Steve's words, sharpening his intolerance.

"At some point in our history it was decided that civil engineers were experts on how to manage rivers," he continued, then shook his head.

"The average civil engineer I meet has the same tools to work on a river as, say, a physician in the 1830s had to deal with infectious disease. That's a good analogy. They don't know germ theory. Policy constricts them. It's not their fault. It's just the way engineering and policy evolved.

"If they sit down with a sheet like this," he said and gripped his fingers along two sides of his illustrated placemat, "to build a bridge over a decent-sized river or creek, they might only survey four hundred feet of the river. They don't know or care what's going on upstream or downstream."

I understood Steve's irritation. Those who changed the Missouri's flow regarded the river as a conduit, not a community. They sacrificed rich ecosystems for the sake of engineering economy. But I also understood that was their assignment. Had the same engineers been told to maintain a semi-intact environment, the river would appear differently today. But over a century ago, what we now consider 'environment' was generally regarded as a wild, dangerous landscape to be harnessed and tamed.

An unspoken understanding in our café conversation was that a river's health pivots on variety, both physical and the variety of opinions of those who manage it. Steve thought that interdisciplinary teams should manage rivers. That way not only engineers, but biologists and earth scientists would look at rivers as integrated systems instead of as narrow barge routes. But the path to that reality was strewn with problems. Some were grave, others pathetic. One was that university 'turf battles' reduced dialog between departments.

"A lot of the best scientific knowledge is in universities. But I've had people tell me — 'I'm in the biology department, I don't work with the engineering department. It can't be done. I don't see how you could do it.' It's frustrating. I find some of these professionals as closed minded as an IRS auditor."

Steve was halfway through his coffee. Frustration clouded his gaze. He was tired of being entangled in the outrageous. He just wanted those who managed rivers to respect their orchestra of life rather than regard flow as some graduate level physics problem. He also realized that progress was slowly underway — that the Corps of Engineers *was* changing its perspective.

"They have to keep in the direction they're going," he said. "In general they're moving towards widening the river, creating backwaters, trying to get back some diversity. It's really all about diversity, velocity, depth, substrate and vegetation. In some sense it's not all that complicated."

We finished our drinks and moved outside. The spring air was sweet. Steve pointed to the Volkswagen Westfalia van outside his home.

"I replaced thirty feet of engine cooling hose last weekend," he told me. " I'm getting ready to fit solar panels on the roof."

When he completed this work, Steve and his wife would take a year long sabbatical to ramble across back roads U.S.A. and explore shores, eddies, and rippling rivers. The notion sounded familiar. I wished him luck.

When approaching the city of Columbia, Missouri, I recalled Steve's admonition to crank more variety into the floodplain. Someone trying to do this was a biologist named Maureen Gallagher.

Chapter 9

REFUGE

Maureen Gallagher works as a biologist for the Big Muddy National Fish and Wildlife Refuge. I stopped at her trailer office south of the town of Columbia. She wore a maroon Fish and Wildlife shirt and sat next to a "Flood of '93" postcard. Her reddish brown hair matched her brown eyes and freckled dimples, a fiery combination that aligned with her zest for work.

"Things were so unbelievably trashed," Maureen said, referring to wildlife habitat along the Missouri River. "We're heading in the right direction now, but have a long way to go before seeing considerable results."

Like Steve, Maureen believed that the confined Missouri River needed 'breathing room,' an upgrade to business class width on its eternal flight eastward. It needed a wider floodplain, more space in which to expend its energy. Yet she tempered her optimistic outlook for the river's future with a pragmatic edge. She went on to explain: "The '93 flood was basically bad timing, a series of unfortunate weather events.

"We had 250 inches of snow pack in the Dakotas and Montana. Reservoirs were so full they had to open floodgates full bore on the Missouri River. We had a day-after-day-record rainfall in the lower watershed. Because of the levee system, there was no place for water to go. No place except to breach levees and get out in the floodplain. The floodplain is the river's opportunity to absorb weather, dissipating energy so it doesn't become so destructive. That's the important thing."

After the 'Great Flood of '93,' scientists from the Fish and Wildlife Service proposed moving levees between St. Louis and Sioux City away from the river. They suggested that the government buy thousands of acres of oat and clover fields, as well as forests and wetlands along more than seven hundred shoreline miles of the Missouri River. The purpose? Breathing space. They wanted to fatten the corridor where floods roam by keeping a strip of undeveloped land a half mile wide to each side of the river's flow.

This visionary, grandiose notion was unrealistic.

What was more realistic than vacating a mile wide collar was a compromise, a collaboration agreed to by the Fish and Wildlife Service, the Corps of Engineers, and the Missouri Department of Conservation. When the river spilled its banks in 1993, it revived an old notion that delivering a part of the floodplain back to the wallowing river could lessen the impact of future floods. One stretch of this revived terrain was created after the disaster — the Big Muddy Refuge. The notion was simple: the government would buy up to sixty-thousand acres of shoreline turf from willing sellers in Missouri state. Those willing to sell their land included farmers jaded by the river's capricious moods. Once refuge acres were bought, levees could be toppled and lands left to flood, recreating wetlands, sloughs and sandbars.

The refuge was to be a unit divided rather than a block of contiguous terrain: a chain of land parcels strung along the river like uneven-sized pearls on a necklace. When I met Maureen, six patches of sodden earth had already been established as part of the Big Muddy refuge. Their colorful names included Jackass Bend, Overton Bottoms and St. Ambert Island.

"The most devastating aspect of the flood was the amount of sediment laid down on the floodplain," Maureen added. "Farmers said — 'okay you beat me. I've had it. Can't fight the floodplain anymore. There's no way to farm in pure sugar sand. Make me an offer and I'll take it.'"

Because land will be bought over time, the total Big Muddy Refuge does not yet exist. Its size was identified; the time to put it into place was not. This makes it a wish with specific dimensions, a vision depending on the willingness of sellers to replace flood mauled land with hard cash.

Trying to suture portions of the Missouri River back to its original floodplain is a quest to find some midway point between the natural and channelized river. I asked why. What practical reason was there to win back this floodplain that had since been transformed to farm fields?

"Like in any ecosystem, species key in on a way of life," Maureen explained. "When all of a sudden that doesn't exist, they've got nowhere to go. Most critters of the world aren't as adaptive as we are. Those that adapt, survive. Those that can't, perish."

Unless part of the river slips into its old jacket and reverts to its behavior from the past, some species are poised to disappear. This includes two species of birds.

"There are no nesting pairs of piping plovers left on the Missouri River, from Sioux City down," Maureen added. "They used to be here. There are no least terns nesting here either."

When the Corps of Engineers reshaped the Lower Missouri, these two birds dissolved like clouds in sunshine. A prime reason they are endangered today is because their sandbar habitat disappeared.

Sandbars can rise after a river surges or floods. But the Missouri no longer runs naturally. Six mammoth dams chop its upper neck and control water running south. This keeps most of its flow as constant as a faucet stream. Unless this flow is changed, few new sandbars will rise in the future.

Creating the Big Muddy Refuge, with its beguiling wetlands and gritty shallows, was an excellent start to remold its lost habitat. But it's not enough to save these two endangered birds. To do that, the Corps has to change the river's flow.

"Getting the right habitat is the first and biggest struggle," Maureen continued.

"If you're looking at sandbar habitat for terns and plovers — you can go ahead and buy the land — but you're still subject to water levels. One could say water levels are determined by God," she said, loosening her huge smile. "But they're also determined by the Corps of Engineers. So we have to deal with Mother Nature *and* the Corps."

The truth that species are thinning out along segments of the river pushed the Corps, instructed by Congress, to change operation tactics. They now tweak portions of the Missouri to run wilder and messier in order to attract and sustain more varieties of reptiles, insects and mammals. But the fingers that adjust the river's flow are not yet spinning the dials as far as biologists would prefer to see. Instead, they keep the Missouri River running steady, maintaining a water depth needed to let barges drift downriver. Yet no matter how many acres are resurrected to marshland — the real gains in resurrecting floodplain habitat will become apparent only after the Missouri River is allowed to flow as it did in the past — varying with seasons. Rather than just change the direction of the flow, the Corps of Engineers has to be given the green light to change the power of this flow — letting it mimic the natural dips and spikes it once gushed with.

Changing the river's flow was beyond Maureen's agenda; her objectives lay with resurrecting wildlife habitat. To do this she emphasized the importance of the word 'recreate,' as opposed to 'restore.'

"We won't be restoring the Missouri River to what it was. It's not possible because the world is not what it was when Lewis and Clark came through here."

The future Missouri River will always differ from that of the past. Before an army fixed the Missouri's course to one channel, more varied wildlife roamed its riverbanks. But this wandering historical river that was so healthy for mammals and reptiles was disastrous to portside towns. To inspect this damage I drove north of Kansas City — to the town of Weston, Missouri.

Chapter 10

WESTON

To reach the Pirtle Winery in Weston, just a half hour north of Kansas City, I drove two miles west along JJ road, passed McCormick's Bourbon Distillery (*"Superior Spirits since 1856"*) and O'Malley's 1842 Tavern (*"If you must drive a man to drink, please drive him in here"*) and parked Six Pac before a red brick church. I then ascended fourteen creaking steps to a hulking wood door. This building that houses the winery was once a bottling works for a local brewery, and later a 'house of worship' where reverent black Baptists caught the wrath of a hell-roaring preacher.

Inside, I sidled up to a wood counter beneath stained glass windows. A grinning lass with a hairdo in the shape of a bucket poured samples of honey wine, apple wine, and raspberry mead into three glasses. I downed each with ease. She told me how the owners of the forty-acre vineyard produced up to ten thousand gallons a year. While swirling more wine in a glass, I picked up a book marker titled *A Little Bit of Romantic History*. It told how Vikings and Norsemen first introduced honey wine (mead) to England. Savoring its crude bouquet, the English deemed the concoction a love potion, then forged a tradition that bride and groom sip the mead for a full moon cycle after marriage — thus the word *honeymoon*.

"We used to ferment honey wine in old whiskey barrels," the chief vintner told me. "When the supplier ran out, we tried brandy barrels instead. The wine tasted much better, so that's all we use now."

The vintner looked indelicate — a character I'd identify more with brewing whiskey than fermenting wine. But appearances are deceptive: my sampling proved that this titan with scrupulous nostrils churned out a zesty product.

I stepped outside with a tipsy head and passed stores along Weston's antebellum Main Street. Most other retailers in Weston hawked antiques. They sold bygone knick knacks: aluminum angels, an Army Vietnamese Phrase book from 1962, and a bottle of *Edna Wallace Hopper's Facial Youth Cream*. Beside alcohol and antiques, Weston's other chief export lay stacked in buildings such as the Burley House at the town's sunken end. A tobacco leaf printed on one wall identified the regional crop inside — which was worth five million dollars a year to Weston.

Weston's town center was a compact and sloping main street, a furrow of time isolated from change since its pre-Civil War buildings were deemed 'historic' and saved from development.

Main Street, Weston, Missouri

Main Street ended beyond the Burley House, where telephone cables shot toward a tangle of brush. These wires crossed arid farmland where the Missouri River once whooshed. But this water that attracted settlers to town later deserted Weston.

In 1836 the Platte Purchase (comprised of land bought from the Iowa, Sacs and Fox Indians) was opened to settlers. William Clark brokered the purchase (soon after ending his transcontinental expedition with Lewis, he accepted the position as Superintendent of Indian Affairs). Chiefs with vibrant names — Bunch of Arrows, Green Lake, Sturgeon, The Orator and Bald Headed Eagle — signed away two million acres of swelling plains for $7500 and for two modest reservations now located west of the Missouri River.

Just a year later, settlers rushed in and founded Weston. By mid-century this hopping metropolis of "West Town" was bigger than Kansas City or St. Joseph. After St. Louis, it had the state's second largest population and constituted Missouri's second busiest port town. Steamboats were anchored by the base of Main Street. Suppliers sold picks, shovels and saddles to settlers aimed west along the Santa Fe and Oregon trails. At any time, six steamboats bobbed before the town's waterfront, picking up passengers heading north or collecting tobacco and hemp destined south.

A painter named Dr. Felling found a vista of Weston sketched by a wandering artist. He liked it so much that he copied it onto a larger canvas in oils. Titled *Weston in 1850,* the painting shows the town as a panoramic haven of red, blue, and yellow brick homes beside the river.

"When that young man painted the picture in 1850 there was no wharf. Steamers put down a gang plank and passengers walked to shore," Etta Brill told me inside Weston's museum. Like the winery, the museum occupies a former church, its interior filled with guns, swords, Confederate one hundred dollar bills and, oddly, modern-day Desert Storm bibles. Clad in brown leather shoes and khaki trousers, Etta was responsible for tending to this collection. A white turtleneck and blue kerchief accentuated her impeccably combed gray hair.

I raised my eyes to the painting again.

"When that picture was painted, there were about five thousand people living here," Etta continued. "By the early 1900s there were only a thousand. The Civil War and the changing Missouri current were a disaster. People came here to cross the Missouri River on the ferry," she explained. "There wasn't any reason to come if we didn't have the river. During the Civil War things were in such an upheaval people moved away. They were frightened. No major battles, but hand-to-hand fights on the street. Desperados went through the countryside robbing people and burning property. They did the same in town until they sent a troop of Union soldiers to quiet things down and keep us safe. People were terrified. They moved off. A lot went to Texas, some to New York. Went everywhere. It lowered our population. That happened before the river changed its channel to the other side of the valley in 1881. You could walk downtown and storefronts were closed. Sellers weren't able to make a living then."

Before the Civil War ended in 1865, slaves harvested hemp around Weston. This was shipped in coils to St. Louis where it was sold to rope makers. When this labor force disappeared, Weston's economy puckered up, then shriveled again when the Missouri River moved away. The flood of 1881 moved the river from the port end of Main Street to the foot of Kansas bluffs — two miles distant.

Etta handed me a four-inch thick book the color of an overripe cherry. A nineteenth century lawyer named Paxton had once compiled volumes of local history. According to Etta, eligibility into his Annals pivoted on three circumstances: you paid Paxton, you agreed with his legal decisions, and you abstained from 'hard liquor.' Hoping to reconstruct a sense of the past, I flipped through the pages of this filtered history. It told how even before the 1881 flood 'robbed' the river from Weston, the current was already tip-tapping back and forth, preparing to make its eventual dash. An entry from June 1858 told how "the port of Weston has been destroyed by a change of the channel of the Missouri River." In 1869 "the snagboat S.H. Long tries to open the channel of the Missouri River opposite Weston, but effects nothing." When the river deserted the town in 1881, the locals should have seen it coming.

"The river changed," Etta added. "A lot of people lost land; some gained land. There were all sorts of lawsuits over whose land such and such was. Nobody could tell for awhile."

Though the river moved, a vestige of its flow still returns to the town at times.

"In 1993 we had a bad flood again," Etta said. "Came to the foot of our Main Street. The river's dangerous. You can't swim it. You can't even swim a horse across it. You have to have a boat. I've talked to people who say there's no way they would fish that river in a rowboat. It's full of whirlpools."

This story of how the changing Missouri River thrashed Weston's economy sours the notion of letting the river run wild and free again. Just as a city is zoned for different uses — industrial, residential, commercial — the Missouri River is zoned into different flow regimes — channelized, dammed, wild and scenic. This 'zoning' mirrors different needs for its water.

Today Weston's population is over fourteen hundred. The town's economy improved in the 1970s when twenty-two blocks of downtown were designated a Historic District. This collection of buildings is now frozen in time, drawing in plenty of tourists.

I crossed the street before the museum and scrunched into a small, cozy bar. There I downed a glass of Boulevard Pale Ale. I enjoyed eyeing sixty nine red and blue plastic strips hung above the bar, each etched with a customer's nickname: Crack of Dawn, French Kiss, Gurgle Butt, Jimmy Cheap Seat. Behind me a woman in a red blouse slotted quarters in a jukebox and played a Jim Croche song.

"Glass of water?" the barmaid asked.

I nodded.

The bar served no food, not even peanuts. This posed a dilemma: wanting to stay, needing to go. I was wondering what to do next when the front door swung open. Three men and a petite brunette walked in.

"Food!" their leader piped. "Free food!"

There was a wedding in town, the woman explained to the bartender. Before the reception ended, the caterer received a phone call revealing that her house was on fire. She ran off, instructing guests to finish platters of turkey, roast beef, ham, salad, pumpernickel rolls, meatballs, pasta, strawberries and the biggest grapes I'd seen all spring. The food was more than they could finish at the reception, so they decided to share.

"Help yourself," the barmaid insisted.

Thankful for this nugget of providence, I gratefully piled a plate high with victuals and veggies. I was mid-bite through a strawberry at the bar when I had an epiphany, a bizarre revelation that was becoming clearer every day: this trip's schedule eluded me. Adhering to dates and a calendar was a waste of time. When I needed assistance, it was provided along the trail. On days when I yearned for companionship, a phone call or welcome stranger came into life. When hankering for information, some person appeared telling relevant stories. And now, when I hungered, trays of food marched through the door. Opportunities, like unseen rain, kept dropping all around.

Chapter 11

THE LOVE OF FARMING

Efforts to halt flooding along the Missouri River have not all worked as planned.

When the long Memorial Day weekend ended, I pulled out of the campground near Weston and drove to a service station at the upper edge of town. There I mentioned my interest in flooded farms to an attendant.

"Talk to Jim Nower," he said and plopped a pressure gauge into his shirt pocket. "Take Highway 45 past the railroad bridge, then the next left at Nower's lane."

Miles ahead, across from the West Sadler train stop, stood Nower's Lane. A half mile later I throttled back beside a lone farmhouse. A spinning silver windmill and a Buick stood outside. Across a corn field, the smokestack of a local power plant punched toward the clouds.

When he saw me park, Jim Nower dismounted from his tractor and smiled. After we exchanged introductions, he led me through his kitchen door.

"I worked for International Harvester for thirty-one years," he declared, meandering across scuffed linoleum. "I'm eighty-one now. My family's been on this farm since Great Grandfather Nower got here in 1856. Today I've got over a hundred acres of soybeans, wheat and corn. I farmed a thousand acres at one time."

Jim had a hardy handshake and a clear mind, though a recent leg operation had alerted him to his frailty. He led me to his living room where his wife Mary Edna sat below huge portraits of toothy grandchildren. Copies of the books *When Miracles Happen, Chicken Soup for the Christian Soul*, and *Holy Hilarity* sat on a bookshelf.

Mary Edna glowed. When she learned why I was visiting she took charge of the scene and extracted two photocopied maps from an expandable file. Each showed the Nower's land and adjacent plots. The care she used to handle the maps showed how she considered the river's history as part of her own family legacy. She lay the maps on a table. In 1877 the Nower's property was riverfront real estate: 220 acres slotted between the Missouri River's jagged banks and a railway line that peeled north toward St. Joseph. Back then green ash, black walnut, and sycamore trees had fluttered along the stubby shoreline. By 1905, the Nowers had chopped their land into two parcels. Both of these were now located a mile away from the river. This land afforded a potent sense of identity for Jim and Mary Edna. Jim had tossed away several opportunities to leave his soil.

"I had the chance to play professional baseball with the Philadelphia Phillies," he said. "I didn't go. I've still got the contract. This was back in 1948. They said: 'You're going to have to be in the majors in two years, or forget it.' They told me, 'We're gonna give you two hundred and fifty dollars a month and expenses.' I figured farmin' was better than that. I only played for the fun of it anyway. I also won a scholarship to go to Fort Collins, Colorado. To veterinary school."

"He didn't go," Mary Edna cut in. "He'd been gone in the war. He wanted to stay home."

"I spent forty months in the service," Jim said. "In the South Pacific, New Guinea and the Philippines. I had to go to Korea for the army occupation. I came back home without a scratch."

What he did bring home was a Silver Star. His achievement: driving a bulldozer during World War II while under enemy fire in the Philippines.

About the time Jim returned from the war the Missouri River started changing its behavior. Evidence of how it changed over decades became apparent during the flood of 1993.

"In two weeks it rained eleven inches," Mary Edna recalled. "That was too much water. On the twenty-fifth of July, Jim had to go to the doctor. After that, our son met us at the highway to bring us here in a boat. We got thirty-three inches of water in this house. On Saturday morning, we started moving stuff out. My son and two boats kept takin' things to the pickup. At noon we could hear water at the basement windows. Kinda tricklin' to start with, then it poured in."

The flood mutilated the Nower's fields and turned their living room into a wet dungeon. This forced the couple to stay with relatives in Weston for three months.

"It wiped out our farming that year," Mary Edna said. "The insurance company came and looked the land over. Of course it was still underwater. Jim told them: 'I'll take you to the crops if you get in the boat.' They said: 'No — I think we can tell it's all gone.' "

For Jim, this flood highlighted how the river changed.

"When I was a kid, the Missouri River cut a lot of farms, then quit to go cut someplace else," Jim said. "That was before the Corps of Engineers took over. They stopped that part of it."

"But in the thirties and early forties, we didn't know what a flood was. Didn't even think about it," he added. "From 1903 to 1943 there wasn't a drop of Missouri water on this farm. Forty years.

The river was wider than it is now. It didn't have a levee. We didn't know what a levee was. For forty years the Missouri was good to us. We didn't have to worry about it. After they started the stabili-, stabo-, sta…"

"Stabilization project," Mary Edna cut in, pronouncing 'stab' like a knife thrust.

"That's it. After they did that to the Missouri's banks, that's when the floods started."

Was the stabilization project worth it?

"Good question," Jim said. "There were more floods, but we got flood insurance. We pay about $300 a year, which is not much. I wasn't worried about it. Just took more insurance out. I'd rather not have a flood though, like during times before they come out with that project for stabi, stabo…

"*Stab*ilization!" Mary Edna yipped.

That channeling the Missouri River increased flooding sounded paradoxical. But in 1979 the Corps itself reported that their stabilization project created today's flood levels along the river. Their project could, therefore, be viewed as "an adverse impact." In the town of Hermann, Missouri, Geological Survey data from a gauging station at River Mile 98 showed that the lavish discharge in June of 1903 produced a river stage (level) more than six feet lower than when the river flowed with almost twenty percent less water in 1986. In other words, less water produced higher floods *after* channelization.

In the year 2001, researchers at Washington University showed that the portion of the flood of '93 contributed by the Mississippi, rather than the Missouri River, had about the same discharge as this same flood that passed St. Louis ninety years earlier. The more recent flood, however, was twelve feet higher. The evidence "indicates that levee construction and channelization on the Lower Missouri and the middle Mississippi have greatly magnified their floods."

Restricting the size of a hydraulic channel decreases a river's ability to handle volumes of water — its 'flood carrying capacity.' Since the Missouri was ratcheted to a third (or less) of its former width, this narrow chute of liquid now rides past many towns and cities much higher than it did in the past.

At the same time that I moved up the Missouri River, an author named Jeffery Rothfeder researched his book about water titled *Every Drop for Sale*. When he heard a spokesman for the Federal Emergency Management Administration complain that flooding in the year 2001 could have been prevented with more levees and dikes, Rothfeder believed that this contradicted reality. His research revealed that floods were worst along stretches of river *with* levees.

"When people are determined to avoid the obvious," he wrote, "not even a flood or thousands of them — can get their attention."

I stood and thanked Mary Edna. Jim led me outside. His energetic thin limbs looked agitated. We stood beneath maple and sycamore trees next to the green walls of his square house. Together we gazed toward his open, silent acres.

"Nice," I told him.

"It's home," Jim said, then climbed on his tractor and drove toward the river in twilight.

SECTION TWO:

KANSAS

Chapter 12

SITTING TIGHT

Less than twenty miles north of the town of Weston, a gangly truss bridge led into Atchison, Kansas. A train whistled and grimy clouds billowed from a town smokestack. Facets of the landscape formed a starker contrast to Missouri. Barns looked shaggier. More cracks checkered tarmac roads. Street centerlines were often deleted and many pickup trucks looked 'income challenged.' Yet community spirit was intact. Atchison residents had turned adversity caused by a flood into a springboard for reshaping their town.

The famed aviatrix Amelia Earhart grew up in Atchison. She later recalled details of the town's floods and wrote of "mud-ball fights, picnics, and exploring raids up and down the bluffs of the Missouri River." For her, the river "was always exciting. There usually were large and dangerous looking whirlpools to be seen in its yellow depths, and the banks were forever washing away. Not that any of us ever got very near the banks, but — a few of us remembered dimly the floods of 1903 when water crept up to the gutters of buildings and swept away bridges and spread out over the lowlands as far as the eye could see."

Like most towns north of Kansas City, Atchison missed the brunt of the 1993 flood. Residents recall an earlier washout instead.

In July of 1958, Don Murray and Diane Varsi starred in the summer movie "From Hell to Texas" (*The story of the day the whole*

West burst into flame!); Clyde Reed ran for Governor (*Says What he Thinks — Does What he Says*); President Eisenhower summoned a bipartisan emergency meeting in the White House to discuss the "Iraqi Crisis," and a ten foot wall of water ravaged downtown Atchison. In forty-five minutes five inches of rain dumped onto the town while ten inches clattered onto the nearby Brewery and Whiskey Creek watersheds. Water swelled through Main Street at 2:30 a.m., gutting a bookstore, slicing open a shoe shop, imploding walls of a movie theater, and unroofing a warehouse. It derailed three freight cars and a locomotive and ladled muck all over the floor of the Daily Globe newspaper office. It rummaged its fist down a basement and squeezed the life out of a sixty-four-year-old woman, then crunched a traveling salesman's car against a parking meter.

One family of three woke inside their trailer home, stranded. The son swam to shore through eight foot deep water while his parents climbed onto the roof of a car and hollered for help. A sixty-year-old neighbor heard their cries. Together with his wife, they tossed the couple a double-duty extension cord and dragged them to safety.

Three weeks later, another flood gushed through Atchison. It pushed a car along Main Street beneath the Sixth Street Viaduct. Two petrified high school girls sat inside, waist deep in water. Workers at the nearby Mill and Elevator Company spied the rotating car as it banged against telephone poles. When its wheels halted at the railway station, the mill foreman, Ed Hearn, fastened a 300-foot rope around his waist and waded out toward the vehicle. He knotted a rope end to the car bumper while his coworker, Charles Contreras, gripped the goldline fibers and waded out to join him. Together the men stood four feet deep in rising brown goo, dodging muddy logs. Each of them then placed a girl on shoulders, clutched the rope and waded back to the loading dock.

In the wake of these July floods, the *Atchison Globe* carried the front page proclamation: "Atchison will Rebuild."

> *"Even among those residents hardest hit there is confidence and bull dogged determination as the arduous, heart-breaking clean up begins. Nowhere is there defeatism."*

> *"Manhattan had a flood as bad as this, and Manhattan rebuilt," one property owner said. "El Dorado had a tornado tragedy but fared up to it. We will, too."*

The paper then boasted:

> *"Out of this wreckage will come a newer, and better Atchison!"*

The prediction came true. As part of an urban renewal program, bulldozers razed a row of houses on Commercial Street and transformed downtown Atchison into one of the country's first pedestrian malls. Yet even though the Missouri River was channeled beside the town, residents of this newer and better Atchison stay wary that another flood could still strike any day.

Before they settled in Atchison in 1857, a band of tenacious Benedictine monks tested various sites along the Missouri River. Once they chose a home, preoccupations about a lack of dedicated men and cash (and the odd crop failure) plagued them. In 1858, a royal pre-yuletide donation of three thousand Florins from the priory's greatest benefactor, King Ludwig of Bavaria, helped the monks launch their college. Nearby, Benedictine Sisters soon opened their own college. In the 1970s both institutes merged.

I drove onto the lush, one hundred-acre campus of Benedictine College above the Missouri River. Well-manicured grounds emanated a sense of tranquility. I soon stood on the second floor of Westerman Hall classroom building and stared at a notice board. Copies of research papers published by college staff lay tacked to a blue corkboard. Their titles included:

Factors that Influence the Gizzard Shad Spawn in man-made reservoirs

Mechanical Analog of the Synchotron, Illustrating Phase Stability and Two Dimensional Focusing

Temperature and Hydrostatic Pressure Effects of the Excitron Spectra of some Lead and Cadmium Halides

Molecular Beam Photoionization Study of $HgCl_2$

Wow.

Among these hung a paper with a drawing of a black and white pheasant beside the simple title: *Sitting Tight.*

Such cool brevity sent me tracking down its author.

In an office down the hallway, Dr. Dan Bowen plunged hands into pockets, smiled his ruddy face and motioned for me to sit. Gray streaks touched this biology professor's curly hair. He was a casual man who looked pleased with where life landed him. Dan supervised students who studied painted turtles, striped skunks, leopard frogs and other creatures that roamed and foraged all over the Benedictine Bottoms floodplain. Like the Big Muddy Refuge, these bottoms were another Missouri River mitigation project, run by the Corps of Engineers rather than by the Fish and Wildlife Service. In science, as in retail, location is everything. The college stood right next to the bottoms, affording a living laboratory only minutes away from biologists.

Dr. Dan Bowen, wildlife biologist at Benedictine College in Atchison, Kansas

"When the Corps channeled the river, they made it 127 miles shorter," Dan explained. "That increased the slope and made it faster."

This change dried up much of the floodplain and pushed wildlife away, reducing biodiversity along the Missouri River corridor. Dan wanted to see life return to the Bottoms. If intelligently managed, ecologic systems on this portion of the floodplain might reemerge with greater diversity.

"What the Bottoms has to do, and I'm speaking personally, is house the biodiversity in a very, very small package that would otherwise occupy maybe a space ten or a hundred times as large," Dan said. "So, managing it intensely is appropriate, because we're not going to get the whole floodplain back."

Dan's reason to preserve species was simple.

"I have a bias towards wanting to preserve all living organisms, so we can figure out what to do before they're gone."

The Benedictine Bottoms was a cageless zoo designed to hold onto life as a snapshot of riverside variety. Students who tended this plot studied fluctuations of trapped species, measured how rainfall repelled mammals and quantified cycles of growth on more than two thousand acres of gummy river bottomland. Dan reaped this scientific data like a farmer harvesting crops.

"They've thrown a lot of money at these bottoms," he continued. "The Corps bought the land and did five million dollars of development, putting in electricity for pumps, roads, a fence, and a maintenance shed. They pump water into wetland cells. I'm an advocate of what they've done, at least of what they've tried to do."

For Dan, time, patience and vision were more valuable than pushing for quick results along the Missouri River's revitalized floodplain. He was in no rush to restore wetlands and wildlife.

"If you could be here in another fifty years, I think we would have a similar conversation. Really. The floodplain is going to be a little bit further along, somewhat improved, a little bit better managed. It's a long-term and political process. Everyone has to represent their interests as best they can — and be patient."

He shared wisdom about where I should visit along the river.

"Last week, I was up in Ponca State Park in Nebraska. It's the most important place to go on the Missouri River to understand what the Corps of Engineers has done. Stand at the lookout. Look down on the unchanneled and the channeled portions of the water. You'll appreciate the change that the Corps wrought in a way you cannot possibly imagine."

The engineered version of the Lower Missouri River begins at Ponca, upstream from Sioux City, Iowa. Visitors there can see two rivers from the hilltop — a tamed downstream version and the more savage, turbulent segment that runs into this from above.

"Last summer I traveled the whole Missouri River," Dan continued. "Ponca, though, it's kinda like the shrine. Visually it makes a very, very powerful statement about the changes we wrought. The river is extremely boring from St. Louis to Ponca. You can't tell where you are because it all looks the same. Other than buildings, there's not an island or feature that would give you a hint. It's been made uniform. It's biologically boring."

"To canoe from Gavins Point to Ponca State Park would be what you want to do. It will give you the best feeling of what the river looked like when Lewis and Clark went up. It's the river that steamboat captains rode."

As he thought about those who first ran the length of the truculent river, Dan leaned back and clasped hands behind his head. His concentration faded and his voice shed its analytical choppiness. His words turned fluid as he described the journey of Lewis and Clark.

"It was hard work. But I'm sure they had fun. What? Forty young guys, pretty damn healthy, working hard but generally not in an extremely hostile situation. What more could you ask out of a twenty year old guy — he's going to get famous, get to party with the Indians. They had fun. They had a sense of themselves too. You get that feeling as you read their journals."

Dan recalled how the expedition first spied prairie dogs near what is now Niobrara to the north. Having never seen the animal, the men spent hours flushing water through burrows ("caught one alive, by pouring a great quantity of water in his hole," Clark wrote on September 7, 1804).

"Can you imagine carrying buckets of water and pouring them down a prairie dog hole all day long?" he asked. "It was a lark."

His words echoed a simple truth: journeying up the Missouri River is loaded with surprises.

Just as journals of the Corps of Discovery captured an essence of past exploration, Dan wanted the Benedictine Bottoms to capture a representation of life that once thrived along the Missouri River floodplain. For Dan, the river bottoms formed their own sort of sentient journal.

We parted in the warmth of late spring. Hours later, I realized I never even asked Dan what *Sitting Tight* was all about.

Chapter 13

DONIPHAN

When the Missouri River abandoned Weston, the town adapted and survived. I wondered what became of less resilient riverside havens.

I decided to find out by visiting what used to be booming Doniphan, Kansas. I first stopped at Atchison's Daylight Donuts to drink a thirty-two cent cup of coffee and ask directions. The counter woman pulled out a road atlas, then phoned the Chamber of Commerce to fine tune instructions. She described the route past levees on old River Road, several miles north.

This hard clay road passed blue herons, egrets and a serenade of bird calls from the Benedictine Bottoms. Miles later a scene evoked memories of how photographer Clint Eastwood asked farmer Meryl Streep for directions to a covered bridge; I spied a white house tilted on a small hill and a tan female working in the garden. I braked and walked over to this tangle of red hair and sagging arms poking through a white cotton frock. The woman was covered by seedlings and dandelion pollen. When I asked how to get to Doniphan, she dropped her rubber bucket and gyrated both hands, creating an aerial map.

"Ain't hardly nothin' there no more," she said. "Go on that road to Carl's farm. There'll be hogs in a pen by the road. Find Carl," she insisted. "You can't find the rock if you don't find him first."

"Rock?"

"About six feet high. Site of the church here before those monks moved downriver. That road you crossed when you were comin' in? Used to mark the river shore before the water moved. They had it all here back then — blacksmiths, wineries, boats."

I puttered in Six Pac a mile south to the crossing of Monument and Mineral Point roads. There were hogs in a hog pen, but no sign of Carl. A tubular Labrador the color of cheddar cheese gave a lame yelp. I drove on.

Before it evolved into the town of Doniphan, Kansa Indians occupied this region in the late 1600s. To avoid conflicts with incoming Sac and Iowa Indians (both stocked with firearms they bought from French traders), the Kansa deserted these plains and migrated up the Missouri River. Doniphan later turned into a settler's port and formed one of the region's larger towns.

I parked and walked across slumbering soil. Tilled farmland before me looked as ripe as fallen pears. Although the Missouri River passed this point over a century earlier, there was no longer any water in sight. A flood had changed the river's course. It seemed strange that steamboat smoke once spilled over this rocky topsoil. I imagined women in skirts and unshaven dock hands bickering and milling around a pungent waterfront stacked with crates. What was now lumpy clay once formed a rendezvous point for freight, gossip and tales of travel. Two warehouses, stocked with cargo from as many as fifteen steamboats, once towered close to Barney O'Driscoll's Doniphan House Hotel (ominously struck by a blizzard its opening day, freezing the first guest to death).

There was no longer a sign of any town. I saw no river. What analogy best described what happened to the Missouri River at

Doniphan? The event was as unsettling as if an interstate highway jumped miles away every few decades. What would that do to those who worked at gas stations, roadside diners and the local highway patrol office?

"This was basically a port city for the interior of Kansas," Bob Nourie told me. He spoke from inside his low-roofed barn.

"For a short period of time it was also a center during the abolitionist's struggle."

I found Bob by stalking the unusual. Near the vacant dirt intersection rose a sign that looked out of place — a crafted wood board beneath a compact red roof. It showed a sunrise, grapes and auburn leaves beside the words *Doniphan Heritage Vineyards — Embracing Sunshine Since 1992*. The sign's incongruity piqued curiosity. I aimed up the adjacent gravel driveway, passed through an evergreen grove and parked beside a marquis ringed by magenta buds. A woman wearing a blue kerchief and holding a garden trowel approached. Without suspicion or hesitation, Kittie Nourie offered a warm handshake and bright smile. Her husband Bob soon joined her. The two invited me inside their immaculate studio, a renovated barn with purple walls and turquoise-tinted window frames.

On the wall inside hung a coat of arms, a painting of a civil war skirmish and a photograph showing Chief White Cloud and son Dan dressed in tribal regalia.

After Bob retired from the Marine Corps in the mid-1990s, the Nouries moved to Doniphan. This was where Kittie grew up. Her father arrived in town in the 1920s, where he met his wife. To provide a sense of this past, Kittie laid a series of black and white photographs on the table. One showed a man girthed by a black apron standing on

Winery sign before home of Bob and Kittie Nourie in ghost town of Doniphan,

the front porch of a two-story shop. The sign outside read E.B. Ford — the name of Kittie's father. This image sparked Kittie's memory and she talked about fugitive floods that occurred while she grew up. She told how the Corps of Engineers built a huge levee nearby that transformed swampy floodplain into tillable land.

"Her family was like many in this community," Bob said. "Her father was Irish and her mother of German descent."

Bob had a round face and clipped mustache. He spoke with a steady demeanor, like a narrator for a history documentary. The combined effect of Bob's diction and the Nourie's well-crafted sign transformed this couple into an anomaly within Doniphan. Their evergreen glen compounded this effect by adding a European tone to the surrounding Kansas terrain.

Bob described how Doniphan had hosted zealots and icons.

"Back in the middle to late 1850s, when the Kansas Territory became a statehood, James Lane was here," he said. "He had been a legislator in Indiana. He was an abolitionist and led Union troops during the Civil War. He was marginally insane. He lived in a local hotel. This community was also of such significance that Abraham Lincoln stopped here on December 2, 1859, when he came through Kansas."

Bob spread a black and white map on the table. Wavy lines indicated where the Missouri River once lapped down the road.

"At its zenith, the population of this town was somewhat in excess of two thousand people," he explained. "The last census of the county shows it at seven or eight hundred. Doniphan had all the basics — hotels, saloons, churches, steamboats. There were three major wineries here producing about 150,000 gallons per year, which is substantial. They were owned by the same family who shipped by river until the Missouri changed channel in the late 1800s. The main channel shifted south and east. Made this a lake."

Back near Weston, Mary Edna Nower had also pulled out maps that illustrated how the crafty Missouri River changed over time. By doing the same, Bob emphasized the esteem given by locals to the history of the Missouri River. For those who work, explore and hunt the land, topographic maps are as integral to daily lives as weather charts are to a pilot. Seeing these pairings of old and new maps emphasized the significance of the Missouri River to nearby residents. Learning how the river's course shifted over decades was essential to fathom the integrity of the place they called home.

Bob pointed to another map hanging next to the door.

"Frank Fogler drafted that," he confirmed, referring to a friend of his living in Atchison. "It plots by latitude and longitude various landing sites of Lewis and Clark and connects them by a red line.

That's transposed over an existing river map to demonstrate that the river channel was all over the place."

'All over the place' was the Missouri River's trait that swallowed steamboats and transformed communities like Doniphan into ghost towns.

"We're told there's about ten steamboats buried near here. Most were small packets, enough to move a couple wagons."

"If you go through the county there's a tremendous residue of abandoned farms," he added. "I mean long-time abandoned. Like since the 1920s and 30s. Others have been amalgamated into newer farming structures. The reason there's nothing left here is that most houses were wood standing on an unmortared stone base. They either rotted or burned. 'They' being one, two, three rooms at most. The stone was then moved and the land tilled. So there's not a lot left. Weston was the same thing," Bob added. "But they survived. This place just dried up."

His words rang with lament. Since withering, Doniphan had turned to a home for bobcats, wild turkeys, unmarked clay roads and random, tumbling farmhouses. The town nucleus was now only a vague memory.

Bob considered this segment of the country as its cultural, social, political and geographical center. Yet the Nouries also kept their minds open to the world: they were thrilled when their son in the Peace Corps met and later married a beautiful Ukrainian woman. Yet although they appreciated the world beyond Kansas, the Nouries considered Doniphan the home they loved. They were content to lacquer doors, garden, or bottle grape juice in a disused winery during free hours.

Enriched by their generosity and wiser about the caprice of the Missouri River, I thanked the couple and set off again in Six Pac.

Chapter 14

THE LEWIS AND CLARK DIET

Missouri River at the town of Atchison, Kansas

Inside a riverside restaurant back in Atchison, I ate a stout burger in a crunchy bun. A lean, bearded man sat on a stool next to me. He looked weary.

"John Mickelson," he introduced himself. "Same name as the Governor of South Dakota. Came down from Great Falls, Montana."

"Boat? Driving?"

He rocked his head and smiled with nomadic grace.

"Eighteen-foot canoe. Tied up outside."

"How long did it take?"

"Forty-eight days so far. Didn't know there were dams on this river when I started off. Six of them. Big! What's the story with these dams? Recreation? Boating? Fishing? That's B.S. Some of these reservoirs are big as an inland sea and have maybe five boats on them. Hell one is 190 miles long. Had to use a compass to find my way near dusk. And finding the main channel? I asked someone how to do it. He told me 'follow the scum line.' It worked. Talk about the value of local knowledge. Good thing I brought an anchor with me. These reservoirs drowned out cottonwood trees. Now the banks are all silt and mud. Nothing to tie onto."

I ordered another beer. John declined the offer. His taut body was poised to rest before another day of paddling. He pinched his gut.

"Started with a thirty-eight inch waist. Now I'm thirty-two. I call it the Lewis and Clark diet. But I'm getting tired of being on this river."

"How long until you finish?"

He waved the restaurant owner over.

"What river mile is this?" he asked.

Larry, the owner, called his granddaughter over. The two conferred and agreed it was Mile 423.

"Canoed sixty-six miles one day, but average forty," John continued. "So in ten or twelve days I'll be at the Gateway Arch. I'm going to meet my wife there. We'll stand on the porch of the Embassy Suites and enjoy the afternoon buffet with a drink."

He drained his frosty mug. His eyes darted back and forth.

John came from Mesa, Arizona. He had spent twenty years working with land titles in Guam. His trip down the Missouri River was a way to get acquainted with his own country. He laughed with corded energy, a restless man obsessed with exhilaration. After six weeks of paddling his tired body writhed with intent.

He rotated one large, but smooth hand.

"Know why it looks like this? Udder balm. Used to lubricate cow teats for milking. Took my wife's advice. Threw away the expensive waterproof gloves, spread udder balm on my hands and pulled neoprene gloves over 'em. Works great."

John yawned. "Going to hit my sleeping bag," he said.

After we parted I walked to the small dock outside to inspect John's scuffed, oxblood red canoe. It was so loaded with gear that I saw little room for a paddler. It was curious that John was not even aware of huge 'mainstem' dams before he began his canoe trip. His determination to tackle a challenge head-on brought him to the river before he learned what might have changed his mind about the trip.

Weeks later in North Dakota I read a *Fargo Forum* newspaper article from June of 1947. It told how a sixty-four-year old newspaper columnist and his twenty-something friend paddled from Montana's Little Bighorn River to Bismarck, North Dakota. The duo took over three weeks to complete their route. With wind at their backs they paddled 125 miles one day, twice the length of John's longest daily haul. Yet their average daily speed exactly matched that of John.

I left the restaurant and returned to the campground at Marnock Lake.

That night turned into a lesson in how water levels along the Missouri River change so fast. It was cold, rainy weather — perfect for a good book and a hot lemonade with a dribble of Jack Daniels. I mixed up this brew and pulled on an "expedition weight" undershirt inside Six Pac. Rain prattles turned to pops and cloud tendrils hung above.

During the next hours a storm ransacked Kansas. Thunder retched and rain turned the land into a mud bath. Wind gusts rustled sheaves of wheat and the temperature dropped so fast I thought my ears would pop. It rained hard, soft, and sideways. The cocktail of water and wind flushed nests from gutters and turned hay bales soggy. I lay beneath a down comforter wearing long johns and wool socks and listened to squadrons of lightning crinkle and crack. They attacked the campground, retreated, regrouped, and charged again. And again. At eleven that night a flashlight beam prodded through the back door.

"Anyone there? My name's Barbara. I work here."

I pulled on jeans and a sweatshirt and swung the door open. A drenched woman stood below a gelatinous sky. A speck of mud clung to her right eyelash.

"Roads coming in and out of the campground are washed away," she said above the rainfall.

"You might not get out in the morning," she added. "So, we'll see you then."

Seven inches of rain fell that night. The morning was low lit and soggy. I walked down a gravel road to where a new lake had formed. It reeked of festering mulch. The roof and half a window of an abandoned cherry red pickup truck jutted out of this pond — a victim of the deluge.

Barbara pulled up again. This time she came with a man named Buck Ross.

"Need to evacuate," he said. "Water's as high as your wheels. Want to try driving?"

I nodded.

"Follow me."

A confetti of olive dark timber covered the road before us like hurricane debris. The sight of scattered tree limbs made the surrounding scene look surreal. One by one we maneuvered our trucks across the inundated trail.

Barbara and Buck then waved before they drove off to help others.

I parked at the Red Cross office on 5th and Kansas Street. A woman inside told me about the condition of roads.

"North is fine. South is fine. Everywhere is fine except here."

This storm came as a message. After spending weeks in the region, it was time to move on from Atchison.

Chapter 15

WOLF RIVER BOB

How strong a pull did the Missouri River exude on those who grew up along its banks? To find out I hunted down a man named Wolf River Bob in northern Kansas. He lived hours north of Atchison, next to alfalfa fields in a puny town named White Cloud. Huddled in the north east of the state, this town celebrated Independence Day of 1857 by ferrying crowds via steamboat in from as far away as St. Louis. The celebration was a ruse. The real intention of the party was to try to sell visitors lots of land. The ploy worked and business soon boomed. New residents erected a mill and White Cloud started producing more lumber than any other town along the Missouri River. At the turn of the twentieth century, its population was four times that of today's, which hovers in the low hundreds.

Once in White Cloud, I walked along the dust rumpled, inclined main street to the only store in sight. A miniature mongrel stood on a bench.

"I'm lookin' for Wolf River Bob," I told the dog's owner. He wore what looked like pilot getup from World War I — goggles and a leather cap with earflaps (this sight made me realize I was getting *deep* into the country).

"In there," he pointed. "Whiskered fella."

I stepped inside to a huge space that couldn't decide if it was a dining room, living room or restaurant. Newspapers lay on counter stools. Tables were piled with stuffed animals, medallions and two Barbie dolls stained brown from tobacco smoke. A man with a tousled Kris Kringle beard and a pony tail stood. He almost saluted when he heard his name.

Wolf River Bob above White Cloud, Kansas

"Yessir, 'at's me," he said. "Wolf River Bob."
He handed me his card:

*Lewis and Clark Trail Guide – Fast Gun –
Bullwhips – Western Historian – Primitive Camping
– Antiques "Till the Wheels Roll No More."*

What's the gig, I wanted to ask: '*Till the Wheels Roll No More?*' Instead, we shook hands. Bob's oversized glasses covered sizzling blue eyes. Layered workshirts bloated his denim jacket; yellow felt gloves waved from a back pocket of his worn jeans.

"Have a seat," a woman at the table said. She had wavy black hair and lean jowls.

"I'm Lois," she told me. "You're welcome here. Nothing too fancy. Really not a restaurant no more. We just kinda get together in the mornin' to talk."

I sat at the card table. It was cluttered with a half bag of corn nuts, one flashlight, a mustard bottle and a coffee-splattered TV guide. Behind me a Pepsi delivery man wheeled his dolly through the screen door and hailed Lois by name. A policeman followed. He sat next to her husband to talk about fishing.

I asked Bob about his past.

"You ask me, I probably done it," he said. "Been there, done that. Born and raised here. Took off in '44, went to California. Missile technician. Propellant crew. Fired me because I had long hair and a beard. Worked stunts part time in TV and movie business. Worked the bullwhips and fast guns, bar room brawls. Met Roy Rogers several times — now I know his son. Slim Pickens? He and I were ol' rodeo buddies."

"I'm pretty happy here. Never run out of work. If I were to die tomorrow, I think I've lived a full life. Been coast to coast and border to border — Florida, New York, California, Montana. Decided those places weren't as beautiful as back home. Came back here years ago, bought my grandparents' home and have kept active since. Traveled the Lewis and Clark trail giving talks to schools and organizations. The news media is pickin' up on this Lewis and Clark now. Millions of people will be flockin' to this area. Let's face it, the secret's out! This area is known as Kansas, Switzerland. Hollywood's comin'. They already shot Paper Moon here, two days along Main Street. Tatum O'Neal ridin' that car and puffin' cigarettes."

Sleepy White Cloud hardly looked poised for the swell of visitors Bob expected.

"I was born here in '26. My mother would paddle my fanny if I was caught near that river. Floods? '93 was a monster. My younger days, when the June rise snowmelt come, we'd see dead cattle and hogs floatin' downriver. Barns too, with chickens riding on top."

"Never had control of the river until the 30s. Then boats went up and down dredging sand to make the channel deeper. I'd seen them workin' the river. It was fantastic. I'm still thrilled by it."

Lois cut in.

"One year ice piled up big on the river. I was on White Cloud Hill when it cracked. Just popped. The ice sheared Cottonwood trees that big around," she said and threw her arms in a hoop.

"Pop! Pop! Pop! Just popped 'em. Early 70s. Would make huge chunks of ice big as an automobile when it cracked. Kinda roared like a freight train when it got to movin.' This river, I'm tellin' ya, she's boss. We can tame her to a certain extent, but 'f she decides she's gonna do something, she does."

These 'ice outs' usually took place in February or March when the frozen river thawed. Ice chunks broke apart and roared downstream. This rush and crunch of ice blocks jamming against each other forced river water to flood onto banks.

"I learned to skin fish because of the river floodin," Lois continued. "In 1952 it got up around trees, then went down again. Left holes full of fish. They were gonna die — so we just scooped them out with a bucket. Everybody had to skin fish. Used to go out with pitchforks to take them out of fields."

Talk of the flood caused all faces at the table to light up. The effect was the same as that at the Glasgow Missourian newspaper office, where the mention of past floods animated faces and made the room pulse with quiet excitement.

" 'Muddy Moe' they called the river!" Bob added. "It was so thick you could almost walk across it at flood times. Nebraska and the Dakotas would lose soil. That's how this bottomland become so deep in gumbo and sand. All the trash and trees that floated down was deposited on river banks."

Lois poured us coffee again. She and Bob told tales about how the Missouri was as much a phenomenon as a river. Like a Kansas storm that does more than drizzle, the Missouri River does more than flow. It floods, freezes, wanders and capsizes the odd rowboat. It also contaminates.

"River is so polluted now. Something you can't see," Bob said. "It's coming off farmlands. We don't have to worry about other countries. I think we're gonna kill ourselves with all the crap we put on our land. Don't like it, but there's no way I can stop it. I'm not powerful enough. Pesticides, fertilizers, everything is put on these crops. The chemical companies of today are interested in the mighty buck."

"Nitrates!" Lois yipped. "You can hardly find a well that's not got nitrates in it."

Frazzled by the subject, Bob changed it.

"Some tribes in this area feel the Lewis and Clark expedition invaded their privacy, invaded their land. It's changing though. Casinos have helped. White people comin' to spend their money. Givin' something back after we took all their lands. I say that's great! We've wiped out the hatred of long ago. Little Bighorn's gone. Let's start today, clean up our act."

He stood like an awakened Rip Van Winkle and flailed his arms with reptilian stealth. We walked outside together to his GMC van and motored up to the Four States Lookout Point. There we picked fat mulberries and looked at the twitching river far below.

"This is loess soil," Bob said. "There are only three places in the world that's got this kind of soil — Germany, China and here. Grows anything. Became farmland after the Corps of Engineers put these trail dikes in. Water filtered through the dikes and deposited dirt behind, then kept the channel over that way. Once you narrow the channel down, where does the water go? Gotta go somewhere. So it climbs over levies. First thing you know, it's all flooded."

Bob moved fast, as though he'd already rehearsed this rapid tour of White Cloud. He next drove to fields of open grass that formed Pow Wow grounds of the Iowa tribe.

"These grounds have been active for 150 years or more. They used to come here in horses and buggies and wagons. It was a pretty picture. This is all sacred area. Chief White Cloud used to go the Dakotas and get horses. They'd break them here during the Pow Wow — their own rodeo.

"Imagine this over a hundred years ago," Bob said. He whipped his shoulder around with the adroitness of an arctic fox. "Hear the birds? Imagine teepees all around. Lot of activity. Horses, buffalo, turkeys, quail. Isn't this peaceful? Tribe has a show comin' up soon. Exchange gifts and put on regalia and dance like years ago. Oh Lord, two or three thousand help put it on. Indians come. White people, too. They have fry bread, tacos, lots of food. Fantastic. Sometimes fifty or more teepees, motor homes, too. You hear tom-toms and drums."

We drove through a roller coaster of dips to a place named Happy Hollow, then stopped to browse at a cornfield near the Nemaha River. Though illegal to collect Indian artifacts, Bob often spent hours hunting arrowheads, then leaving the pieces where he found them. The search, he explained, was "like spring plowing. You have a rain and all your artifacts come up where they could be seen real easy. Arrowheads, knives, tommy hawks."

The process was as important as the find.

"Get my therapy coming here, lookin' for pieces of flint. Walk out and first thing you know you find yourself four or five miles from the car. Close your eyes and gaze around. Imagine this place two hundred years ago. The Indians were here. We're handling what they handled. Isn't that fantastic? Sit down. Relax," he insisted. "That's the thing to do here. Just forget all your troubles."

I crouched in this empty field. Wind rolled through hair and thoughts. Temperature — warm; work pressure — zero; health — good; friendship — present; exploration — in action. Bob was right. Forget all troubles.

Sunshine emerged and the sky tightened. Life felt grand. After Bob moved toward the edge of a thistle field, we spun around and returned to his van.

"Let's go!" Bob bellowed. "We'll take the scenic route along the river."

I hopped inside, thinking: *till the wheels roll no more!*

Minutes later we stopped at a small graveyard and stood in hushed reverence before a row of tombstones.

"Peaceful, ain't it?" Bob asked. "Now, here's Chief White Cloud. I take care of his gravestone now and then. Brush it up so it can be read. White Cloud was chief of the Iowa tribe. Born in 1840 and died in 1940. I knew him. Had a wounded hand, had to carry it a special way."

According to legend, an earlier Chief White Cloud was directed by the Great Spirit to climb Council Hills and seek advice after whites announced that they wanted to buy his tribe's land. When the chief looked to distant hills and saw them covered in plantain weeds he interpreted this as a sign that settlers would soon cover the land in the same way. White Cloud then realized that only by relinquishing control of their territory would his tribe avoid battles. They sold their land. Today what remains of the tribe's territory lays west of White Cloud in a 2,100 acre reservation with about as many members.

We returned to a wood building on the main street just uphill from the Missouri River. Bob unlocked the front door and we sidled inside. Until trains stopped running in 1933, this old train station was used by CBQ — the Chicago, Burlington and Quincy line that ran next to the Missouri River.

Bob bought the building five years earlier. Its cracked plaster walls smelt of bat urine. He had laid out antiques on tables — fuel gauges, vacuum tubes, milk bottles, belt buckles, telephone bells, date stamps and scissors. I gazed at cairns of obsidian chippings, petrified wood, glass bottles, gold watches, bone dice, buttons, hacked pottery, even a rubber horseshoe. Big black and white photographs hung on a wall showing handsome young Bob standing in Santa Barbara, California. He held a whip in one hand and a 41 Colt in the other.

This room was Bob's private museum. It formed part of his love of seeing chaos put in order: antiques arranged, gravestones cleaned, the river stabilized. When he replaced his baseball cap with a straw hat, he looked like a pious, invigorating gent, a man who had worked and laughed with movie icons before he realized that White Cloud, Kansas, was his favorite live picture show. He felt at home beside the Missouri River. The land he fled in youth had pulled him back.

We stepped outside. Two dogs raced up the street to Bob. He stooped to pet them, then shook my hand and winked.

"Happy trails to yeh," he said.

"Happy trails to yeh," Bob said.

SECTION THREE:

IOWA
AND NEBRASKA

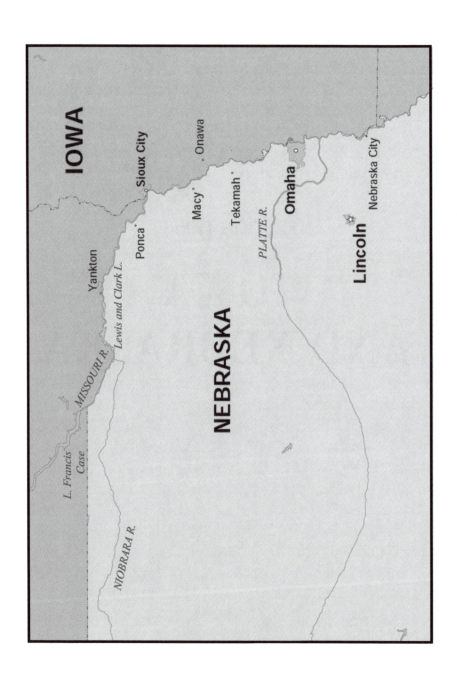

Chapter 16

RESTAURANTE MAMASITAS

The Missouri River became a stream of stories about life, landscape and geography. Many voices repeated a similar message: watch and care for our rivers, educate the young about how these waters nourish the land. Strangers shared insight, opinions, history and wisdom.

I also heard rumblings of disillusionment.

The problem with the 'endangered' Missouri River turned out to be its flow. Steve Gough and Maureen Gallagher had talked about this. Political manipulation caused six dam gates poised above Sioux City to be adjusted to ensure that a monotonous, even stream of water rolled toward St. Louis. This artificial flow was steady enough to keep barge pilots plying water throughout their navigation season — but erased the natural spikes, dips and floods of the river, obliterating sandbars and gravel beds. The flow now endangered plover, tern and sturgeon species.

Was regulating the river for the sake of barge traffic economically worth it? Two men shared conflicting opinions.

Chad Smith sat inside his office in the Mill Towne Building on 6th and J Street in Lincoln, Nebraska. Old advertisements for Peter's

Ammunition — images of a stunned pheasant and a noble dog — hung on a wall.

Chad directed the local field office for American Rivers, a nonprofit organization dedicated to protecting and restoring rivers in the United States. This group had twice listed the Missouri River as the most endangered waterway in the nation. Chad spoke about the river before it was channeled — the way he might talk about a dog before it was castrated.

American Rivers advocated that the Corps of Engineers begin altering the Missouri's flow at least twice a year, letting water gush wildly so that swirls and vortices might resurrect the habitat of endangered species. Chad criticized the practice of maintaining the steady level of the Lower Missouri to keep barge companies afloat.

"There's no economic justification for it," he told me. "The Corps of Engineers' own numbers say there's an average of something like one to three barge tows per day on 735 miles of river. Barges on the Missouri River each year only carry three tenths of one percent of all the grain harvested in these lower states. Navigationists talk about this huge boon to agriculture; how the river's a vital artery for moving grain. But 99.7 percent of grain grown and harvested in these lower four basin states goes by truck or rail. Navigators don't quibble with that because it's true."

Chad's voice vibrated with irritation. "It's never panned out. People like Bill Beacom say that even the presence of one barge on the river holds rail rates down and, if you take that away, there's reduced competition. Agricultural economists from Iowa State, the University of Nebraska and Kansas State have all said that's just hooey."

Chad rocked back and forth in his chair. He believed this argument about competition was a facetious betrayal of common sense. His body language radiated disdain for the almost mind-blowing stranglehold barges still kept on the Missouri River.

"If you have that little traffic, why would it even be conceivable for rail lines to pay attention? The analogy is this: if I were to go home today and open a hamburger stand in my front yard, then McDonalds and Wendies and Burger King would suddenly drop their prices to compete with me. That's the kind of scale we're talking about. The navigation industry has a broken leg to stand on.

"A lot of people with powerful friends in Congress still believe that the Endangered Species Act doesn't apply out here; that science functions differently on the Missouri River. Some entrenched interests have owned and operated the river for fifty, sixty years. They don't want change. In this part of the country, change is bad. We have to break through that, ultimately."

Was he optimistic about the future?

"I'm a Cornhusker football fan so I think in terms of the running game. What we're doing is kind of running the ball forward three yards in a cloud of dust. Eventually we'll get into the End Zone. That's the kind of the process we're engaged in now. Slow and incremental. But we'll get there."

Chad had mentioned the opinion of Bill Beacom. I tracked Bill down at a conference about the Missouri River in Great Falls, Montana. He stood hawk-nosed and robust in a bright Hawaiian shirt, reminding me of other boat pilots famous for wearing bright clothes (one nineteenth century steamboat pilot named Joe Oldham was known for his "extravagance in personal adornment," including fur mittens that reached to his elbows and "kid gloves of the most delicate hue").

Bill consulted on navigation issues. He began immersing himself in the subject in 1955 when he started driving piles and building dikes on the Missouri River.

"I was out on the river when I was just a youngster," he said. "It's like a shoemaker's son grows up in a shop. He learns to make shoes. Or if you grow up on a farm, you farm. I grew up in a river family and went to the river."

Once there, Bill was attracted to the prospect of navigating.

"It provides a challenge. Kind of an adrenaline thing. Like flying a jet airplane. There wasn't that many people that could do it successfully. Current's swift, it takes a lot of time to stop when you're southbound."

Bill's voice was deep. His opinions were outspoken. During the conference Bill had no fear of challenging speakers during question sessions and did not hesitate to share his viewpoints.

"As population increases the necessity for using waterways increases, because they're so user friendly to the environment," he said. "It's something apparent in Europe and other developed countries. Pollution-wise they're much more friendly. You don't have noise because generally rivers are in remote agricultural areas where you don't have to listen to 'em.

"From an environmentalists standpoint, you could make a good case that all interstate highways should be removed because of deer that get killed trying to cross them. If deer were an endangered species, would you take out the highways? No, you wouldn't. You'd figure out a way to keep the deer from getting hit, and I think that we're in that situation with rivers. I don't think that any country that has waterways can economically afford to ignore them."

Any proposal to wipe out barge traffic irked Bill.

"If we do something to regulate navigation like what is being proposed by environmental groups, we'll destroy navigation. It doesn't make sense for one economic opportunity to completely cancel out another. If it wasn't for rivers, railroads probably wouldn't be where they're at today because competition is the mother of necessity. Railroads had to adapt or get better. And they did. And the U.S. citizen and the U.S. economy is the beneficiary."

Although erecting dams on the Upper Missouri flooded out thousands of acres, Chad appreciated how recreation along the reservoirs generated tens of millions of dollars for state economies.

"Dam removal is not an option," Chad told me.

Bill thought otherwise.

Historian Steven Ambrose, author of *Undaunted Courage,* a book about the Lewis and Clark expedition, spoke at the conference in Great Falls. When Ambrose applauded the notion of dismantling all dams along the Missouri River during the next century, Bill asked him pointed questions, challenging the prospect. He considered dismantling dams akin to severing a national tendon. Upstream dams, after all, control downstream flows vital to barging and boating interests.

"You saw Stephen Ambrose get up there and speak," Bill said.

"His idea of what the Missouri River needs to be is American Rivers' idea. Even though they might posture themselves and say 'oh no, we don't want to take out the dams,' they do. If you take out dams there will be no fishing or navigation. Or flood control. We're going to have a whole lot of people come from the east and west coast and ride down there like Stephen does in a canoe and camp at night and get eat up by mosquitoes. That's where they want to go. And I don't think that's where the nation should go."

Irrespective of dams, did barges really provide necessary competition to lower rail rates? While enjoying a cold beer and a taco dinner outside Lincoln, the answer turned irrefutable.

After speaking with Chad, I drove southeast of Lincoln past the Country Bible Church while listening to a harp rendition of *Nightingale* on National Public Radio.

While driving, I reflected on the barging situation. It seemed ridiculous to sacrifice three endangered species in order to maintain a water level that kept a dwindling handful of barge pilots employed. This traffic was shrinking along the Missouri River. Was it worth sacrificing a sturgeon species that had existed for more than seventy-million years to keep barging alive? During the following weeks, both experienced biologists and dedicated Corps of Engineers staff convinced me that the answer was no. But economics and competition were other matters.

I stopped in the snug rural town of Bennet and walked inside Mamasitas Restaurante. The atmosphere was a blend of banter of city visitors and the drawl of local retirees. I spread past newspaper articles on the table before me and sipped a Dos Equis beer.

The restaurant owner walked over.

"Hi," he chimed, then sat in the booth.

"I'm Dennis," he began.

"My mother's Mexican. My dad's German," he said. "I got tired of the bad food in Lincoln and decided to open this restaurant. We've been running almost ten years. My mother still makes our tortillas."

Dennis was obliquely sniffing out what I was up to while I chiseled away at his own life, prying into his history, his future, his story. We were like spies gathering information about each other.

Dennis Gardner's Latin features did not poke through his appearance but emerged from his manner instead. He was hospitable without brandishing any overt agenda, was curious about the doings of other men. Dennis sat at the table ravenous not for facts, football scores, or statistics, but for surprise. He was on the prowl, a man seeking plot or drama to light up his Mamasitas. He yearned for the outré because it reflected the reality of his own restaurant — a successful, semi-secluded foreign nook in a small Nebraskan town. Seeing a stranger scrawling notes on loose napkins and poring over newspaper clippings hinted at an interesting story.

He asked about my trip.

"You're a writer! Need pictures? A National Geographic photographer lives three miles up the road."

"Thanks, but I'm okay. Is business good?"

"Sure. There's a one or two hour wait on weekend nights."

"What did you do before this?"

"Railway engineer."

"Where did you work?"

"City of Lincoln's a big hub. I worked all sides. Near the river, I worked as a brakeman on branch lines. That was '77, '78. Became an engineer in '80. At 2:15, 2:30 in the morning, I'd be riding beside the Missouri River and see a barge coming up with its lights on. Only other person out there. He'd toot at me, I'd toot back. Saying hello in the dark. Not two boats passing in the night, but two people hauling goods. Same business, same line of work."

A waitress appeared.

"Another beer?" she asked.

"Sure. Menu, too."

Dennis studied my map of the state, recalling his own memories.

"Was flooding a problem when they built the railway lines?" I asked.

"They tried to avoid it," he said. "Hugged the bluffs. There were still washouts. Burlington Northern ran the east side of the Missouri. Our rail line was on the west.

"I worked branch lines," Dennis continued. "Rock Port to Shenandoah. Corning to Fairfax. Now all closed. Now that roads can access grain silos, semi trucks do it. The towns out in eastern Nebraska are all about five miles apart, twelve at most. That was the distance a farmer could haul grain to a silo in his buggy."

Graceful feminine fingers set a Mexican cerveza on the tablecloth.

"Anything to eat?" she asked.

"Small taco," I answered, while thoughts raced away.

Minutes later, I bit into a Mamasitas' taco. It was as thick as a mature pine cone, a steaming welt of cheese and ground beef pellets as well sorted as river sand. This combination of rich food and reminiscence with Dennis formed a little vacation for the evening.

All other customers had left by ten in the evening. I looked outside. Corn stalks reflected the sprinkle of star glow. Unrushed countryside surrounded the restaurant. Darkness lay two minutes in either direction. But true illumination came from what Dennis revealed that evening. How could barges provide 'essential' competition to railroads when trucks hauling grain did the same?

In the space of two beers and a beef taco inside Mamasitas, the argument that barges offset rail rates shattered into fragments.

I thanked Dennis. When least expected, the trail of travel had delivered another insightful encounter.

Chapter 17

IMAGES FROM VANISHED CULTURE

I tried to imagine riverside life in the nineteenth century before smallpox decimated tribes along the Missouri River. Where imagination failed, art succeeded.

Even before smallpox ripped through the high plains, artists and authors expressed fears that the onslaught of immigrants to the West would change Indian culture forever. In 1814, author Washington Irving wrote of the Indians: "they will vanish like vapor from the face of the earth. Their very history will be lost in forgetfulness."

His words were prophetic.

Soon after Lewis and Clark's expedition cracked open the Missouri River to extended exploration, an unlikely duo moved upstream in the midst of fur traders: the German Prince Maximilian of Wied-Neuwid, and Swiss artist Karl Bodmer. Maximilian was fifty years old, an officer experienced on Napoleonic battlefields. He came to the Missouri River to record the natural face of North America and its "aboriginal population." Indian customs first caught Maximilian's interest fifteen years earlier when he explored South America. That trip had partially incited him to launch his new adventure. While the prince wrote about what he saw on the trip, his twenty-three-year-old accomplice Bodmer painted scenes of all they encountered. Today, Bodmer's depictions of a vanished lifestyle form their trip's strongest legacy. Many of his paintings hang in the Joslyn Art Museum in Omaha, Nebraska. To learn more about their trip, I stopped at the museum to see the paintings of Western tribesmen.

Before these two men reached St. Louis, they stayed at the town of New Harmony on Indiana's Wabash River. There, Maximilian visited biologists Thomas Say and Charles Alexandre Lesueur while Bodmer began painting. His scenes included a vista of this simple and stately village: broad streets, painted wood homes, picket fence, a man in a top hat mumbling to a friend and a shuffling woman draped in a shawl. The scene's tranquility contrasted to the rugged, howling universe they were to meet further west up the Missouri River.

When Maximilian and Bodmer finally arrived in St. Louis in March 1833, they contacted William Clark, who was now superintendent of Indian Affairs for western tribes. Clark convinced Maximilian that the best way to meet tribes was by traveling along the river and staying at fur trading posts. Maximilian agreed. He secured permission to enter Indian Territory and then booked passage on the *Yellowstone*, a steamer belonging to the American Fur Company (one of Bodmer's paintings shows the boat floating on the snag-laden Missouri River).

Their journey upriver turned into a visual smorgasbord. The duo traveled to what is now North Dakota where they slept before fireplaces inside Mandan huts. Bodmer painted a tenebrous scene titled *Das Innere Der Hutte Eines Mandan Hauptlings*, or the *Interior of the Hut of a Mandan Chief*. Light from a ceiling hole illuminates a family of five, three dogs and two snorting ponies.

Bodmer painted even when temperatures plunged so deep that mercury solidified in Maximilian's thermometer. His works included his gray blue *Mandan Village Mih-Tutta-Hang-Kusch* showing Indians huddled in blankets lugging firewood across the frozen Missouri River. I shivered just looking at the image of an anguished dog huddled against a chilled horse.

At Montana's Fort McKenzie in the fall of 1833, Karl and the prince awoke one day to a volley of musket shots. They peered over the fort walls at a prairie coated with Assiniboine and Cree Indians. Bodmer's painting of the battle shows warriors fighting to the death. One Indian aims a spear at point-blank range while another peels off a dripping scalp. Others rush at enemies with their tomahawks, bows and arrows while soldiers on fort walls pump rifle shots toward more than six hundred intruders. This battle tableau was reminiscent of a war movie.

Maximilian and Bodmer were so shaken by the sight of this battle that they abandoned their journey to the Missouri River headwaters and instead returned downriver. Maximilian eventually returned to his castle on the Rhine and Bodmer went to Paris. Neither ever returned to the U.S. This pair foresaw the coming demise of the days of Indian glory along the high plains. Incoming settlers, importing disease with them, soon infected the Indian population along this wet Missouri River corridor.

During decades following Lewis and Clark's upriver journey, settlers who used the Missouri as their highway to the interior came into growing contact with riverside tribes — including the Hidatsa, Arikara and Mandan — and brought with them deadly consequences.

In Pennsylvania in 1763, a commander of the British forces named Sir Jeffrey Amherst suggested, in one of his letters, infecting certain Indians tribes with smallpox by 'means of blankets as well as to try every other method.' Whether or not this rudimentary biological warfare was ever launched is disputed. But smallpox eventually did spread west. In 1837, a steamboat chugging upriver from St. Louis picked up three Arikara women and their children at Fort Bellevue, above the confluence of the Missouri and Platte Rivers. These women contracted the smallpox virus from an infected deckhand. By the time the boat reached Fort Clark, some Indians had become ill, but recuperated to a degree. Near the Knife River, these Arikara disembarked for Mitutanka village where the tribe recently moved to live with the Mandans. Meanwhile, inside their bodies this 'rotting face' sickness as they called it lay coiled and ready to spring. When smallpox did strike, it hit hard. In three months the disease killed fifteen hundred Mandan. Within two years, the smallpox spread throughout the villages of Hidatsa, Arikara, Assiniboine, Blackfeet and other tribes and killed twenty-thousand. Immune to herbal remedies, smallpox cut a swath of misery across the high plains.

Artists, among others, lamented the speed with which tribes were extinguished along the Missouri River. In 1841, the painter George Catlin wrote in a book summarizing his life's work: "I have, for many years past, contemplated the noble races of red men who are now...melting away at the approach of civilization."

Catlin was a lawyer who was so inspired by seeing a group of tribesmen visiting Philadelphia that he dedicated his life to studying American Indians. By 1837, he had produced 470 paintings which captured both dignified and harrowing scenes within cultures on the verge of collapse. Some of Catlin's paintings show life in tribal villages, including his *Mandan Buffalo Dance,* in which a band of dancing men wear bison heads and necklaces.

Catlin was appalled at how greedy land speculators and asinine government policies helped wipe out Indian cultures. An image illustrating this was the hand colored lithograph *Wi-Jun-Jon, an Assinneboin Chief.* It shows two images of the leader. On the left the chief is "Going to Washington" and holds an ornate peace pipe and wears a robe, moccasins and headdress regalia. To the right he is "Returning to his Home" fitted with gifts from President Jackson: a black top hat and dapper blue suit with gold epaulets. He also carries an oriental fan and gray umbrella. A scabbard dangles from his waist and he puffs a cigarette. The story goes that when Wi-Jun-Jon returned home wearing this new finery with silver buttons he ranted about his encounters in the city. Neighbors tolerated this new behavior at first. Soon, finding they could no longer trust their chief, they supposedly murdered him.

After smallpox ravaged tribal villages, a Lakota Indian named Spotted Tail told of his tribe's desperate struggle to survive on dwindling reservation lands in what are now the Dakotas.

"There is a time appointed for all things. Think for a moment how many multitudes of animal tribes we have destroyed; look upon the snow that appears today — tomorrow it is water. Listen to the dirge of the dry leaves that were green and vigorous but a few months before! We are part of that life and it seems our time has come."

In 1919, the artist N.C. Wyeth painted a brash, poignant scene epitomizing the eclipse of Indian culture. His large oil image advertising Fisk Cord Tires showed Indian parents dragging a child and belongings on a crude wooden travois along a road. A passing automobile kicked dust in their faces, forcing the adults to wince and cower.

When Indians were forced onto reservations, part of their identity vanished. In what became the state of Nebraska, one reservation boundary was defined by the Missouri River. When the river changed course, it caused a lengthy court battle. The pivotal question was this: if the Missouri River defines property boundaries, who owns land when the river moves? The answer turned out to be a matter of timing.

Chapter 18

BLACKBIRD BEND

As I approached Macy, Nebraska, a spear of lightning divided the view. A squall line hustled overhead. With a Corps of Engineers Navigation Chart in hand I walked through wet, pungent grass above the Missouri River and aligned the map to the landscape. I then stared down toward Blackbird Bend.

In the 1700s, the Omaha Indians migrated along the Big Sioux River and established their 'Big Village' south of where Sioux City lies today in Iowa. By 1750, the tribe occupied a large mesh of land in what is now northern Nebraska and Iowa.

In contrast to their aggressive Chief Blackbird, the Omaha were peaceful people who never fought European immigrants moving west. They wrought their sustenance from hunting and agriculture and believed in an inseparable union between earth and sky. They laid out lodges within bisected circular villages. 'Sky People' lived in this circle's northern half and attended the tribe's spiritual needs while the southern half of the tribes' physical welfare was managed by 'Earth People.'

When Lewis and Clark navigated this section of the Missouri River in 1804, they visited Blackbird's grave.

"After the rain was over Captain Lewis, myself, and ten men ascended the hill... (under which there were some fine springs) to the top of a high point where the Maha king Blackbird was buried four years ago," Clark wrote.

"From the top of this knoll, the river may be seen meandering for sixty or seventy miles."

The men strapped a white flag on a pole and hoisted this over the grave mound, leaving a souvenir of their visit.

Three weeks after leaving St. Louis I arrived and parked in the reservation town of Macy, Nebraska. A huge man, the color of a chestnut, radiated calm certainty from a bench. I told him I was looking for 'Wayne.' Days earlier someone provided Wayne Tyndall's name as a source of Omaha tribal history.

"Take this road uphill, then right on the highway," he said and nudged an elbow. "First house on the left. Maroon."

Minutes later I approached Tyndall's home. It lay in a sea of uncut grass. From a corner perch, Wayne nodded.

"Come on up," he said in a low tone. He motioned to his deck bordered by a green trellis fence. Wayne was wearing gray trousers and sat perched on a cast iron stool, his eyes dark, and his presence calm. Two diffident dogs at his feet lapped their tongues at nothing.

Wayne Tyndall was born in the town of Winnebago in 1935. He grew up in a log cabin near the Missouri River, which the Omaha called *Neshuda* — Smoky Waters. Big Elk, his great grandfather, was the last full-blooded Indian chief of the Omaha; his father trapped and sold furs in Sioux City. As a youngster Wayne met many distinguished visitors who visited his family's home, including his mother's friend John Neihardt (author of *Black Elk Speaks*) and anthropologist Margaret Mead, who stayed with his grandmother when she studied the Omaha in 1932.

Wayne Tyndall in Macy, Nebraska

After graduating from university, Wayne spent six years working for the Navy. While based in Georgia he came to believe that blacks were often treated with a disrespect similar to the people on his own reservation. This observation helped him embark on a journey to improve the lives of the Omaha Indians. Yet when he returned to his own reservation, his peers' attitudes troubled him.

"It's hard to live on the reservation," he told me. "Not an easy thing. Too often people make wrong choices. 'Be proud,' I told them. 'Stand up for yourself.' "

Before he became vice-chairman of the Board of Directors of the Omaha Tribe of Nebraska, Wayne worked with the Bureau of Indian Affairs. These years of work took him to Hawaii, Cuba,

France, Italy and Spain; he had retired less than a year before we met.

"Poor health," he said. "Quit working. Got no exercise and gained too much weight. Used to weigh 140, then it went up to 280."

Clouds smoldered above us, uncertain of whether to rain or disperse. Wayne rattled off dates and shards of history. He talked with an urgency, as though cleansing past tensions from himself. When I asked about the Missouri River, Wayne insisted on sharing history about the Omaha's land. Only by knowing this, he insisted, could I appreciate his tribe's determination to solve the problem of Blackbird Bend.

The Omaha tribe's original land stretched from the Platte River in the south to where the Niobrara River meets the Missouri River in the north. Its western boundary cut through Elkhorn River. A treaty ratified in 1854 set new boundaries for the Omaha people, reducing their traditional land from four million acres to a reservation of only 300,000 acres. This new home was defined by five straight edges on its western side and by the Missouri River to the east. Once informed about where they would live, families gathered their meager belongings together and moved. When relocated, Wayne said, "they put in gardens and put up earth lodges."

In the 1840s, Brigham Young and his traveling band of Mormon followers stopped in to stay with the Omaha.

"Gave us sickness. Used our wood," Wayne complained. "After two years they went to Utah. Built an empire. Never thanked the Omahas, never helped us again."

Unlike the Mormons, some visitors to the reservation never departed. After the Santee Sioux War in Minnesota, displaced Winnebago Indians sought shelter with the Omaha.

"They built rafts of cottonwood, came downriver," Wayne said. "After they landed their boats nearby, they came ashore, sick with tuberculosis. The Omaha gave them food, corn, teepees, robes and let them stay here."

This influx led to another treaty in 1865 that sold the northern third of the Omaha Reservation to the Winnebagos.

This action bewildered Wayne.

"They spoke a different language, had different customs — we never really did get along. There's still problems. The Omaha gave up 100,000 acres to them."

Soon after this, the Omaha learned of 'allotments.'

According to an 1870 Quaker Peace Policy in Nebraska, whites had two means to 'civilize' the Omaha. One was to enforce the concept of private property; the other was to encourage agriculture. Fine print within the 'lofty' 1854 treaty contained a provision allowing the U.S. President to send teams out to survey the Omaha Reservation and distribute its land to residents in allotments. Based on this provision, the 1882 Omaha Allotment Act divided the reservation into patches of land for each member of the tribe. There were about a thousand Omaha Indians at the time. Couples were given 160 acres each and single people older than sixteen received eighty acres.

"However, the Omaha didn't want allotments," Wayne told me. "They wanted to hold land in common."

Allotments resulted in disaster: crop production took a nosedive; cultural bonds eroded across the reservation. Allotments eradicated the common land essential to tribal identity. Once allotments were created the Omaha were free to sell or lease their turf to non-Indians. This shrunk the tribe's property base, threatening the integrity of the reservation. Sixteen years after the law was enacted, a report showed that 112,000 out of 140,000 allotted acres on the Omaha and Winnebago reservations were being leased to whites. Even six years before this report was issued (before he took reign as U.S. President), Theodore Roosevelt assessed the problem and complained about allotments. He suggested that non-Indians be evicted from the Omaha Reservation.

By 1887, the truth was clear: allotments were a failure. But lawmakers in Washington, DC, reluctant to pay attention to this truth, used this Omaha subdivision as a springboard to launch another act with wider scope: the Dawes Severalty Act, imposing allotments on *all* reservations. Ironically, those lawmakers who created this act referred to allotments on the Omaha Reservation as an example of their success. Most who proffered this travesty never visited the land they divided and spoke with its residents.

By the century's end, the government granted permission for railroads to be laid through the Omaha Reservation. Each line required a half-mile wide easement, more land taken away from the tribe.

"Reduction, division, allotments, easements. What else impacted the Omaha's land?" I asked Wayne.

"This is what really messed us up," he said and tilted his head, befuddled by the act.

"In 1910, a bill was introduced to tax allotted lands. Sudden taxation put many Indians in debt. Delinquent taxes cost the Omahas thousands of acres."

To get out of this financial logjam many families sold land to non-Indians. The result was incredible: by 1976, fully eighty-two percent of land on the Omaha and Winnebago reservations was owned by non-Indians.

Finally, drought.

"The Omahas sold land cheap because of the drought of the 1930s," Wayne said. His own grandmother was a white woman of

Irish descent who lived in a splendid home with four scrubbed porches, an oak paneled interior and stained glass windows. The drought thrashed even this relatively well off woman.

"She lost everything. Moved by the river and lived in a log cabin my uncle built for her."

This slicing and dicing and selling of land led to much legal wrangling: who should have ultimate authority over laws on reservation lands? Non-Indians said the states should. The states agreed. In 1953, Indians in Nebraska were brought under state jurisdiction.

Wayne opened up a cream colored album of clippings. One article showed a photograph of him holding a telephone and quoted him saying: "No Indian can receive a fair trial in Thurston County."

Upset at what he considered a corrosive system that led to unfair treatment of the Omaha, Wayne spearheaded an effort to take tribal matters away from both state government and county control and hand them over to federal authority. After battling the issue for two years, his tenacity paid off. In 1970, the Secretary of the Interior signed an order of 'retrocession,' removing criminal jurisdiction on the reservation from the state and returning it to the federal government. The Omaha were jubilant. It gave the tribe their own judicial and law enforcement agencies and criminal jurisdiction over their land. Except for thirteen major crimes, including kidnapping and homicide, all crimes would be tried on the reservation. Others would be brought to a federal court in the city of Omaha.

Clouds still lurked above the porch. Wayne shifted in his seat. His somber history of tribal land formed a prologue to a story about the Missouri River and the case of the Blackbird Bend.

In February 1966, Omaha Indians complained that part of their original reservation land was stolen. Decades after the reservation was surveyed in 1867, the tawny Missouri River shifted course and cut onto reservation land to the west.

"The river shifted, leaving land on the Iowa side," Wayne emphasized.

Between this new flowpath and the dried up old riverbed lay land that once belonged to the reservation. Because it was now across the river, non-Indian farmers assumed the land was outside the reservation and up for grabs.

"Farmers squatted, making money off it. Gettin' rich for years," Wayne complained.

But the Omaha were adamant that the territory still belonged to them. This brought up a pivotal question: if the Missouri River formed the reservation's eastern boundary, what happened when the river moved? The answer was that it depended on how fast it changed course.

In the fall of 1967, when newspapers ran Dick Tracy comic strips and advertised Elizabeth Taylor and Richard Burton starring in the movie *The Taming of the Shrew*, articles also told how Omaha Indians took their grievance to the U.S. District Court. They said that between 2,900 and 3,100 acres of land, assigned to them 'in perpetuity' by an 1854 treaty, were now owned by white farmers.

The simple land dispute went unresolved in courts for six years. This delay incited a group of Omaha men to move onto this riverside turf. They set up a teepee and tents along the riverbank to demonstrate against what they considered the illegal use of Omaha territory. An injunction soon forced them off the land, based on a simple technicality: none of the seven men belonged to the Tribal Council.

Two years later, the group returned. This time the same legal tactic could no longer work: their leader Eddie Cline had joined the Tribal Council in the interim. The men set up camp, planted crops, swapped stories and waited while litigation plodded ahead. In 1977, after twenty-one days of testimony, a U.S. District Court Judge ruled that the land at Blackbird Bend no longer belonged to the Omaha. Judge Andrew Bogue sympathized with the Indians' loss and called it a "seemingly unfair situation," yet insisted that the culprit was not white interlopers but the Missouri River's meandering ways.

The outcome of the case pivoted on whether this strip of land was created by 'accretion' or 'avulsion.' Did the river move in a slow, gradual and imperceptible way to its new alignment, letting new land 'accrete' on the opposite bank? Or did it make a fast, rampant jump to its new course during a flood, gouging an avulsion into riverside acres like incisors chomping into an apple? The defense claimed slower accretion as cause.

Cline's reaction was swift.

"We certainly say from the attitude of the Judge during the trial that he is a real redneck," he stated. "…he is absolutely anti-Indian."

The case was appealed.

Meanwhile, a group of police, including six tribal officers, drove onto the disputed land. They dished out a fresh injunction: the Omaha again had to vacate the three thousand acres. The group ignored this, supported by another ruling that let them stay put until the case was finally settled.

This nonviolent showdown ended in 1980 when the Circuit Court of Appeals ruled that the Missouri River changed course not because of accretion, but avulsion. After fourteen years of effort, the Omaha took back their land at Blackbird Bend.

"Everything's been an uphill battle for us," Wayne lamented. "I'd fight again," he coughed. "Fight the rest of my life if I had the energy."

Wayne stood. He pulled his squeaky screen door open and stepped inside to put his album and articles away. He returned to sit with folded hands.

For the balance of the afternoon Wayne stopped talking about land disputes and court battles and transformed to a man seeking peace on his porch. When I stood to leave, he encouraged me to stay. He had stories to tell.

Having no timetable and only a vague destination, I sat back to listen. What was to have been a thirty minute talk with Wayne stretched on for more than three hours. He told stories and shared memories. He read a short story he once wrote, titled *Shoes from God*. The story went as follows:

One Friday, when he was ten years old, Wayne's mother told him she was going into town. She wanted to kill time until her husband finished his work stabilizing the Missouri River for the Corps of Engineers. Although he had no shoes Wayne ran after her. It was June. A light wind blew a scent of wild roses past hedgerows. During this walk, Wayne's intuition told him to move to a field. He stepped that way, looked down and saw a pair of brown penny loafers. Although they had been in the rain all night, the shoes still smelt new. He put them on and ran after his mother, showing what he found. She smiled and suggested that perhaps greater powers helped him because he was always a good boy.

"From that day," Wayne told me, "I've always tried to follow God's footsteps and be a loving, caring human."

I stood to thank Wayne, a venerable and unsung hero of tribal progress. He shook my hand and asked me to visit again.

Dusk crept in. Under the sky's crimson light I got ready to leave, feeling a little wiser than hours before. Another life had revealed itself to me, passing on its smattering of knowledge and insights. Just before I stepped away, Wayne mentioned a world beyond this, a universe greater than any victories that he or others helped bring the Omaha people.

"I'm ready to leave," he told me with a sigh. "If there is a place to go, I know I have a space there."

Chapter 19

BUFFALO BILL

After a damp week in Nebraska, finally, sunshine warmed the state.

In the town of Tekamah, less than ten miles west of the Missouri River, I stopped at Greg's Barber Shop, nestled beside Dick's Western Store. While Greg wrapped a cool towel around my neck, another customer clattered inside. He wore mud crusted boots with zigzag treads. He sat and fidgeted, then stood again.

"Got to get my glasses to read this magazine," he mumbled.

"I got a pair you can use," Greg offered.

"Yeah? 'Bout 150s?"

"Somethin' like that. Try 'em."

He took the glasses, sat and read.

Life was not complicated in Tekamah, Nebraska.

North of Tekamah in Decatur, Nebraska, I pulled off Highway 75, paid a seventy-five cent bridge toll and followed Highway 175 to the Lewis and Clark Center across the Missouri River in Onawa, Iowa. A sign below its tilted flagpole announced that this was the second campground of Lewis and Clark in what later became Monoma County.

At the lakeside, a huge man with peeling pink hands stood on a dock. He volunteered to tell visitors about the Corps of Discovery expedition and stood next to a replica of the original Lewis and Clark keelboat that bobbed in Blue Lake. He wore buckskins and a hat even in eighty-degree heat and called himself 'Buffalo Bill Sanders.' The fact he had not already passed out from heat exhaustion was more intriguing than the boat he described.

Replica of keel boat used by Lewis and Clark to ascend the Missouri River

"Blue Lake was the main channel of the Missouri when the expedition passed through," Bill told the ad hoc group that meandered across the dock. A thin physician from Tucson asked how the Corps of Discovery fared with Indians.

"They had presents," Bob explained. "Fish hooks, mirrors, tobacco, blankets and peace medals. They handed out flags, telling the Indians of the great white father in Washington and encouraged them to get along with their neighbors. Well they already did get along with neighbors — most of 'em anyway.

"Course, like today, there was hanky panky in Congress back then. President Jefferson acquired cash for the trip before title to the land had even been appropriated. And the Louisiana Purchase? I've got an Omaha Indian friend who says that this was the greatest land grab of all time."

Bill rocked his wrapped body sideways.

"I think it's the greatest expedition our country ever went on," he continued. "I include the World Wars, Desert Storm, even going to the moon. When we went to the moon, we knew where we were going, knew where to land. These guys went into the unknown. They were makin' maps every day of where they had been. They met with over fifty different tribes on the way out and back and only had a confrontation with two of 'em. Minor one with the Teton Sioux up at Pierre in the Dakotas, a fierce testy bunch of Indians, and later with Blackfeet further west.

"It was a great feat of exploration. Scientific wise, we learned of 122 different animals unknown to white man before this trip, including the prairie dog, magpie, antelope and mountain goat and 178 different plant species. The captains were good at drawing and descriptions. Put in meticulous detail of what they saw. They reported on rocks and minerals, plants and animals. Were able to do celestial navigation. They had brand new mercury thermometers, recorded temperatures up in Mandan, North Dakota — like 40 below zero some days."

I asked Bob where he would join the expedition if he could go back in time.

"Top of the Great Divide," he answered, referring to the Continental Divide. "Lookin' both ways in the mountains, where water flows towards the Mississippi or towards the Pacific Ocean. Would have been a marvelous sight. Or when they first spied the Pacific Ocean, breathtaking moment. Or meeting with different

Indian tribes, like when they met the Shoshone out west and were able to trade for horses they needed to get over the mountains. Exciting time that."

After the others left, Bill led me inside a small rotunda store that sold souvenirs, such as copies of *The Wild Critter Cookbook* and *Best Cookin' within a Jillion Miles of Des Moines*.

Bill then described building the replica of the Lewis and Clark keelboat. Over a decade earlier, up to twenty-five volunteers called "The Friends of Discovery" spent weekends on the job, keeping the design of the boat faithful to William Clark's original drawings. They also constructed copies of the expedition's two pirogues, flat-bottomed boats fashioned from cedar planks and oak frames.

"Kinduva labor of love," Bill admitted.

After hearing about floating along the Missouri River, I was ready to get on the water. To do that, it was a time for company.

Chapter 20

CAPSIZE

A friend named Dave Grove spent thirteen years suing contractors for a law firm in San Diego. Jaded by depositions, oral arguments and summary judgments, he awoke one dawn and decided to cleave away from his partnership position. He sold his suave house and SUV, bought a backpack and Eurail Pass and spent months in Europe freebooting past alps, fjords and drizzling glens. When he finished, he joined me back in the U.S. to canoe a segment of the Missouri River. A month after I left St. Louis, we met in Nebraska and decided to canoe a 'wild and scenic' river segment.

The two of us crowded our belongings into Six Pac and drove less than a half hour northwest of Sioux City to Ponca. We parked on a hill and walked to cliffs that overlooked the Missouri River at the point where it transforms from a loping liquid wolf into a leashed hydraulic greyhound. Both aspects of the river were visible here — its wild northern torrent and its more channeled southern section.

Tornados ripped through Nebraska that night. Hailstones the size of ice cubes cracked against the roof of Six Pac ("Twisters Hit," blazed the next day's headline in the *Omaha World Herald*).

In the morning, we went to a restaurant that opened at 5:00 am for farmers. A homely tapestry on one wall showed the town's eleven principal buildings. Five of these, Dave pointed out, were churches.

Outside, flags flew before each home. If Nebraska was the heartland, Ponca formed its ventricular valve.

After breakfast we drove to a grocery store and stocked up on supplies: Snickers bars, salami, peanuts, beef jerky, Pop Tarts and a bottle of Bacardi. We then followed directions along a convoluted trail to a patch of riverbank land that belonged to a man named Marlin who agreed to rent us a canoe. From here the river looked rough and gorgeous as it wound toward craggy bluffs. Dave was so pleased with our remote campsite that he twisted open the Bacardi. By dusk, both the sky and our faces were glowing.

Our campsite location was strategic; it was located midway between the put-in and take-out points for our fifty mile canoe trip. When the first day of paddling ended, we only had to haul our canoe onto grass where boxes of food and a firepit waited at the campsite.

Marlin roused us the next dawn with a friendly shout. He pointed to a silver canoe strapped to his battered pickup truck — our downriver transportation. To get to the put-in-point I sat in the torn and half stuffed passenger seat of his truck. Dave squeezed into the back bed between a pile driver and a Flintstones lunch pail. Marlin then motored north toward Gavin's Point Dam.

"I bought this truck for twenty five bucks," he bragged. "If it goes to heck, why I'll just park it under a tree and walk away. Bought another truck like it for twenty dollars," he added. "For spare parts."

The designated fifty-nine mile-long 'wild and scenic' segment of the Missouri River begins below Gavins Point Dam and forms part of the border between the states of Nebraska and South Dakota. This snag-riddled water, untouched by engineers, is as glorious and malicious as the day it choked the life out of the steamboat *Arabia*.

Once we arrived at the dam at Gavins Point, Marlin backed his truck down a concrete ramp and unhooked rubber bungee cords to release the aluminum canoe. A minute later Dave and I sat inside the wobbly craft and started paddling downriver. The weather was clear and our task was simple: to float and paddle and gnaw beef jerky and cell phone friends pouting in distant traffic jams. After twenty-two miles on the river, we would nudge against Marlin's shore, strip off sunglasses from our burnt faces and pop open beers.

Marlin Roth (left) and Dave (in truck) about to set off to the Missouri River.

Dave was the experienced canoeist. He sat in the rear and talked about 'J turns' and 'baling methods.' During our first minutes afloat he mistook the sight of catfish for snags and sent us paddling in zig-zags to avoid fish swimming in S curves. We next dug our aluminum paddles deep and headed toward midstream. Miles later we spied two bald eagles weighing down the parabolic branch of a cottonwood tree. We pulled over to a pebbled beach to inspect the pair. There were no humans in sight for miles around us.

For an hour we paddled through gooey blonde eddies without seeing another boat. The waves were pert and sunshine kept the temperature optimal. We laughed at our fortune — glorious weather on a vacant river. Life was bliss. We paddled toward a roiling eddy line.

"Right! *Right!*" Dave hollered.

I eyed a coin-sized snag poking out of the water ahead. No, I thought. Left. No, no, Dave's the *expert*. I snapped off two strokes to the right. Too late. The meeting of bow on bough ruined us. What looked like a wood knot the size of a trench coat button jabbed the aluminum and pitched us out of the canoe like a sneeze. Muddy water flushed inside and we waded groin deep in the river pulling our transport to shore. The truth was as transparent as disagreeable — our canoe was as vulnerable to snags as an eggshell to a Vibram boot sole. A flounder in deeper water would have ended our trip.

After putting in again, we covered two dozen miles in five hours, passing crimson petals of Indian paintbrush flowers, jammed driftwood and magnificent eddies. Dave recognized the clump of loose cottonwoods that marked Marlin's land, distinctive because our host had felled no trees along his shoreline soil. Before hauling our canoe ashore, we paddled to a sandbar across from camp. There we stepped up to a red nylon rope where a sign warned us to stay out of this arena of protected tern and plover eggs. We watched these skittish birds dash across warm sand grains, then paddled back accross the river to a slough that cut into Marlin's land.

That night we ate beef jerky and drank lukewarm beer. Soon, Marlin joined us again. He sat at his own riverbank picnic table, half buried in tall grass.

Marlin's shaggy land was filled with forests that looked rum dark and haunted. Gnarly weeds bloomed in fields. The state of the land mirrored the wild river massaging its banks. Why did Marlin leave his riverside acres unkempt? Could he sell them?

"If I had, then you and I couldn't be sittin' here enjoyin' it," he replied. "I've been offered a couple hundred thousand already and I've been broke a long time. Could've used the money. But it's just too nice. I'm trying to make it a park — give it to the state. 'Cause you can't take it with you when you die. And what you can't take with you, you can't control."

His words sounded familiar. Wolf River Bob repeated the same mantra back in White Cloud. I was to hear this same salt-of-the-earth manifesto repeated many times during my months along these waterways: in the long haul, we can't take the goodies we accumulate with us to the grave.

"This land is 120 acres," Marlin claimed with upbeat pride. "I put a little alfalfa out of the trees for deer. Somebody else might come here and bulldoze those trees, put a center pivot irrigator down and farm it. Not me. Just too nice, that's all."

Except for small personal gardens, Marlin was finished with farming. After twenty years of working the land, he was tired of boom-and-bust cycles.

"I farmed five hundred acres at different times — corn, soybeans, oats, alfalfa, hogs, cattle. Whole works. Basically how it always goes is you overspend. Then I had to sell out. We own about a thousand acres, so the land's there. I could spend more money on fuel and repairs and time and break more skin than I could ever get back off it."

He pointed at the protected sandbar. "That's my island," he told us. "I own to the middle of the river."

'My Island' was a sandbar three quarters of a mile long that didn't exist a few years earlier. The same floodwater that scoured Marlin's riverbank had deposited this oblong stretch of beach.

He looked toward the water.

"This is a wild part of the river," he said. "Doesn't get any Corps money or work or rock. It's left to the erosion. Normally the flow is around, say, 32,000 cubic feet per second. When you kick it from thirty-two up to forty-two, that adds quite a bit of water. Dirt and sediment settle out, sort of like a ragin' river. In fact they could turn on the water at Gavins Point Dam and wash this whole island right the heck outta here."

Marlin was just shy of forty, a boyish and upbeat character always on the go — tinkering with his double-dump truck and fleet of half-intact tractors or running his canoeing venture. Marlin hauled antiques to Tucson to try to hawk them, harvested red grapes from his small vineyard and leased out his family acres above the dam at Gavins Point in Nebraska. He welded for cash and grew a smattering of corn at his home along the Missouri River. His tourism venture raised both money and local suspicions. Even after ten years of operating a canoe and tour business, local farmers begrudged his exploits.

"Tourism," he explained, "is just people lookin' around. Not everyone in this area likes that."

That mattered little to Marlin.

"I could have moved to Denver, or Phoenix or Tucson, but I stayed here," he told me as we drove. "No rat race, you know. And it doesn't cost much. Livin' cheap's what it's all about."

By seven the next morning, we were on the river again. The flow was reduced from the day before. We shouldered our paddles tighter to improve progress. The sky turned fractal: splintered crystals and kaleidoscope chips. Farmers and fishermen roused early. A red-tailed crop duster pulled tight above Wynot. An angler wearing an orange cap throttled his skiff past Goat Island and waved.

"Look at the houses," Dave said. He pointed his paddle toward a strip of shoreline trailers. "Marlin could done this. Subdivided his land and sold off chunks."

But he didn't.

This unspoken realization notched up our esteem for the man. Marlin balked at buying a car for more than twenty-five dollars but never considered selling scraggly riverside property for six figures. He'd rather give it away to have it protected.

Marlin's attitude added perspective to the reasons for making this journey. Instead of conforming to the black and white, digital paradigm that divides adult life into two distinct segments — work and retirement, Dave and I had quit our jobs to spend over a year roaming around and to consider alternate ways of conducting this business called life. Encounters with people like Marlin bolstered confidence in our choice. His decision not to follow mainstream attitudes was a dash of chili pepper in the bland soup of predictable lifestyles surrounding him. What made his life attractive was not galactic sophistication, but a determination to live as he liked without giving a hoot toward what the neighbors thought. The river's creed — the truth that Wolf River Bob, Dan Bowen and Marlin all emphasized through their words and actions lay spread before us in washed sunlight: that variety is as essential for healthy rivers as it is for lives of integrity. In both ecology and life the shortest distance between two points rarely forms the most advantageous route. Instead, reality's most vivid and flickering avenues, those packed tightest with vigor, color, wisdom and precious moments, lie along unchanneled, unpredictable routes.

Hollow booms sounded from our left.

"Stay away from the South Dakota side," Dave said, digging his paddle deeper. "Huntin' season's started."

The river widened and narrowed at Cranberry Bottoms. Navigation became confusing from our low vantage point. Islands looked like riverbanks; rivulets resembled the main channel.

"Current's building a sand bar," Dave said ten seconds before we ran onto one. We stepped out and hauled our aluminum pod a dozen yards ahead to deeper water, then repeated this frustrating chore ten times within several miles.

A mile before Ponca, we heard the sound of churning engines and noisy families. We maneuvered between motorboats and hauled the canoe onto a rocky shore. Marlin arrived an hour later. He was groomed for his upcoming dentist's appointment: he wore a clean shirt and sported a freshly braided ponytail. Together we strapped the canoe on his pickup truck.

His truck was a chintzy shebang that smelled of mustard. The dashboard was stuffed with wire cutters, a box of bullets, an empty Visine bottle and a pair of black spectacles without glass. A coffee pot smudged with residue was wedged between seats. His antenna was a rusty coat hangar, and the truck floor surged with tides of loose nuts and bolts. The whole package reeked of entropy. But for twenty-five bucks, who was complaining?

The truck huffed over Nebraska hills. Marlin was rattling on about county history when a plume of smoke darted through his air vent. I yelled, he braked, and we threw the doors open and scrambled outside. The dashboard vanished behind cocoa colored smoke, and we stared inside to see if flames munched at the gear shift. Marlin reached in toward the odometer and tugged a cable. The fire died within seconds.

"Guess my wiring job wasn't so good," he complained, fanning a blue-white cloud away. After getting the heap restarted, we climbed aboard again and Marlin maneuvered down Wynot's Rattlesnake road to the Wiseman Monument. We parked and inspected this stone on a patch of shaded grass. The monument was erected in 1926. The story it commemorated put the uncertainty of frontier life into context.

At forty-five years old, a gallant frontiersman named Henson Wiseman left his wife and five children in Cedar County, Nebraska, to foray into Dakota with the 2nd Nebraska Calvary. His children had pleaded with him not to leave them, lest they be vulnerable to attack. Wiseman urged them to stay calm. He assured them that other troops were on their way to keep vigilance over local farms. After Wiseman departed, these substitute troops never arrived.

The years from 1862 to 1864 were a time of nasty frontier warfare in this heartland region. Hundreds of settlers perished during an attack carried out by Sioux along the Minnesota River. The repercussions of this drama were felt out west. In July 1863, after Wiseman rode north, his wife Phoebe returned to their country home on foot. When she arrived, she was astounded to see blood on the door and one of her sons sprawled dead on the grass. Terrified that her other four children might also be dead, she ran three miles through soaked wheat fields to solicit help from neighbors. Fearing that marauders still lurked nearby, the party dared not approach her home until morning, when they found three Wiseman children dead and two barely alive.

The massacre had been brutal. The dead children were stabbed and their limbs smashed. A barely alive five-year old boy muttered enough to identify his attackers before he fell into a coma. He died two days later (though the deaths were blamed on Yankton and Santee Sioux, this is still disputed). The fifteen-year old girl was pierced with arrows from her genitals to her hips, and a rifle cartridge had been detonated in her mouth. She lived five more days without saying a word, looking wildly at anyone who came into sight.

Wiseman heard this outrageous news while he guarded horses near a camp in South Dakota. He rode one hundred miles to Fort Randall where he learned more gory details before he headed home. In the meantime, his delirious wife had fled to Sioux City. It was a month before the couple reunited. They later returned to St. James. Haunted by the massacre, Wiseman spent years sleeping with his Colt revolver. He paid a sentry to roam their property and look out for trouble. When the couple bore another child, the girl screamed without provocation each night, as though the horror in her mother's memory had seeped into her consciousness.

We left the Wiseman monument and returned to Marlin's peaceful acres. There we sat at the picnic table and Marlin opened his 'family bible,' a collection of photos and stories. A black and white picture showed Phoebe Wiseman, a stern woman without a trace of levity. The album lacked photos of Wiseman, but Marlin described the pictures he had seen of this frontier man, who was his "cousin Alice's great-great-grandfather."

"He's got an old beret. 'Bout my size or dang near. Beard and kinda long hair and he had a pipe, corncob pipe, and a big old musket, forty five. So he was a tough old bird.

"After the massacre, Wiseman lived up in the hills," Marlin continued. "His daughter and her husband built themselves a new house, oh, three-hundred yards up in the hills by the river. He'd go up on the bluff and sit there and wait until Indians floated by in canoes. Then he'd shoot 'em. Shot so many he got to be a dang nuisance."

The years rolled by. Wiseman grew even more bitter when the government for whom he volunteered his service never provided money to help compensate his loss. When he was seventy-seven, more than three decades after the killings, he wrote down a history of the event. Wiseman lamented that he was "forced in old age to hard labor; my life miserable; my family buried in blood."

His old homestead was sold to the state of Nebraska in 1985 as a wildlife management area. I considered old Wiseman, rifle in hand, hunched over the bluffs we canoed beneath that day. I wondered whether time and space had provided any peace to the land tainted by slaughter? I wondered whether the sound of the Missouri River swishing against frail banks offered any serenity to the man in his old age. Did its murmur help ease his entry into a long, final sleep?

As we sat on Marlin's land, Dave and I looked out toward ochre bluffs and riffled plains. Our appreciation for this wild segment of river, and for life in general, was suddenly huge.

Chapter 21

RESERVOIR CONTROL

Dave departed for Utah to spend his summer at a highland cabin. I decided to meet gatekeepers of the six dams along the Upper River basin — guardians of the river's flow. It was time to learn about the men who controlled the mighty Missouri River.

In Omaha, Nebraska, I punched a four digit code before a metal door at the Northwestern Division of the Corps of Engineers building. When the door clicked open, a hydraulic engineer named Bob Keasling led me down a hallway into a plush Briefing Room.

Bob Keasling, Hydraulic Engineer with the U.S. Army Corps of Engineers Reservoir Control office in Omaha, Nebraska

We sat at a polished boardroom table surrounded by ten chairs. This was the 'war room' of the Reservoir Control Group, the nexus for cooking up strategies and hammering out decisions about how water would be moved between six dams along the Missouri River. The decisions agreed on at this table held floodwaters at bay, kept barges gliding, electrified power grids and ensured that chicks and eggs stayed unruffled by river level oscillations.

Graphics were plastered on a wall across from me. I read the titles beneath these colored images: *Main Stem Power Generation, Missouri River Commercial Tonnage, Satellite Data Collection Network, Summary Hydrograph.*

The opposite wall showed a dove-white map riddled in red, blue and green triangles. These pinpointed gauging stations throughout the half-million square miles of the Missouri River watershed. From these, weather and hydrologic data were relayed from river tributaries — such as Red Willows, Glen Elder and Turtle Creek — and used to paint numerical models to predict the river's future behavior.

Bob was a lean, organized man who appeared to thrive on exactitude. His blue workshirt was tucked into pressed white slacks and he spoke with a mild southern twang. His responsibilities included managing how the cascading Missouri River produced power, a job that seemed to mate with his natural interests (his license plate read *H2O PWR*).

A second engineer joined us. This was Bob's heavier-set accomplice Larry Murphy. Larry was the Team Leader for regulating reservoirs, a position that required him to stay two steps ahead of details.

Inside their air cooled fortress these men divulged to me how they controlled discharges along the Missouri River's upper miles. This segment of the river was blocked by six 'mainstem' dams (each capable of generating hyroelectric power) stacked like dominoes between Fort Peck in Montana and Gavin's Point, South Dakota.

Bob pointed at a wall map and explained.

"This is the largest system of storage reservoirs in the country. The Columbia River basin on the west coast couldn't even compare. They have a lot more hydropower capability and about ten times the flow," he added. "But they don't have the large reservoirs we do."

The six 'mainstem' dams stacked along the Missouri River are listed below, along with names of reservoirs they impound.

Name of Dam & Location	Name of Reservoir Behind Dam	Reservoir Capacity in Millions of Acre Feet (MAF)
Fort Peck, Montana	Fort Peck Lake	18.7 MAF
Garrison, North Dakota	Lake Sakakawea	23.8 MAF
Oahe, South Dakota	Lake Oahe	23.1 MAF
Big Bend, South Dakota	Lake Sharpe	1.9 MAF
Fort Randall, South Dakota	Lake Francis Case	5.4 MAF
Gavins Point, South Dakota	Lewis and Clark Lake	0.5 MAF

The sizes of reservoirs along the Missouri River are impressive. The three largest, northernmost dams of Peck, Sakakawea, and Oahe (pronounced OH–wa–hee) can accommodate nine tenths of all water that is stored behind these six huge earth dams, the total quantity being enough to flood the state of Missouri a foot and a half deep in water. After lakes Mead and Powell along the Colorado River, Lake Sakakawea forms the third largest reservoir in the United States.

All six mainstem dams generate electricity. Like a team of climbers ascending a peak, the dams and power plants function as a coordinated system. Each has strengths and weaknesses, yet all work together to fulfill a collective mission. Within boundaries set by Congress, engineers at Reservoir Control decide what that mission is.

At 10:30 a.m. on Monday, Wednesday and Friday morning, Bob, Larry and a group of engineers gather around the polished briefing room table to determine crucial numbers. Larry's 'Reservoir Regulation Team' decides how to balance flows between all six reservoirs. Bob then decides on the 'System Release' — how much water to let out of the lowest dam at Gavins Point.

To nourish their day-to-day decisions these engineers inspect results of hydraulic studies and computer models. After they agree on how water will move within and out of the dam system, Bob or Larry phone Watertown in South Dakota and pass this information on to the Western Area Power Administration (WAPA). What I imagined to be intensely sober men wearing plaid trousers at WAPA then use this data to retool energy schedules for each dam power plant, brandishing optimal electricity for each cubic-foot of water released from the dams.

Although the Flood of '93 was called the granddaddy along the Missouri River, few talk about the larger flood of '97. The reason is simple: the Corps was able to successfully control the raging waters.

"In terms of damages prevented, the biggest year was '97," Larry explained.

No photographs show choppers evacuating stranded mothers from rooftops, because the '97 flood never took place. Its water, instead, was captured behind a half dozen dams.

In 1993, most flood water pirouetted into the Missouri River from locations downstream from dams. Torrents slipped inside the river from tributaries such as the Platte River that were seated low, south and beyond the grasp of men from Reservoir Control. In contrast, the floodwaters of 1997 barreled right into Bob and Larry's domain — the Upper Missouri River basin.

Melted snow water enters the Missouri River from two sources — high plains and craggy mountains. In January of 1997, Bob and Larry inspected data from snowpacks in both locations. Larry's group then calculated how much meltwater could gush out from the Rocky Mountains during the forthcoming spring and feed into the Missouri River. To fine tune their estimates, teams dressed in wool socks and winter parkas huffed over frigid inclines to measure the depths of snow packs. Larry also studied online information from the Natural Resources Conservation Service obtained from 'snow pillows,' sensor equipped cushions buried beneath snow drifts. Both plains and mountain readings were abnormally high that year.

"It was kind of a one, two punch," Larry said. "Lot of plains snowpack, plus lot of mountain snowpack. Almost all that was captured."

Captured as in 'stopped.' When snow melted, all six reservoirs along the Upper Missouri were poised to halt the incoming deluge.

Bob flashed a diagram across an elevated monitor before us. It showed the height of water in each reservoir divided into four zones. The upper zone formed a thin red line — the Zone of Exclusive Flood Control, or what Bob just called 'exclusive.' According to the Master Manual (the 'bible' of operating procedures used by the Corps along the Missouri River) exclusive water needs to be jettisoned out of reservoirs as soon as possible without causing more damage. Only in 1975 and 1997 had all six dams been in 'exclusive' status at the same time. Water was then lapping at the top of spillway gates.

"One storm with wind and wave action washed water over the top," Bob said, recalling high water at the Garrison Dam in 1997. "The dirt road with access to a camping area was washed out. We had Fort Peck Dam clear full. Oahe Dam was within about a foot and a half of being clear full. That's when you start getting nervous."

By adjusting water flows between dams, the flood of '97 never occurred. Through their technical élan and late nights slurping coffee, engineers at Reservoir Control outmaneuvered disaster.

" '97 was a big one," Bob confirmed. "If the dams hadn't been in place the levees in Kansas City would have been overtopped, causing significant damage."

How significant? Each year the Corps prepares an estimated value of flood damages prevented by these dams. In 1997, the Missouri's mainstem dams prevented an estimated $5.2 billion of destruction.

When Bob and Larry are not taming potential floods, their work pivots around classic water resource dilemmas — how to juggle flows for different interests. Downstream of the dams barge companies demand high river levels to keep their cargo floating while water skiers and fishermen on upstream reservoirs moan when lake levels dip. The reservoirs have to stay full enough to churn out decent hydro power, but low enough so they can take on potential flood waters.

Engineers rely on runoff forecasts and annual operating plans to tackle these problems. Yet the men still face a spectrum of the unknown each workday.

"We respond to what Mother Nature gives us," Bob stated. He then leaned back in his chair to elaborate on "Mother's" latest delivery. Although channeling the Missouri River erased most sandbars south of Sioux City, a stretch of river untouched by engineers still runs between Gavins Point Dam and Nebraska's Ponca Park — the section Dave and I canoed. Each year endangered plovers and terns stake out sandbars along this stretch of water.

Bob constantly assessed telemetry data and information obtained from emails to protect these birds' eggs from rising water levels. He often ran 'unsteady flow routing models' on his computer to determine how to control dam releases to avoid flooding out clutches of eggs.

On the day we spoke, Bob's target was to maintain a discharge flow of 28,000 cubic feet per second (cfs) past Sioux City, adequate enough to grease a slick path for barges. Yet the actual flow was slightly higher: Gavins Point Dam was releasing thirty-thousand cfs. The problem was that fine tuning the flow to meet the lower target involved lowering, then raising, the water level. This could possibly send a surge of water onto a sandbar.

"Chicks that haven't fledged are still running around sandbars," Bob explained. "If we go down too low with releases, then come up to meet this 28,000, they can be swept away."

I was surprised to learn how much Bob knew about the location of the birds' nests. Not only did he know *exactly* how many terns and plovers nested on sandbars along the Missouri River, he knew how many eggs they laid, how many chicks fledged, and how many dappled nests lay poised within eighteen inches of the shoreline (a week later, while visiting Gavins Point Dam, I would learn how he knew this).

Certain aspects of the Missouri River cannot be controlled. One of these is a silent storm that brews within the river's flow.

"We occasionally have problems due to sediments on upper ends of reservoirs," Bob explained. "Because they're claims are forty, forty-five years old."

When river water enters a reservoir it slows down and dumps sediment, like an arriving passenger dropping bags on a train station platform. When engineers drafted blueprints for each of the mainstem dams, the Corps had the foresight to predict this sediment problem. They calculated how much silt the Missouri would drop onto the floor of each reservoir, then tabulated the time for this accumulated 'luggage' to render each reservoir obsolete.

Bob lay a spreadsheet on the tabletop before us. He ran his lanky finger down a column covered with digits. This showed that each year the river secretes 18,100 acre-feet of sediment on the base of Fort Peck Lake, giving the reservoir another millennium before it will clog up with silt, reeds and sniffing muskrats. The life span of Lake Sakakawea is shorter — a hair less than a century, while in 180 years puny Lewis and Clark Lake will turn into a corrugated plain, probably honeycombed with prairie dog burrows.

Two offspring of this sediment problem are ugly marshlands and ice. Accumulating sediment steals depth out of the lakes. It first flattens the shallowest portions of reservoirs, then riddles these with reed-coated marshes and acres of cattails.

"Creates a swampy area," Larry explained. "Not like having a lake or river. It's a type of habitat I don't think anybody gets really excited by."

The Corps studied different strategies to deal with this challenge of sediment and vanishing lake levels. Dredging was considered excessively expensive; there was too much sediment to haul off to a few dump sites. There was also the problem of stirring up pollutants. A Missouri tributary named Cheyenne River, for example, runs east to Lake Oahe. Its sediment is filled with arsenic and mercury from previous mining. Because dredges would stir up these heavy metals, the Corps decided not to try relocating sediment from that region.

Larry seemed to enjoy this sediment scenario about as much as an inflamed jawbone.

"Going to take a lot of money to solve the problem," he sighed.

This sediment also creates another problem with ice.

Beside the city of Pierre, South Dakota, sediment clogging the upper reaches of Lake Sharpe has raised the lake level three feet. This means that when temperatures spiral below freezing, ice spreads to upstream shallows.

"It's backed through storm sewers and flooded streets," Bob said. "Vehicle tires were frozen to roads. If we get severe cold temperatures, twenty below with wind chills at sixty and seventy below, ice will build rapidly. We'll have to restrict releases."

'Restricting releases' means keeping Lake Sharpe low by reducing how much water enters it from Oahe Dam upstream. But doing this creates another problem: spilling less water into Lake Sharpe during winter means Oahe Dam generates less power.

Sediment keeps building with time. In the future when temperatures drop, water releases are cut, and power production plummets, what will happen to the city of Pierre?

"Do you have a brown out, a rolling blackout, or do you flood these people?" Bob asked.

Flood these people? His words jolted me. The message also held the men's full concentration. Bob and Larry have left this big problem to a distant person briefed on the scenario — the Division Commander of the Corps of Engineers in Portland, Oregon. When the day comes when either power has to be cut or homes flooded, this general will have to make the call. Meanwhile engineers work to solve this problem before it occurs — in the same way they prevented the flood of 1997.

The worse case scenario will leave a simple choice — flood homes or cut off electricity. The Corps tried tackling this problem by vacating flooded property — they bought low houses that got soaked during high waters. But they could only buy so much property.

"But there's no practical way they could buy to where we have full power plant releases out of Oahe," Larry confirmed.

We spent hours before screens and monitors, inspecting prim graphics, purple matrices, calendars, detailed maps, pie charts and statistical correlations. I listened to these voices of experience describe the river's attributes. The men took their jobs with deadly seriousness. They set up lap top computers at home so they could check data on lake levels during nights or weekends. Their thought processes formed an allegiance to monitoring and controlling the changing moods of the Upper Missouri River. This truth was emphasized a final time during my last minute at Reservoir Control. Before I left the Corps building and walked into the brutal summer heat of Omaha, Bob accompanied me in the hallway. He was a compact, eager man who looked excited about performing the work he loved. When we plodded across the shiny hall he let loose a simple understatement, an affirmation intended to banish any doubts about the Corps's grip on the Missouri River's flow.

"You see," he said, emphasizing the obvious. "There *is* control."

Shoreline of Lake Francis Case near Fort Randall Dam in South Dakota

Chapter 22

FLOODGATES, TERNS AND PLOVERS

Before leaving the Lower Missouri River, I wanted a final briefing on the acrobatic duo so many riverside dwellers spoke about — the piping plover and least tern birds.

In a Corps of Engineer office adjacent to Gavins Point Dam in Nebraska, biologist Greg Pavelka sat before a spacious computer monitor. An adjacent Nature Conservancy calendar blasted out an image of velvety wetlands.

Greg sat facing generous windows on the east wall. A set of binoculars mounted on a windowsill tripod was aimed toward whirlpools near the base of the slate gray dam. Though a biologist, Greg's reserved demeanor reminded me of an engineer from the Corps. His brown hair was clipped above ears. He hushed a light cough in his fist as though it might introduce an element of the unknown into our conversation. He was eager to talk about the endangered birds he helped protect.

The bird subspecies known as the interior least tern flocks to wilder segments of the Missouri River still lined with sandbars. During their journey, Lewis and Clark categorized this bird as 'frequently observed.' In the nineteenth century the bird's number diminished when its feathers and skin started adorning hats. In 1918, the Migratory Bird Act clamped down on this trade in avian plumage. But this protection did not last. After the Missouri River was confined to one channel the bird's sandbar habitat was virtually eliminated. By the 1970s the population of terns dropped to twenty percent of its numbers during World War II.

Six Pac crosses Lewis and Clark Lake, South Dakota

Piping plovers flutter north to the Great Plains in late April, a month before terns glide in from the tropics. Males the color of sand stake out territory along naked sandbars that form lookouts against predators. From there they surge into rituals of courtship, displaying graceful and intricate overflights. After mating, birds stay united to defend their young. If a predator looms near their eggs, the orange-legged male will lurch onto the sand in a ruse, dragging one wing while moaning to distract the intruder.

Biologists like Greg hope to prevent either plovers or terns from going extinct. If these birds are to survive in the long haul they need homesteads — sandbars. To grant them this, Reservoir Control engineers need to be able to *create* this habitat by letting more water spill downriver from Gavins Point dam; they need to allow at least one sizable pulse of water to roar through the river's course every few years. Unfortunately, the very floods that create and maintain sandbars are those that the Corps is supposed to eliminate. The result is that the river's flow, regulated by upstream dams, only surges when some of that control is lost.

Floods not only create sandbars; they clean them. Although the high water of 1997 cleaned vegetation off sandbars between Gavins Point and Ponca, weeds blossomed and covered these again. This created a problem.

"The birds like a little vegetation so chicks can hide," Greg said. "But if there's too much vegetation, they desert the area."

Another high water pulse was needed to shave these sandbars clean again. But how to do this without waiting for a flood?

"Generally the river's flood pulse has been eliminated," Greg said. "That's part of the reason the birds are endangered. They're adapted to a system that changes, but now the system is more or less constant."

The unchanneled section of the lower river that Dave and I canoed remains sprinkled with the sandy habitat these birds love. To protect terns and plovers there, they need to be monitored to ensure their eggs don't vanish. Staff from the Fish and Wildlife Service and the Corps have developed a plan to accomplish this.

During months when these birds visit the river, teams of biologists traipse along sandbars to record the location of each nest.

Missouri River near Niobrara, South Dakota

They then pass this reconnaissance intelligence onto Greg who pastes a summary of this data (including exact GPS coordinates) onto the Corps' internal website.

Greg pushed his coffee mug aside with the back of his hand. He rotated his computer monitor my way. The sheet read: *Threatened and Endangered Species Data Management System*. He scanned the data.

"We've had a total of 112 piping plover nests so far this year: ninty-four hatched, fifteen destroyed, three — fate unknown," Greg said.

"The crew surveyed from river mile 785 to 805 yesterday," he added. "They'd observed twenty-three chicks. More than a hundred have fledged the river from near here."

Even a small rise in the river level can wash onto a sandbar, flushing eggs downriver. Heedful of this danger, field teams note which nests sit within eighteen inches of shore. Greg then 'red flags' these waterside nests on his spreadsheet.

He tapped his highlighter against the monitor. The screen identified four nests perched along this foot and a half wide danger corridor at River Mile 839.5. Once Greg entered this data onto a spreadsheet, Bob from Reservoir Control inspected the figures, phoned Greg to get an estimate for when the last chicks would fledge, then fine tuned water releases from dams to protect each precarious nest.

This truth was refreshing and amazing. The distribution of millions of kilowatts of energy and the flow of over twenty cubic miles of impounded water depends, at times, on whether a single tern weighing less than a demitasse of espresso has flapped its wings and flown south in the direction of Guatemala. Until this final chick makes its departure, the interaction between dam flows, nest data, field teams and power output remains as coordinated as a four-chambered heart.

The day before, Reservoir Control wanted to increase water releases from South Dakota's Fort Randall Dam. They phoned Greg to find out the status of all nearby birds. Greg retrieved fresh data from field teams on five nests near Niobrara bridge, then phoned Bob to discuss water levels.

"I told them if Lewis and Clark Lake stays at 1206 feet above sea level, it shouldn't effect nests. It was at 1205.8 yesterday, so they'll be watching their gauges."

Based on Greg's data, Reservoir Control then unshackled identical quantities of water from both Fort Randall and Gavins Point dams to maintain a steady level along Lewis and Clark Lake.

Within days, when the last birds fledged and headed south, Greg would let the engineers at Reservoir Control know.

"We'll tell them the reach is clear — that they can change flows to their heart's content."

"Are there other threats to birds beside flow?" I asked Greg.

"Big things are weather and predators," he explained. "Hailstorms, heavy rains. If a mink gets onto a sandbar, it could wipe out an entire colony. You also have avian predators — hawks, owls, gulls, crows. And there's the possibility of human disturbance. These birds nest on sandbars. People with dogs can destroy nests without knowing it."

"Their adaptation is camouflage," Greg explained. "If disturbed, they freeze in place and try to blend in with the surrounding area. The idea is if you can't see me, you can't eat me."

Greg turned a group of photographs over on his desk. White pebbles around the perimeter of one nest looked like rock salt on the rim of a daiquiri glass. Camouflaged eggs lay circled inside this ring.

"Nests are just depressions in sand," he said. "Eggs are colored to blend in. In the old days a flood coming down the Missouri could wipe out a colony. The birds would then renest again because they're adapted to a constantly changing system."

When fall weather blows in, plovers flap as far away as Laguna Madre and the Caribbean isles while terns hightail it to the sunny Baja peninsula, Central America and Venezuela.

Perhaps, Greg added.

Biologists were unsure exactly *where* birds went when they migrated. Such uncertainty is critical.

"There's a big emphasis on birds up here on the breeding grounds," Greg said. "But one thing kind of overlooked is that they spend the majority of their lives, from nine to ten months, down in wintering grounds."

In other words the Endangered Species Act helps protect these visitors for the quarter of their lives they spend raising families on temperate U.S. terrain. Meanwhile in other countries smoking chain saws may be garroting their tropical rainforest homesteads. If the birds are to survive, other nations will have to recognize the need to protect them.

I was curious about the future. Did Greg think there would be more nests on the Missouri River in ten years?

"Not sure that's possible; that channeled segment of the river is going to stay channeled. There are big plans to restore some side channels," Greg said, referring to mitigation sites such as the Big Muddy Refuge and Benedictine Bottoms. "I'm not sure that will benefit the birds though. They prefer sand bars in the main river."

Mitigation sites might, however, help buy time for a species that is also vanishing from the Missouri River — a bullet shaped fish with a deep genetic memory.

SECTION FOUR:

DAKOTAS

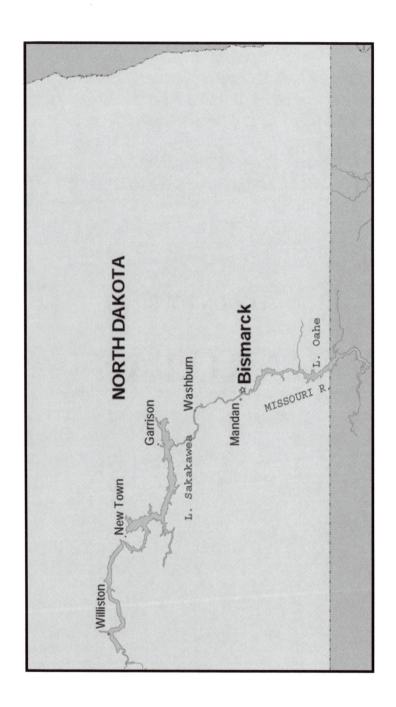

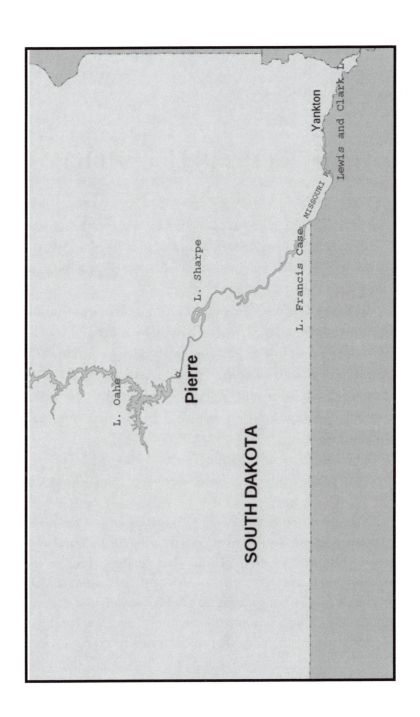

165

Chapter 23

LAST OF THE TROOP

allid Sturgeon. I pulled out a dictionary to check the meaning of pallid: lacking in color or intensity. Had to be color. Who could accuse a species that has survived seventy million years of lacking intensity?

In South Dakota I drove west along Lewis and Clark Lake and turned down a semicircular drive named Hatcheries Circle. Inside an adjacent fishery building was a damp world the color of cold oatmeal. A notice slapped on a concrete wall explained how fish were bred: staff slid a 'rigid plastic tube' up a female sturgeon's 'gynopore' to remove eggs before injecting the fish with a hormone.

This sounded rather painful.

"You gonna read this," a deep voice asked from behind, "or you want to talk with me?"

The afternoon before Mark Grodish promised me time and information. He now came to deliver, wearing his Fish and Wildlife Service shirt and smiling behind dark glasses. He looked an amenable character, like a trustworthy guitarist from an offbeat blues band. Mark led me outside to a field of rectangular ponds, each a hundred yards on a side and filled with walleye, saugeye, blue gill, bass, and trout. A strapping wind shook a nearby elm tree, ejecteing crows like tossed confetti. While we walked, Mark dug a plastic scoop in the bucket he held and heaved brown pellets into ponds with practiced flicks, as though throwing grain to chickens.

"Raisin' fish is pretty satisfying," he said. "I equate it with farming. Similar rewards."

A problem with these huge open air ponds was that ravenous osprey swooped down to snack on fingerlings. Mark couldn't afford that with more fragile fish.

"Let's look in the endangered species building," he told me. "That's where we keep pallid sturgeon."

We entered a cool yellow warehouse. The sound of flowing water chattered inside the dank interior. Mark flicked on a light and aimed toward a matrix of thirty-six stomach-high circular tanks and two larger reservoirs. Each small tank was eight feet in diameter; the reservoirs were twice that.

"Facility's got some high tech equipment," he explained. "Lake water is filtered and disinfected to kill bacteria or viruses that might sicken sturgeon. All water comes through that big blue box." He pointed to the back of the room. "Filters it down to seventeen microns."

After that, ultraviolet lights killed whatever diseases remained.

We shuffled to a smaller tank. Using a triangular net the size of a shoebox, Mark scooped out a young fish.

A sturgeon is a species most people have heard of but few have seen — sort of like a boysenberry. Its spade shaped head and tubular torso resemble a slimy dustbuster vacuum cleaner. The creature looks sleek, pruned by evolution over thousands of millennia.

"Feel this," Mark said. He held an eight-inch long fish in his palm.

I rubbed my finger across the prickling, notched backbone.

"Little bony structure," Mark said. "Mostly cartilage. They're not very active. You don't see 'em up swimming around like rainbow trout. They're a bottom feeder, built for a river. Head looks flat. They lay right on the bottom and the current flows over them."

His words made me wonder — was the key to surviving 70 million years the ability to lay low?

We moved to a larger tank (tanks were circular instead of square because corners confuse sturgeon). The tank held 125 fish from five different families, a lineage designed by fishery staff. The squiggles we looked at were brood stock — bred to be future mamas and papas of what might be the last pallids to swim on earth.

Mark drained water from the tank, giving us a closer look inside. When water dipped to a level of two feet, we peered at a squad of careening fish that resembled hyperactive sperm cells hunting ovaries. Each was between one and two feet long, with backbones darker than flanks.

I squinted at the sight. Each fish looked as odd as a four-winged fruit fly, a taut mixture of virility and fragility harboring genetic memories from a time before the Missouri River existed. Could these few pallids preserve a species so old that it thrived in rivers where dinosaurs once drank?

"We're developing brood stock from different genetic crosses," Mark told me. "We can identify every fish back to its parent because of a fin tag. The fisheries manager has a data base so we can say, okay, that's from this female. Or this female. Down the road we don't want to be crossing brother and sister."

Sizes varied.

"These are all the same age. Like people. You got some five, six pounds and some that are two. And you got runts."

Parents of these sturgeon were captured further upriver near Montana's Fort Peck Dam, a task no less difficult than hunting boar in a French forest. Each half-century old parent weighed sixty to seventy pounds. This age told a critical story: there may not *be* any more young pallids in the river. The elders might be the last of the troop.

The dammed Missouri River now flows with such artificial steadiness that spawning cues — seasonal changes to temperature and flow — have vanished. After six mainstem dams were raised along the river, silt and clay replaced fine sands and gravels that formed spawning grounds. Meanwhile, low dams along the Yellowstone River blocked movement of fish. The result: pallids became endangered.

"Between dams, channelization and pollution, man's influence is destroying a lot of reproductive habitat," Mark said. "Water quality's gone downhill too."

"We've never seen any small or young fish in the upper and lower river. Upper River, all we're seeing is big fish. Thirty to fifty years old. Last female we spawned was sixty-six pounds. So you're looking at a big fish. Old fish. Probably at the end of her reproductive cycle.

"There are a limited number. And they're difficult to find," he added. "On low water years like this, we had a pile of pallids. I'm not talkin' thousands. I'm talking twenty, twenty-five. That's a bunch. We've had years where we've only found one female on the river to work with. We have a problem dealing with these fifty to seventy pound females. They're old, susceptible to handling stress. Ten years from now if there's no improvement, those fish are gone: we don't have that genetic material any more. We lose that, that's the big one."

The Big One. An image flashed into mind: a departing aircraft retracting its undercarriage. The landing gear pulled from view was a reminder that the entire species was vanishing from sight. The few remaining pallids swish along a quiet trail toward extinction.

Mark and his coworkers were well versed at breeding captive pallids. But unless flow changes along the river, these fish may never breed again in the bubbling Missouri; those raised in captivity will be as clueless about life in the wild as pandas in a zoo ("just an artifact of some genetic material," a biologist named Allyn Sapa later explained).

Mark and other biologists had penned out the mathematics of genetic variation, the stochiometry of sturgeon survival. Yet unless the river's flow changes so it floods again, he had doubts about the species' future.

"Think it's pretty iffy. There are a lot of things working against this species," he said. He wheeled around and waved at the tanks.

"You can do this forever," he said, referring to artificial spawning. "But I don't know if we're going to save the species. If we could get habitat improvement, that would be ideal. It's part of the plan. Propagation, habitat improvement."

Habitat improvement means changing the river's artificial flow. Downstream mitigation sites at the Big Muddy Refuge, Hamburg Bend and Benedictine Bottoms were attempts to reformulate a semblance of the pre Pick-Sloan Missouri River, a stab at recreating the liquid savannah where these legless wildebeest might once again roam. I was again reminded that although altering flows may not be in the financial interest of downriver barge companies, it is essential if these fish are to survive.

"Corps of Engineers has been supportive," Mark said. "Lot of help with different projects. Monetary support. These kinds of projects? You better work together on them. There's no small group that's going to save the fish on their own."

After leaving Mark I drove past a field of prairie grass dotted with bison. Knowing 125 fish from a species that outlasted most life on earth was like looking out of a plate glass window toward a future we do not want to visit.

I recalled the story of how an activist watched a harpooned whale roll over and die. At that moment, eye contact between the two transmitted a message, a flash of communication that sent this man in later years to cold, lonely oceans to try to protect these mammals. Although I'd looked no sturgeon in the eye, the minutes spent regarding these pools of swishing fish mesmerized, then haunted me during coming months. Seventy million years, I thought. Seven orders of magnitude beyond seven. Were pallid sturgeon to become another gutted lineage?

Weeks later in North Dakota I spoke with Mike Olson, the Missouri River Coordinator for the Fish and Wildlife Service. Mike was a stocky redhead who shared a story about an encounter with a tribal elder in Rapid City, South Dakota.

"He pulled me aside after a meeting," Mike told me. "Said he appreciated comments I'd given, but that I didn't understand the significance of the sturgeon to his culture. To him the eagle represented the sky, and the bison or wolf — either one — the land. The sturgeon represented the river, the aquatic world, because it lives to be sixty or seventy years old, the river's oldest living resident. To Native American cultures, those types of long-lived species are significant. The elders in the tribe are extremely important to their culture; the sturgeon is the 'elder' of the river.

"I think," Mike added, reflecting on the tribe's outlook toward the fish, "they have an appreciation that maybe we don't have, at a level above ours."

Losing pallid sturgeon will not fan out the flames of the earth's ecological machinery. I thought it would, however, be like drilling a sizable core out of a Sistine Chapel fresco, then trucking it to a landfill.

Chapter 24

JOE DAY BAY

O ver two months after leaving St. Louis, I stopped to peer at spill gates of Fort Randall Dam in South Dakota. The earthen dam itself curves like a boomerang for a mile and a half, with brawny power lines marching beside it in parallel. Beneath these wires flash miles of perennially mowed grass, trim as a Marine haircut. Seeing this came as no surprise. Each facet of the dam's layout and operation appeared military: polished, organized, without emotion.

Earthen Fort Randall Dam in South Dakota stretches almost two miles long

A sign at the viewing area read "Fort Randall Dam — a Unit of the Pick-Sloan Plan." These terse words revealed plenty. A 'unit' was a part, a piece, a component in an assembly too big to describe on a plaque. Pick-Sloan was more than a project; it was a paradigm. Here, at Fort Randall, it changed the Missouri River into a lake.

The viewing point looked at a divided panorama. To the northwest, Lake Francis Case was a hundred miles of sinewy liquid. To the southeast ran a ribbon of river.

I drove past the dam powerhouse. Two burly fishermen cast opaque lines into water coming over from the power house. Behind me a mechanical beep blared — the power plant's internal message code. With its own language, the dam site forms a country unto itself. Yet, in bizarre symmetry, an adjacent empire spreads beside this plant: over five hundred acres of the Karl E. Mundt National Wildlife Refuge. This refuge, off limits to humans, crackles with ring-necked pheasants, sharp-tailed grouse and great horned owls who flock in for provender and solitude. The ecological pistons of this genetic engine thump according to their own unwritten Master Manual. When winter tosses bald eagles out of Canada, they glide to this refuge to hunt rainbow smelt which become stunned after they flush through dam turbines.

From the dam I drove Six Pac toward Lake Francis Case, passing hay bales and descending a steep, tortuous trail toward Joe Day Bay. A sign warned that the final half mile might be impassable. This sounded grand. I passed a wind wheel without rotors before parking at the shoreline's dirt circle.

Finding this empty campsite was unexpected. There was no thirteen dollar fee to park next to a row of campers lined up like customers at a barber shop. A crude wood fence circled a lot beside a lone picnic table that curved like a banana. The grass was uncut. Good, good and better: empty, wild, slightly messy. I ate a bowl of musky vegetable soup at dusk, then hiked along the shoreline. Here the lake stood beside bristling grass under a peaceful concert of raw starlight. This was a grand place — no fee, jetskis or worries. There was no barbecue pit or shower or clanging RV generators or gift store selling key chains shaped like sullen buffalo. I would spend the evening alone, first sitting in a lawn chair outside the camper by starlight, then sleeping on a foam mattress inside. During these months on the road, I came to regard Six Pac not only as home, but as an ally. Its interior was compact, bright and cheerful and provided solid refuge during strong winds and thunderstorms. During evenings I worked at my computer below its bright ceiling light, while on cold nights, pulled a thick down comforter over myself and drank sweet tea. Its spacious upper bunk had been filled with boxes of books and documents collected during the trip, and I slept on a lower bunk. Although there was little extra space in the camper, its interior rarely felt cramped.

Outside this small castle, I sat and read a newspaper article about the nearby Yankton Reservation. This was shown on the road map as a pink parallelogram adjacent to the Missouri River. When the Fort Randall Casino Hotel opened on the reservation, tribal unemployment shrank from seventy-five percent to zero within a year. An unexpected side effect of this new economy was that it roused old traditions.

In Yankton Sioux culture, White Buffalo Calf Woman introduced seven rites to the tribe, including the *Isnati* — Becoming a Woman Ceremony. This ritual that once thrived along the Missouri River's banks vanished over time. Yet a segment of the wild river still touched the reservation; if the tribe decided to resurrect their ceremony they could perform it once again, along the shoreline.

The Yankton Braveheart society was created to carry wounded tribal warriors away from battlefields. With no wars in sight in the 2000s, Braveheart women decided to use their free time to revive this *Isnati*. At first, tribal elders were wary of the decision. Yet the society pushed ahead. They held their ceremony near Greenwood, where the river flows by wooded banks. Young female initiates camped in a tepee and spent days singing songs, chatting with elders and immersing themselves in the lore of traditional rituals. The success of the ceremony re-established this lost rite.

Small waves sloshed against the disfigured shoreline. What little I learned about the *Isnati* was satisfying. Variety was returning to the Missouri River, not only in terms of ecology, but also culture.

Evening near Joe Day Bay along Lake Francis Case in South Dakota

Chapter 25

CIRCLES OF POWER

Black Elk, the Lakota Medicine Man, said the power of the universe always works in circles. Much of the power in South Dakota also originates from circles: spinning turbines, shafts and generators at Fort Randall, Big Bend and Oahe dams are poised to milk energy from the Missouri River.

If you fold a map of South Dakota in two, touching north and southern borders, the crease cuts through the Missouri River five miles north of Oahe Dam. This dam staggers a mile and three quarters long, stands as tall as a twenty-four story building and holds back the swell of Lake Oahe, fourth largest reservoir in the U.S. The lake waters above this dam scramble northwest like a spindly millipede — linking the Dakota's state capitals of Pierre and Bismarck.

Inside the power plant at Oahe Dam, I met an operator named Don Miller. He wore matted jeans and a cap the color of cantaloupe. Don wore air cushioned sneakers to keep him agile on the plant floor. Before he took me on a rapid tour of the plant, he led me upstairs to the control room, a bright fortress of gray panels stacked along tall walls.

"The man who is on the six o'clock at night 'til six in the morning shift is by himself. He leaves the control room twice in that shift," Don explained. "Makes inspections on the floor. Makes sure equipment is running right. He's running this thing all by himself."

This 'thing' is the seat of power, the jade throne of electricity generation along the Missouri River, the provider of more watts than any other mainstem dam along the river. Each of Oahe's seven turbines produces 112,000 kilowatts of power. Combined, that is enough juice to power the homes of more than a half million people.

When Don spoke about synchscopes, set point loads, phase differentials and breaker failures, my brow clenched.

"Have I thoroughly confused you?" he asked, then toned down on the technicalities and summarized his work.

"An operator's main job is watching seven turbines. He starts and stops them, changes voltages. He's monitoring nine transmission lines, plus all power plant equipment. In a nutshell, that's what that one guy does. These units," Don added, "are basically maintenance free."

There were exceptions, he admitted. If a breaker failure stopped one generator, operators needed to react before other generators started clicking off like street lights at dawn.

"If you don't take care of that problem it's going to snowball on you," he said. "It'll go far enough to the point where you eventually lose the whole plant. This is the biggest hydro facility on the river. Do that in the middle of the afternoon and take seven hundred megawatts out of the system and you really made a mess."

It had been years since an operator 'made a mess.' Don recalled the last time when a flummoxed novice stood on the plant floor phoning other operators for assistance. Fortunately, Oahe was not generating power at the time.

Other minor problems cause headaches in the control room.

"A bad thunderstorm or ice storm in wintertime will put you on your toes most of the night. Power lines start trippin' out. Nothing you can't handle, because you can put the line back in. But you're always worried about losing something."

Other men walked in the room. They wore hardhats and coveralls and bantered with Don before moving out again to perform assigned tasks. This gave the well ordered room a sense of liveliness.

I asked Don how the power plant interacted with Reservoir Control. He walked to a table in the control room corner, reached past a can of Mountain Dew and Dilbert funnies and clicked a computer mouse. The monitor flicked alive and showed one colored column for each mainstem dam.

"Bob Keasling doesn't call us from Reservoir Control. He calls Western Area Power Administration in Watertown, South Dakota. He basically tells WAPA what flows he wants. Then their computer sends that number to us."

The computers then sent that power from Oahe to WAPA.

Don tapped the green column representing Oahe Dam.

"Right now, Watertown is telling us we need 400 megawatts."

Another monitor showed targeted flows, actual flows, and power outputs, numbers updated each half second.

"Just targets," Don said. "Sometimes we don't hit them. Sometimes we're higher, sometimes lower."

"We" was the world of computer commands that linked the power plant's hardware together.

"Want me to run you through the plant quick?" Bob asked.

I nodded.

Quick was an apt word. Don jogged down the hallway.

Water enters the dam powerhouse through seven parallel tunnels that lead in from Lake Oahe. Each one of these sloping, reinforced concrete 'penstocks' gapes with the diameter of a two story high building and careens for more than a half-mile beneath the lake's water. Seven parallel penstocks lead to seven generators.

Faced by an emergency, Oahe staff can shut this flow off, stopping it from gushing through penstocks. But halting a ten-mile-an-hour, two-story-high flow of water at the end of a half-mile-long tube generates a bit of pressure. If water is suddenly stopped, the pressure is absorbed inside the dam's strangest looking feature.

Outside the powerhouse, fourteen silver cylinders stood clustered in a rectangle — with two rows and seven columns. They looked like tennis ball cylinders, except that each towered as high as a fourteen-story building. Two such 'surge tanks' were attached at right angles to each penstock. If water flowing into the powerhouse was suddenly cut off, these monstrous tanks gave the backed up water a place to surge.

"Gigantic shock absorbers," Don described them. "If you have to close gates real fast, water goes up these, taking pressure off penstocks."

Water normally courses through penstocks, enters the power house, thrashes through an assembly of circular turbines, then spits out the dam and continues rushing downstream toward St. Louis. Imagine the capital letter I, or a barbell turned on one side. This is the geometry of power generation — two discs linked by a vertical inner shaft. The bottom disc, the turbine, catches water and spins. The upper disc is the generator that converts this circular motion to electricity. Joining these spinning plates is a glimmering shaft of stainless steel.

Don dashed down a set of concrete steps and opened a restricted access door. This led to a hallway that passed seven churning turbines.

"Going to get a little noisy here," he warned me.

We entered a hot, loud bay in whisky colored light. Vibrations oscillated my kidneys. We stood above one turbine, a horizontal water wheel surrounded by 'wicket gates' that opened and closed in unison. By changing the angle of these gates — like adjusting a circular Venetian blind — a computer controlled how much water flushed through each turbine to make it spin. Once past the turbine, water spewed outside the dam to the river again, frothing above walleye fish.

I stepped over to where the whirring shaft connected the turbine and generator. Its three-and-a-half-foot diameter column whirled one-hundred times per minute.

"Touch it," Don said. I splayed fingers against this spinning lukewarm steel, and recalled words of Black Elk again: *"The Power of the world always works in circles."*

Oahe Dam merges mechanical and organic systems. Until the Endangered Species Act was passed, this and similar dams served as water barriers and generators, divorced from the surrounding riparian ecosystems. Those days are over. Today, maintaining tern, plover and sturgeon habitat is already as integral to plant operations as buying lubricating oil or scheduling spillway repairs. Through a process of federal law, power generation must defer to the protection of speckled eggs on sandbars.

We spent an hour pacing through dank tunnels and walking past rumbling machines. Hungry for fresh air, Don led me outside the generator room. We stood in wind on the face of the dam and looked at water splashing below. I asked Don if they ever shut the plant down fast.

"We've had drownings on the river, where we'll shut it down right away. As long as you have a flow, bodies just keep on goin.' Lost a little Indian boy two years ago. Never did recover him."

Don pointed at the water.

"Let me tell you what happens when you get inside this flow. Looks like it's going downstream, right? But on the bottom, that concrete pad sits at a slant to angle water up. It'll suck you back against this wall and keep you against it. Every once in a while it'll push you down. You get beat up pretty well. We've had divers here. About four years ago one was pulled up against the wall and couldn't get away. We ended up shutting down the plant to get him out. The operator threw a buoy ring and pulled him around to the side. Wouldn't have made it much longer. Don't think he wants to dive in the water again."

"Another time a boat tried to come up here and capsized. Found a body seven miles downriver."

We moved inside again.

In a vast, immaculate room the size of an airport hangar we passed seven circular generators, then descended a staircase next to two wire cages. Each held twenty-two red cylinders filled with carbon dioxide for putting out fires. One set was a backup. Don wheeled his hand in their direction.

"Two of everything," he said. "Two wicket gates, two cooling systems, two sumps. Two swivel motors. All for backup. You'll notice there's an AC and DC pump to keep bearings oiled. Something happens to our AC, the DC kicks in. With the oil sumps there's a lead pump and a lag pump. One's a backup."

Oahe power plant was more than a nation to itself — it was also an organism. Just as a human body has backup systems — two eyes, legs, lungs and nostrils, so did each generating system. Like an organism, Oahe responded to sensory input. When an Indian boy fell in the river, the staff shut down gates; when downstream plover eggs lay within a foot and a half of water, wicket valves froze or closed.

We returned to the lobby. The stalwart hum of distant generators vibrated our shoes. Don said farewell and dashed off, a man cognizant of the unforgiving demands of details. In contrast I crept along the road outside the power house in second gear, viewing electric lines that spat out from the switchyard and fueled the lifestyle of a vibrant nation. I considered penstock, surge tank, turbine, shaft and generator. Monumental foresight and focused intelligence gave birth to Oahe Dam's power plants. Considering the feat produced a lasting respect for the intricacy of what determined minds can create.

Chapter 26

WASHBURN

I drove past the Lewis and Clark Saloon, Lewis and Clark Café, Lewis and Clark Senior Center and a full size Lewis and Clark mural slapped across a prominent brick wall in Washburn, North Dakota. At the town drug store I bought a raspberry flavored Sacajawea chocolate bar. Washburn was capitalizing not only on its position and history, but on its curious lack of competition. Most of the Missouri River that Lewis and Clark traveled along in what is now North Dakota has since vanished beneath reservoirs. Two dams that created lakes Sakakawea and Oahe inundated 250 of the state's 348 miles of Missouri River. The result: the river in Washburn runs as a legacy to its past flow. Yet this legacy is rich.

An unchanneled segment of the Missouri River runs downstream from Garrison Dam and through Washburn. Like other similar wild sections, recognizing this was a breeze. The river bank was a morass of noxious weeds and stunted bushes while its inner shore was comprised of boulders, gruesome deadwood and a scuffed up forest.

I stepped into the Bergquist Gallery west of Washburn, inside the Lewis and Clark Interpretive Center. A displayed Carl Bodmer painting was titled: *Hundeschlitten Der Mandan Indianer*, translated as *Traineaux a Chiens des Indiens Mandans*, translated again as *Dog-Sledges of the Mandan Indians*. I inspected the painting's sky — filled by prehistoric looking birds with angular wingspans. Two scrawny dogs hauled a sled across the frozen Missouri River behind a woman draped in rough buffalo hides. The image conveyed a sense of brittle cold and hard labor; it also portrayed dignity in a land where death lay just a few degrees, a dose of smallpox, or a tribal raid away.

From the center, I drove two miles away to a reconstruction of Fort Mandan, where the Corps of Discovery spent their winter from 1804 to 1805. At this camp, the captains promised local Indians that President Jefferson, the 'great white father,' would care for them if they were 'good red children.'

Reconstruction of Fort Mandan in winter, North Dakota
(Courtsey, U.S. Geological Survey)

The fort's triangular exterior was hewn from vertical timber posts. Each post was pencil sharp and twice the height of an adult. This 1972 reconstruction sat only ten minutes downriver from where the original fort lays buried below the Missouri River today.

Lewis and Clark selected the site because of its proximity to five Mandan and Hidatsa villages at the mouth of Knife River. These clusters of huts once housed thousands and included Rooptahee (Black Cat's Village) and Matootonha (Big White's Village).

The fort sat next to a baggy reach of river. Little splashes touched a blush colored shore. In seventy degree heat I ate a plum on the riverbank. A man with a handlebar mustache and gray ponytail sat on a nearby boulder. He ran a hand through the water.

"River looks wild here," I said, stating the obvious.

"Yes," he quipped. "However briefly."

His economy of words was powerful. Sections where the Missouri River roared at its natural pace were rare. Recalling this made me wonder: if a peoples' identity is linked to a river, what happens when the river disappears?

The answer lay further north.

Chapter 27

INUNDATION

Almost fourteen hundred river miles from the Missouri River mouth, I sat on a sharp talus bank of its Knife River tributary in North Dakota. The earth behind was coated with depressions that resembled dimples on a golf ball. Each shallow divot was between twenty and forty feet in diameter. If a Cessna flying above tilted its wings, curious passengers could spy how the hungry Knife River munched into this field of earthen circles over time. In 1798 an explorer named Thompson counted fifty-two depressions in the earth; by 1990 only thirty-one remained. These holes, remnants of villages from the past, were lopped off by the wandering Knife River. The sight was another reminder of how changes to a river's shape and flow can obliterate communities.

Each shoreline divot outlined where an ancient Hidatsa earth lodge once arched toward the sky. The Hidatsa erected timber framed domes a story and a half high next to the river, then plastered damp sod against these semi-globes made of bent wood. Huts were packed into villages as tight as ball bearings in a bucket. A single hut held up to twenty people and at least one pony (safeguarding it from being robbed at night). During daytime, men escaped these huts by clambering onto roofs and watched vagrant buffalo trudge toward water, or else kept a lookout for troops of raiding Sioux.

During the nineteenth century, artist George Catlin captured the atmosphere of these villages in painted images. He found the people "fond of fun and good cheer, and can laugh easily and heartily at a slight joke." He described one hut as a 'potash kettle inverted' and climbed on its roof to see what lay on top. The brik-a-brak included buffalo skulls, canoes, pots, and groups of gabbing men. Catlin spied trophy scalps tethered to poles and marveled at the "newness and rudeness in every thing that is to be seen," and strangers who "carry an air of intractable wildness about them." He described how the Mandan did not bury their dead, but wrapped corpses in fresh buffalo hides, then hung these cocoons on an elevated scaffold to "moulder and decay," with feet aimed toward the rising sun.

Buffalo and agriculture formed twin pillars of Hidatsa community life. When ice broke on the Knife River during spring, Indians stood on banks spotting dead buffalo that bobbed downstream. The carcasses provided meat, hides, even tools: buffalo scapulae were strapped to wood poles and used as hoes to till riverbank plots. In spring, the Hidatsa planted beans and squash and lined sunflowers along trail perimeters. Months later villagers worked in unison to harvest each family's crops.

This region around this Missouri River tributary was home to humans for eleven thousand years. Legend even tells how the Awatixa, a sub-tribe of the Hidatsa, were created along the Missouri River. In truth, the Hidatsa settled at the mouth of the Knife River in the sixteenth century, from where they traded valuable river flint ('the Porsche of flint,' one park ranger described it) as far south as Texas and eastward to what is now Maine. But flint was a bonus of the site. Tribes chose to live near rivers not for scenery or flint, but for survival. The environment provided rich soil, fresh water and a steady supply of fish. Curling avenues of wild berries and trampling game dotted trails near the moist banks.

During later decades when smallpox and war thinned Indian populations, tribes along the Missouri River amalgamated to survive. The combination of smallpox and raids by Sioux warriors pushed the sedentary Mandan Indians, "people of the pheasants," to move up the Missouri River to live alongside the Hidatsa. The Arikara followed in the 1860s. Such moves demonstrated that tribal survival depended not only on proximity to water, but on safety in numbers. Eventually the Mandan, Hidatsa and Arikara settled close to each other and Fort Berthold Reservation was established to protect them. Their Three Affiliated Tribes Government was officially recognized by the U.S. government in 1943.

Before this gathering took place, a tribe named the Arikara lived in three distinct villages south of Hidatsa and Mandan Indians. They also built sod homes (nicknamed 'potato holes' by Europeans). More than two decades before Catlin walked through these villages with his paintbrushes, Lewis and Clark visited this nation of six hundred Indians named the Rickerees (also called Ricares, or Rickerries, or Rickores by Lewis and Clark. Consistent spelling was not the expedition's forte). There the captains gave a speech to the tribe about the power of the U.S. government and how the Arikara should make peace with their neighbors. They then doled out portions of sugar and salt to the listeners. With not unusual condescension, Lewis noted there that the Arikara women "collect all the wood and do the drudgery as Common amongst Savages."

Once the expedition parted, a grateful Arikara man sent two attractive young women ('squars') up the riverbank to follow them. Their instructions were to follow the expedition's boats and enter the men's camp. About this incident Lewis only wrote that they "persisted in their civilities," not embellishing on what imagination can supply.

Further upriver and inside a Hidatsa smoky lodge, a French Canadian visitor relished the trophy he recently won in gambling: a teenage Shoshone girl named Bird Woman. Named Toussaint Charbonneau, this man then stepped outside the lodge and exited the village to find the group of explorers axing down tress to build a winter camp. Once there, Charbonneau offered his services as an interpreter to Lewis and Clark, requesting that they take him and his wife upriver in the spring. His offer was accepted. Charbonneau and Bird Woman, Sacagawea, were allowed to join the expedition.

Later that day and less than twenty miles north of Knife River, I sat on banks of Lake Sakakawea behind Garrison Dam. The grass smelled sweet. Clouds formed a tartan cover over lake waters and a motor boat ripped the foreground in a staccato of revs. While seated there, I sifted through articles from the past, trying to learn more about how the Missouri River changed and how such changes impacted those living beside it.

On July 3, 1945, newspapers spread urgent news: U.S. military forces had entered the German city of Berlin. The first American soldier inside the capital was a Ute Indian named Harvey Natchees. A recipient of the Silver Star, Bronze Star and Purple Heart, Harvey drove eight miles through Berlin in awe of not seeing any intact block of buildings.

On that same day in North Dakota, the Bismarck Tribune ran a story about a local battle zone. The Three Affiliated Tribes had gotten word that a dam was to rise across the Missouri River. Their Tribal Council asked for a hearing and soon six of their representatives met with the Army Corps of Engineers. A former Indian judge named Daniel Wolf stood before the Corps in tribal regalia and spoke in the Gros Ventres tongue. Though translated, the complaint was clear from his tone: taking away Indian land to build any dam constituted another treaty infraction.

"Same old story," he said. "First we were assigned a big reservation, then it was made smaller, then smaller. Now it is proposed to take more of our land by putting it under water."

Wolf complained that the tribe could never find and relocate their ancestor's unmarked graves before the reservoir rose. One of his Arikara colleagues was less specific. He just called dam construction "a vicious project."

Others added words of protest.

In January of 1946, seventy year old Ms. Byron Wilde from the Affiliated Tribes met North Dakota's Governor Aandahl in Bismarck. A Fargo newspaper described her as "a quaint little Arikara Indian housewife." Ms. Wilde said the dam would bring electricity for lights and appliances, but believed those were useful only for whites.

"We are content with our kerosene lamps," she said. "All we ask is to be left alone."

She reminded the governor that the land to be flooded was given to her people by the Treaty of 1851. She told how her tribe valued its cottonwood coated shoreline. She then added a final complaint. It irked her that the Bureau of Indian Affairs never informed her about any dam. Instead, she learned about it when she saw surveyors planting red and yellow flags on reservation land, then walked over and asked the men what in the world they were doing.

Her words had no effect on the governor. Though sympathetic, he told her the dam was going up, and that relocating the tribe was his priority.

Both white and Indian landowners fought against dam construction. They lost. On May 20, 1948, leaders of the Three

Affiliated Tribes signed a paper that sold more than a quarter of their reservation land, 155,000 acres, to the U.S. Government. The poignancy of the moment was captured in a splendid AP photograph showing Secretary of the Interior Krug signing the contract. To his right George Gillette, chairman of Fort Berthold Tribal Council, covered his face and wept. For the Arikara, the rising dam formed a tear-stained conquest, a victory of mind over heart.

In 1949, the combined companies of Peter Kiewit and Morrison and Knudsen joined forces with Garrison Builders to begin constructing Garrison Dam. These companies unleashed a platoon of heavy equipment that moved twenty-one million cubic yards of dirt, an accomplishment the Engineering News Record described as 'fantastic.' During the following years contractors broke every earth moving speed record to build the dam embankment, a two mile long earthen wedge two hundred feet high and a half-mile thick at its base. Machinery scooped away a quantity of soil that could build a five-foot high, three-foot thick wall that girthed earth at the equator. The dam's base was so large that today its sloping downstream wall is used as a farm field; dozens of hay bales lay beneath electrical transmission towers. Each concrete spillway gate stands forty feet wide and twenty-nine feet high. Combined, these gates can discharge eight tenths of a million cubic feet of water per second — as easily as flushing a latrine, but at seventy-five miles per hour.

The project's first step was to build Riverdale, a new town for administration staff (a housewife from Granville won twenty-four dollars by naming the town in a competition). While the dam rose, an incoming flux of visitors from out of state turned little Riverdale into North Dakota's cosmopolitan center.

When it was completed, Garrison Dam formed the plug that transformed part of the Missouri River into Lake Sakakawea, third largest reservoir in the U.S. (with a coastline that stretches 1,530 miles long). To mark the closing ceremony for dam construction, thirty thousand special 'Souvenir Editions' of the Bismarck Tribune were printed for June 10th and 11th of 1953. Their front page showed a collage of black and white images: an irrigator hunched over Dakota soil, a boy wearing a beanie cap and baggy trousers dwarfed beside the rubber wheel of an earth excavator twice his height. On page three a photograph of the dam's powerhouse under construction stood above the words "Welcome to the President of the United States — Ike Eisenhower." Other images embodied optimism: a sailboat, one squatting fisherman, women in prim bathing suits strutting along a wood dock, and picnickers shaded beneath cowboy hats.

Yet not everyone celebrated.

Judge Wolf told the Corps that in order to remove him from his land they would have to kill him and cart his body away. He died before any deputies showed up at his doorstep, leaving others to inter his remains in a new cemetery located above the rising waterline.

Although a relocation plan was never agreed upon, the Affiliated Tribes were paid for their land. Nine Indian villages were flooded beneath Lake Sakakawea, forcing eight tenths of Fort Berthold's tribal population to move. Reluctant families packed up and abandoned villages with such names as Charging Eagle, Red Butte, Beaver Creek, and Elbowoods. They moved to higher land, including a site named New Town created out of a stubble field. By 1955, a total of fourteen hundred residents filled this town. Today it holds two thousand. Although most of the tribe and white farmers moved off their land with cool obedience, the loss of houses demoralized many residents.

"For the old people it must have been terrible," Marilyn Hudson told me. "They had lived in one area. The young people had not formed any real sentimental attachment to that land. Myself, I was seventeen years old. I was in the last graduating class from Elbowoods and in the process of leaving home anyway."

I met Marilyn at the Three Tribes Museum in New Town (next to the more crowded Four Bears Casino). Marilyn was a Mandan / Hidatsa woman who had worked for three decades for the Bureau of Indian Affairs in Montana and California. She then volunteered on the Board of Directors of the museum. Marilyn was open minded and effuse with welcome. When we sat together, I asked her how she remembered the river and the coming of the dam.

"There were nine children in our family. We lived about a mile from the river. That's where we would get ash and pole for fence posts and corrals, and firewood and timber. That was all owned by everyone on the river. That's where the deer were. It was a natural shelter for cattle in the winter. There was a lot of dependency on the river and what it provided. You never knew from one day to the next what type of bottom would be there, whether there'd be a sand bar, or whether there'd be a completely sharp drop off. It would change rapidly. Overnight. We couldn't go in the water as children. Too dangerous. Nobody knew what to expect. If we did go in, we'd have a rope tied to a tree around our waist."

Marilyn's eager words disclosed a simple past, an age where landscape and community were as tethered together as a Hidatsa family to its earth lodge. She pointed to an old photograph on a wall.

"Picture shows where we picked juneberries. Called it the sheep pasture," she said, adjusting her hand. "Down around here is where you would cut fenceposts. This is about where we would try to get in the river. And here, coal mines. This is what we call Saddle Butte. All this is under water now.

"Indian people understood the Missouri River. They understood beavers, willows, cottonwoods, ice breaking up. All of these were factors that affected the river and where it went. That's understanding it purely from a point of view of nature. But they knew you're going to destroy it the minute you put a dam past it."

The government gave the Affiliated Tribes a choice. They could either have their land appraised or condemned. If condemned, a value would be ascribed to it. To get a fair market price the tribe chose appraisal.

"People were paid for their land. We had some good attorneys that litigated and prosecuted claims. They did a remarkable job testifying. It's amazing. We submitted testimony on the value of coal, game, timber, and cattle ranching so that we could gain as much compensation as possible. About five million dollars for the lands that would be covered and five million for the actual relocation."

With her round face, round glasses and a rounded way of perceiving events, Marilyn did not consider that raising a dam and creating Lake Sakakawea had any single 'effect' on her people. Each evacuee recalled different impacts. For her the world was not divisible into culprit and victim. There was no objective reality as to whether building dams and flooding the land was right or wrong. The answer, she explained, depended on who looked at the process, when, and from what angle. There were other factors, ancillary and mainstream, that pressed against her culture over time — war, missionaries, attitudes, economics. I realized that her tacit skepticism toward equating a single cause with one effect reflected a holistic way of thinking that the stewards of the Missouri River are only beginning to learn today — that a river cannot be managed in the same way that an algebraic equation is solved.

Three years after Garrison Dam rose, more fanfare hit the press when the powerhouse started running. A consortium of three companies from California, Boston and New York secured and executed this ten million dollar contract. On January 21, 1956, the *Minot Daily News* gave a headline tribute to the Garrison Dam's "Power-On-The-Line" ceremony. Five hundred people attended this blowout to inaugurate the first flow of the plant's electricity.

Other articles in that day's paper painted a mood of the times. One described how the State Department argued with Red China after they demanded that the U.S. abandon Formosa (now Taiwan). Another detailed how the communist East German government chose a defense minister to direct its new 'People's Army.' This was a time of uncertainty on the world stage, when the United States vied for power against socialist and communist ideologies. By controlling forces of nature at home, the country oiled its muscles with self confidence. Lauded in newspapers as the "behemoth straddling and chaining the once unconquerable Missouri River," the Garrison Dam turned into one of these projects. An article told how the dam "tamed the turbulent old Missouri" and how electricity it generated was to illuminate homes, ring telephones and "milk thousands of cows."

On the day the Garrison powerhouse first cranked out kilowatts, a farm wife penned a newspaper column recalling the drudgery of life before electricity. She moaned about days of pumping water by hand, washing clothes with bent knuckles and filling kerosene lamps to provide a meager glow for her children crouched over homework. It was no surprise that Mrs. Majeres wrote "God bless Garrison Dam...for the many blessings and comforts that Rural Electrification brought us. Let's not stop there," she demanded. "Let's have many more Garrisons as the years go by."

Marilyn regarded the project with more ambivalence.

"I don't know if anyone really sits and evaluates the worth of a dam," she told me, considering the problems with sediment. "It's too early. Eventually the reservoir will hold a few feet of water. You can't even navigate without getting stuck in silt that's now around Williston. Where does all that silt go? Just starts to gather. We hear that eventually Lake Sakakawea will only be four feet deep."

Did losing the river affect tribal culture?

"It wasn't only Garrison Dam, but a lot of federal policy, not only with American Indians but immigration," Marilyn replied. "All of the sudden it was — everyone should be an American. Throw away your foreign accents. During World War II anything that was foreign was bad. When I was going to school there was little emphasis on preservation of culture.

"In the early forties, you could go to any one of these little towns and hear Russian, German, probably Swedish languages spoken all over the street. And Indian. You don't hear that any more. That happened during the war. Keep in mind you didn't call it sauerkraut then, you called it 'victory cabbage.' People got rid of their Indian names and took what they considered more American names."

Her words were a reminder of a powerful lesson from biology class — that diversity breeds adaptability and that specialization makes a species more prone to extinction. I shook my head, wary about glorifying any sort of monoculture.

I left New Town to return to Lake Sakakawea's shore. The campground was so big that I had to use a map just to find a toilet. A lone cloud sat above Six Pac. I was happy and cool in the shade on an otherwise searing ninety-degree-day. The wind swept my hair back, tossed yellow leaves down my shirt and pushed lake waves in parallel, deformed lines. I sat in a sagging lawn chair and considered recent conversations.

In the city of Bismarck days earlier, the Fish and Wildlife Service coordinator for the Missouri River named Mike Olson told me about healthy economies and healthy rivers being interlinked. Mike's work involved traveling along the Missouri River and encouraging communities to understand the importance of maintaining a healthy river. In the meantime the museum where Marilyn worked informed visitors about how changing the Missouri River affected communities. I realized that both Mike and Marilyn shared two common traits. Both taught the public about the Missouri River. Both also regarded history as a teacher, not as a source of blame.

Chapter 28

DIVING THE TAILRACE

To learn more about the Missouri River I decided to peek at it from the inside. At Lake Sakakawea I woke to the sound of wind, pulled on jeans, swallowed three handfuls of blanched peanuts, then drove to a Conoco station at Riverdale. At 8:00 a.m. sharp, a new silver XLT vehicle sidled close with the license plate: ADVENTUR. It hauled a trailer with *Adventure Divers — Minot* painted on one side. I stepped outside to greet the driver, then shriveled with fear on realizing that I had forgotten to set the hand brake. The truck started a forward roll. I retreated, slipped inside and stomped the pedal. The passenger wearing sunglasses sitting in the XLT threw a glance my way that read: 'So that's how you park, buddy. Let's see how you strap a scuba tank on.'

The driver, meanwhile, walked around his truck. He wore denim cutoffs and purple sunglasses and a T-shirt that read: *Actions Speak Louder than Words.*

"Aaron," he introduced himself. He was so clean cut that he looked aerodynamic. After shaking hands we drove below Garrison Dam.

The passenger was Aaron's younger brother Chad. Once we parked, Chad opened the trailer door, picked through piles of neoprene and dropped my gear into a heap.

Aaron's 'mobile dive shop' was impeccably ordered and ready to suit eighteen divers. It was no wonder that his business soared —

his was no loose-wheel organization. Aaron had quit his job as a heating and cooling technician to take over the local dive shop in Minot, further north. He was twenty-six years old and charged with enthusiasm, having completed over 350 dives in the region.

Aaron reversed his truck down the slipway and dropped a flat pontoon in the water. We stepped aboard it, then motored to mid river.

This section of the Missouri River below the Garrison Dam formed the 'tailrace' where chilled water ran away from the powerhouse through a 750-foot wide corridor. Chunks of hacked boulders armored both banks, halting erosion. The stretch of frothing water between the tailrace and Lake Oahe further south formed the Garrison Reach, almost one hundred miles of non-channelized, wild Missouri River. The difference in hydrology from one side of the dam to the other was immense. A drop of water took a year and a half to travel close to two hundred miles through Lake Sakakawea, but less than a day to bobble through more than ninety river miles of the Garrison Reach.

"You prefer this to diving in the lake?" I asked Aaron. The pontoon puttered in slow motion.

"Lake Sakakawea? We've done dives there. Usually visibility isn't good, even in winter time. Stirs up easy. Lake Sakakawea is a backed up river. There's a lot of water moving, so you get a lot of silt coming in from the river. Up towards New Town you can stick your arm deep in mud and never hit solid bottom."

I asked what the diving was like near buried villages, including Elbowoods.

"Most villages were wood, some block. Not much to see anymore. Most structures have fallen in. You can find foundations and debris. No different than lookin' at a bunch of rocks."

I started to put my wetsuit on, backwards.

"Haven't used a wetsuit before?" Chad asked, no doubt recalling my facility with the parking brake.

"Learned to dive in the Middle East," I said, having been certified in Dubai. "Never used wetsuits."

Chad shook his head as though to say: *right, buddy. Middle East, Midwest. Whatever.*

I suited up in booties, gloves and a neoprene hood so tight that it bruised ears, then punched arms through the sleeves of a buoyancy compensator, fought heels into a pair of yellow flippers and breathed through regulator valves to check that both worked. One was speckled with river silt and I jerked the mouthpiece away and spat out granules.

"How are conditions downriver?" I asked.

"Zero vis," Aaron said. "After three miles you get algae blooms."

He cut the motor beneath the spillway.

"Water's fifty-six degrees today," he told us. "Little chilly. Don't swim when you get in. Just drift. Ready? Jump at five."

I clasped a hand on the mask and jumped splay footed into the Missouri River. The water was the color of asparagus stems. After bubbing up, I gave Chad an OK signal, pushed a knob on the buoyancy compensator and sank — unaware of moving until seeing rocks on the river bottom, like burnt potatoes, whooshing past my ankles. My torso lunged downriver like a soap bar squeezed through a wet fist. Cold water squeaked inside the neoprene suit. I felt chilled, awake and free — happy and disoriented in a universe of blurred images of catfish and flicking grass.

The current bowled us over rocks. We could see only seven feet ahead. Chad shadowed me as I prodded at pillars of clay and cavities filled with coal. The flow was tame —eleven thousand cubic feet per second squirting from two floodgates — and we shot through a froth of air bubbles, moving head first to avoid clobbering shoulders on clay columns or catching our ankles in gaping cavities.

I turned behind. Chad reached down and grabbed a lost lure. He carried a fistful of other lures he had found — green bobbles and angled blades. His collection was part of a trove hunt: he would sell the salvaged booty back in Minot. I grabbed low and pulled a lure from the river bed. It had a rusty hook, an oval head and one Cyclops red eye. Chad, mercenary of the deep, thumped my shoulder and pointed at my chest. This meant *keep it.*

The depth gauge showed that we were between ten and twenty feet below the water surface. Propelled by the cold tailrace we washed through the Missouri's innards. Chad held onto a yellow line attached to a red buoy that floated on the surface with a sign reading *Diver Below.*

The current pushed us past pockets of coal into a twenty-eight-foot deep 'Honey Hole' between creamy clay towers. I kicked to the chasm's bottom. Chad followed. There we stood unmolested by currents in water the hue of salad oil. I then kicked legs and entered the current again. It was like swimming in gazpacho. After a half hour in this movable soup, my twenty-eight-pound weight belt sank from waist to rear and the pressure gauge flicked from yellow to red. Chad motioned upward and we ascended through a liquid strata of colors from pumpkin-pie-orange to opaque blue. Our heads burst above the water surface and we leaned our necks backward, marveling at the clarity of the sight of riverside bluffs. Once on the pontoon we unzipped wetsuits and let our shriveled flesh tighten in sunshine.

Below the water we had had seven feet of visibility, because water flowing out of the Garrison Dam was partially decanted from sitting in Lake Sakakawea. Even just another mile downriver the visibility dropped and water changed to the color of shriveled prunes. I realized that the relative clarity of this stretch of the Missouri River was artificial, a 'gift' of dam contractors.

"Look south," said Aaron. "The steep cliff? It was once an Indian kill site. Used to run buffalo off it into the river. If you were to look in the records for Jacques Cousteau, they came back here in the sixties and seventies and found up to three hundred buffalo skulls. They spent a week and a half bringin' em up."

Those days of treasure hunting were over.

"That's no longer legal. They're considered artifacts and property of the Corps of Engineers because the Corps maintains this land. We've found some parts — jaws and horned caps. Heard of people finding complete buffalo skulls. There's a big fine for that, it's either a $500 or $750 fine to take 'em from the river because they can be sold to the black market."

I looked at Chad's fist.

"Course fish hooks," Aaron added, "lots of those."

He pulled a cover off the engine and thumped it, then drove upriver for a second dive.

"Can't remember the date but they had a jet fighter crash in the river north of New Town," Aaron said.

The 'river' there formed Lake Sakakawea.

"Crashed through ice. Found it within twelve hours. Navy SEALS were there. They stripped the plane bald and took all the equipment out. One story is they demolished it, blew it up underwater. Other people said the plane's still intact with its wings broken off. Talked to guys who said there's nothing left but fragments. Too many stories. Probably been buried by five feet of silt since then. You could find it with metal detectors but you'd have to dig deep."

"Corps of Engineers won't let anything stay at the bottom of the lake. You have to have it out within seventy-two hours. Otherwise it's theirs and you have to pay them to get it out. Cars, snowmobiles, pickups. Anything that falls through ice or sinks has to be out within seventy-two hours for EPA and Corps regulations."

Aaron sighed. For the first time all morning his shoulders slumped.

"We're a little tired," he admitted.

At 8:23 the night before, he and Chad were called to recover the body of a missing eight-year-old near the town of Minot. The boy had lost his shoe in a river, sauntered in to find it and strode into a world beyond ours. The dive rescue team arrived forty-three minutes after getting the call, suited up and then recovered his body. I asked Aaron about searching under murky water. Was it difficult to see?

"We never open our eyes underwater when we're searching for people. You have the odd case of coming up on their face. There's a pretty good chance their eyes may be open. That will stick with your mind a long time. So we train in black masks, using duct tape or neoprene to cover the masks. It's all by feel."

He stood mid-pontoon, then swung his hands to demonstrate the dragnet technique.

"We're tied off with a rope on a pivot point. Just like a horseshoe. We learn signals and the guy who's holding the rope is your pivot. You keep the rope tight. When you get to a certain spot he'll give you two tugs, gives you three feet of rope. You tighten that rope back up, turn and change directions."

He recalled the night before.

"I swept right," Aaron said, feeling before an imaginary line before him. "Ended up grabbing the top of the little boy's head. Can't mistake the feeling of that."

Would searching the Missouri River be different?

"Searching gets pretty tough anytime there's current. Just depends on how bad it is. You might have to anchor. If the river was going north to south you'd anchor a boat in the east and west. Run a rope between 'em and have a diver move back and forth on that rope. Then lift up the anchors, drift six feet, and do it all over again."

Aaron and Chad dove during the warmth of summer and throughout long Dakota winters. When Lake Sakakawea froze over, they chopped holes in ice and plunged in. This sounded as inviting as circumnavigating a subpolar island by bicycle in winter. But the cold did nothing to detract this pair's love of the Missouri River.

"I don't think a lot of people know about this area. Everybody thinks North Dakota, oh, that's land-locked. There's nothin' to dive in. Well," Aaron said, looking out at the rough current and exquisite riverbanks. "That's just wrong."

Chapter 29

CHARLES DICKENS

The town of Garrison, North Dakota, prides itself as Walleye Capital of the World. The local radio station brags it's "got more tunes than the lake's got walleye" and the town park boasts Wally the Walleye, a twenty-six-foot long yellow and brown timber fish that bends its body beneath a trio of flagpoles.

When Garrison Dam rose, Lake Sakakawea turned into a sport fishing haven stocked with walleye, northern pike, sauger, yellow perch, crappie, white bass, and chinook salmon. This drew in fisherman and lit up the local economy.

I stepped inside a cinder block laundry center where a woman was making the transition from washer to dryer and from youth to middle age at the same time. Her glorious smile was endearing.

"From out of town?" she asked

"Yeah, you?"

"Spent my whole life in North Dakota. People say there's nothing here, but I like it. Don't have to lock my home or car or worry about where kids are. Somethin' else — I know my neighbors. You come for the lake?"

"Sort of."

"That lake and dam help this 'conomy in a big way. Affects everything when the water's low. Less visitors. Less people in the grocery store or laundromat."

She folded both arms, registering my silence as a cue to continue. "We have the Dickens Festival in winter. I participated last year."

"Charles Dickens?"

She nodded.

The town of Garrison scoots back in time each year for three weeks after Thanksgiving. During afternoons, a special market opens where vendors dressed in dated English costumes serve High Tea and scones on bone china. During evenings, a parade wafts down Main Street to where the Christmas Carol plays at the Kota Theater.

"Dickens," I said. "What's the connection with Garrison?"

"Isn't any. But we do it anyhow."

I threw my soiled socks and a cup of detergent into the washing machine, then pumped in quarters.

"I tried to get inside the library, but it was closed," I said. "There were no hours posted out front."

"Oh, yah," the woman said with a voice as bouncy as her cheeks. "Librarian, she takes lunch from 12 to 1, usually."

"It's 11:30, " I countered.

"Like I said, usually."

Back in the truck a radio singer bragged about his sexy tractor. I stopped and bought a quart of chocolate milk and tub of strawberries, then drove to Wolf Creek recreation area.

Once there I waded into Lake Sakakawea's waves. Two sunbathers lay in skimpy bikinis earning a deserved tan after eight months of Dakota chill. A nearby jetski whined and sent gulls rattling away. Globs of mud coated the shore and the geological trio of erosion, transportation and deposition performed their concert inside the lake's water, gumming up the reservoir bed with strands of sediment.

The thinner Missouri River had run before Lake Sakakawea rose. And before this river flowed, a hulking glacier pressed the bald earth down. When the glacier shriveled to a blue prune and retreated toward Canada it dropped a trail of holes in its wake, deeper and sparser than depressions left by any Hidatsa hut. Each hole formed a special type of habitat, one I decided to visit the next morning.

Chapter 30

PRAIRIE POTHOLES

The Audubon Wildlife Refuge in North Dakota is a land of ferruginous hawks, marbled godwits and chestnut-collared longspurs. Moorland surrounds a lake. The land looks like it would entice shamans hoping to recharge their magic and holds the same 'inarticulate character' that author Laurens van der Post used to describe the South African veld.

Before Garrison and Oahe dams rose, surveys predicted how their reservoirs would displace close to a million pheasants. To help compensate for this loss, the Snake Creek Wildlife Refuge was established in 1956. This included a pool singled out from Lake Sakakawea east of Highway 83, a cluster of water that resembled a hitchhiking left hand. The refuge was later renamed after John James Audubon. Today its 160,000 boggy acres provide refuge to whooping cranes, peregrine falcons and bald eagles.

Audubon was born on a sugar plantation in Haiti, the son of a French Naval Captain and his mistress. His father took him to France as a child and concocted stories to hide his illegitimate birth. Audubon later moved to the U.S. near Philadelphia to manage his own plantation. There he met and married a woman named Lucy who helped push him on to his eventual success as an artist. After Audubon published drawings of birds, he decided to depict mammals for a book titled *The Vivarious Quadrupeds of North America*. By then he was in his mid 50s. This goal took him on his last great adventure — through the Dakotas along the Missouri River. In the summer of 1843, he lodged at Fort Union and spent days crouched on a riverbank, sketching images of wildlife.

I roamed by foot over miles of prairie. Grass rustled against thistle. A lone doe scuttled past mating blue dragonflies. The land was not only diverse, but sneaky; stalks of grass unlaced both shoes.

Islands lay inside Lake Audubon. After Garrison Dam rose, the lack of predators drew waterfowl to these isles. Because unweathered shorelines are exposed to erosion, huge divots of earth slough away from isles after each storm, committing this little archipelago to a life that will be measured in decades rather than centuries.

The Fish and Wildlife office in Coleharbor is a low, comfortable box plunked on dark soil. Two biologists named Greg Hultberg and Mike Grabow greeted me inside. Greg wore a thick cotton suit. His dark glasses resembled shields.

"We've got four seasons up here, although I think the prairie changes season every two weeks," he said. His words and smile unmasked affection for the land.

"I grew up on a farm two miles away. My family homesteaded here in 1882," he added.

Decades before the refuge existed, Canadian geese nested in nearby cottonwood trees. Zealous hunters then blasted these fowl. By the 1930s, the savvier geese abandoned this region. In a later effort to recover their numbers, captive young were let mingle with migrating birds. This project paid off. Free young then returned to nest in the refuge.

"We've got lots now," Greg said. "Wherever there's water in this country, there's Canadian geese. So our efforts are now more focused on eco region areas. I'm talking about the Northern Coteau, the prairie potholes."

The Coteau system is a massive expanse of prairie wetlands containing 'potholes.' These are described by the U.S. Geological Survey as pockets of 'hummocky, rolling stagnation moraine' (moraine refers to debris deposited by glaciers). When it comes to draining the state of North Dakota, the Missouri River is the main channel. The total flow of the Red River at Fargo, the Sheyenne in Valley City, the James at Jamestown and the Souris at Minot add up to a scraggly four percent of the Missouri's flow at Bismarck. But three million years ago, instead of moving south toward where St. Louis now throbs, the Missouri River ran northeast. Four separate periods of glaciation reshaped the landscape, transforming the geography and giving the Missouri a new river valley to flow through along one glacier edge.

Greg reveled in his proximity to the Coteau. Knowing this was essential. Fathoming his love of this land put his viewpoint toward the changing river into context.

Ten thousand years ago glaciers receded from North Dakota. When the last ice blocks liquefied they created potholes east of the Missouri (the river's course formed the glacier's western frontline). This was the terrain I walked over earlier, soggy wetlands that formed tread marks of glaciation — considered delicious by wildlife. A hundred wetlands per square mile provided habitat for hundreds of species.

The process of building dams and changing the Missouri River to a chain of lakes irked Greg.

"Catastrophe is what it is," he said. "Eliminated five hundred thousand acres of a natural system. To me that's huge. Our legacy is that once these dams have fulfilled their use, we've destroyed a lot of land. What's that land going to look like? Look at everything it's displaced. All those species have moved out. These dams aren't going to be here forever," he said, referring to the ongoing buildup of sediment.

"This is called the walleye capital of the world. Yet when the lake first came up we never even heard of catching walleye."

His reaction toward altering the Missouri River was typical — emotional anguish about losing a landscape combined with rational acceptance that dams brought benefits: power, jobs, flood control. But would Greg favor dismantling mainstem dams along the Missouri River decades in the future?

"We might see the end of the Missouri River dam system. I don't know. I don't have a crystal ball. It'll keep going as a controversy 'till the dams disappear. That's my opinion.

"We're all governed by economics. You start changing economics, there's going to be controversy. Does Garrison want to see the river run wild? Probably not. Does somebody that doesn't live around here want to see the river run wild? They might enjoy that. People are self-interested no matter where you go."

Whenever I asked someone to identify the 'most significant' change brought about by pouring concrete dams across the Missouri River, their head shook with incomprehension. The question was worthless. It was impossible to pick out one single effect after entire systems of life and culture were severed from their surrounding. Yet Greg did respond, producing an answer that revealed an attitude as ancient as civilization.

"I would say landscape is the biggest biological factor that changed," he declared.

By calling landscape a biological entity, Greg unwittingly brandished his allegiance to the Gaia hypothesis, the belief that earth itself is a living, self regulating being — not just a collection of disparate ecosystems. If true, then all forms of life as well as inorganic matter form part of Gaia. The whole shebang of the natural world is considered part of Gaia: elephants, wrens, goldfish, cumulonimbus, festering algae, monkey puzzle trees, slithering chunks of lithosphere, cantering oryx, toxic bacteria, argon gas and truffle spores. When asked what they think of this 'hypothesis,' many farmers regard it as common sense, while more skeptical scientists — devotees of chopping reality into segments — shake their heads with disdain. This is because Gaia is not a quantifiable entity; it is a paradigm.

I thanked the men and stood to leave. Greg spoke again. His parting words revealed not only his allegiance to Gaia, but his untrammeled faith in her power.

"Mother Nature will always prevail," he stated. "We might screw things up a little, but it all comes out in the end."

Chapter 31

WILLISTON

Williston Bridge

Town streets in Williston, North Dakota looked sinister and immutable, as though frozen in time. The brown brick walls of J.C. Penney and the New Grand Cinema (*Our Screen Talks*) came from another era.

In a corner bar I spoke to a forty-year-old man who acted twenty-five. He had blue eyes, a red face and a silver necklace. He ordered a dollar bottle of Bud.

"Buildings around here look preserved," I said.

"Founding fathers don't want to change things," he explained. "They own the buildings. Want to keep everything the same. Keep new people out. That's what I think. You passin' through?" he asked.

I nodded.

"Good thing it's not winter. It gets too cold here. Thirty below for five days at a time. I have to chain up to drive out to the oil rigs to work. The older I get the harder time I have with it."

A lean man with deep eyes entered the bar. He was a darkly handsome fellow who looked toughened up from living in a town governed by the fist. He inserted himself on a stool next to me with the stealth of a bobcat. He looked in his early thirties.

"Hello sir," he said.

"Hi."

He eyed me like prey. In turn, I swigged down beer and asked him about camping.

"Going upriver? Doin' the Lewis and Clark stuff? Don't camp on that reservation. Don't do that. All alone? They'll kill your ass. You pull over for the night and somebody'll slit your throat. Don't go up there. They kill ya' unless you got local blood. Like me. My name's Winston. I went to school in Missoula, Montana, then came back to the rez."

I decided to pull into a town parking lot to sleep that night.

"You want to learn about the river? Then you need to talk to tribal elders," he said. "Always bring tobacco if you visit. If they're old, sixty, seventy, take unfiltered cigarettes. Remember, when an elder comes into the room, stand and offer your chair, even if there's a hundred empty seats. And don't speak or interrupt. Just listen."

I nodded.

"Another thing. If you go into a room and get a bad feeling, step outside. If it's quiet out there, if there's no sign of birds, squirrels or animals, then get out. Fast."

We talked for an hour. After he stepped away another man staggered in. He scratched his crotch and shook a shank of black hair as though he were a teenager in a shampoo commercial. A mashed green X was tattooed on his lower neck. He sat close. He gave a vicious scoff at a half heard joke and managed to convince the stranger — me — to buy him a drink. I asked for a beer and he changed the order to a shot of whisky. He gripped his glass with fingers resembling talons. This accentuated his image as a thankless harpy.

The conversation turned black fast.

"Whatcha doing?"

"Passing through. Researching the river."

"You strangers built that dam," he snarled. "Maybe tonight, maybe I kill a stranger. So, eh, buy me another drink," he demanded.

His jabbering was a nuisance. Yet eager to avoid confrontation thousands of miles from the nearest known face, I complied.

He eyed my notes.

"Journalist?" he asked.

"Engineer," I said before realizing that was worse — my ilk erected dams.

"Where you stay?"

"Camper."

"That one outside? You keep notes, tapes? What if something happens to your camper? Maybe it burns up," he said, and smiled a row of serrated brown teeth.

"Let me see these," he said and grabbed papers from my hands.

"Hey!"

"Gonna see what you're writing," he blurted, "Else maybe you don't leave this town. *Not alive*."

Lovely, I thought. Though I wanted out, timing was critical.

He opened the papers and read. His face oozed with enmity.

"You write like a doctor. But I can read it," he said.

He lied. No one could read my scribble.

"Write this down," he demanded.

Considering the pen-mightier-than-the-sword option as a peaceful exit to an asinine situation, I wrote down what he dictated.

"This was a life of a friend that I met in a bar talking about Williston. Name unknown, but he was a good friend. Thank you."

After I wrote this he thrust the papers back and slithered off to the bathroom. When he disappeared from sight I breezed out through a corner door. Under starlight I looked sideways, then listened. There was no sound of bird, squirrel or any other wildlife. Winston was right. It was time to leave. Fast.

SECTION FIVE:

MONTANA

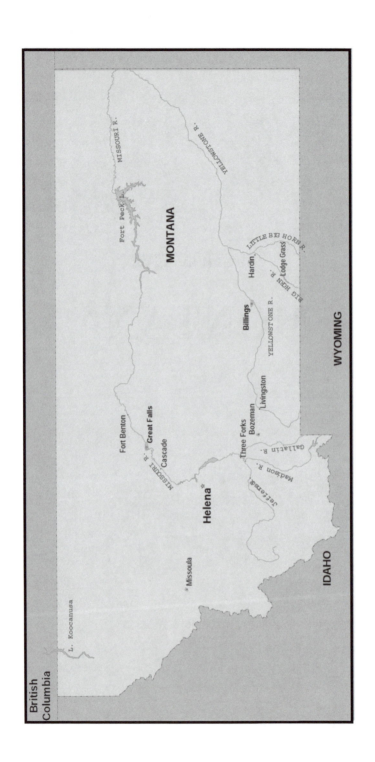

218

Chapter 32

BOOM TOWN

Road signs near Fort Peck Dam, Montana

Constructing Fort Peck dam not only changed the Missouri River's flow, but altered the fortunes of thousands of workers who completed the task. The dam sits on a hunk of badlands in eastern Montana. Until 1933, this location of searing summers and brutal winters epitomized desolation — a place where wild wind gusts crunched into misshapen hillsides. That changed when President Roosevelt launched construction of this gargantuan dam to attack Depression unemployment.

A local farmer named Sam Richardson recalled the dry era. "Our family hadn't had a crop in four years. When you went to lunch, the grasshoppers would gnaw at the salt from your hands on your pitchfork."

Fort Peck's earthen dam was drawn, poured and pumped into shape as 'a symbol of hope's ultimate victory over despair' during a severe economic slump. From its moment of inception, progress raged forward. In 1936, ten thousand workers dwelled in rattletrap shantytowns close to the construction site, eking their livelihoods by working in both marrow-chilling and sweltering temperatures. In 1936, temperatures oscillated between a summer high of 114 and a winter low of minus sixty-one degrees. The cold spiraled so deep that concrete had to be heated before it was poured. Winds up to seventy miles an hour whistled through shirt collars, clogging workers' ears with sand.

The Old Fort Peck trading post was built in 1867 on a shale ledge abutting the Missouri River. The following decade the river changed course and devoured the site. Today the 'new' town of Fort Peck forms the administration seat for dam operations, a quiet nook erected from what look like the same blueprints used to build Gotham City.

I drove into town on a hazy morning. The rectangular Corps of Engineers office was roofed with red and black tiles in a town as still as a coal shed in summer. Today its number of residents constitutes one percent of those who lived there when the dam rose. The 'General Store and Café' was abandoned. The local sixteen hundred-seat theater looked a tad large for town.

Inside the nearby Fort Peck power plant I stood on red floor tiles, my toes vibrating from generators underfoot. A black and white wall photograph showed a circle of men wearing aluminum hardhats and dribbling ash from Lucky Strike cigarettes while a hefty turbine rotor was lowered in place.

A young woman named Callie Riggin with long blonde hair and a hint of blue eye shadow met me in the lobby. She was guiding plant tours between semesters of studying biology in Helena. She wore clean new sneakers, a tartan dress, blue socks, white blouse and a sleeveless sweater. Within this pinnacle of engineering (an effort so exalted that the dam's photograph commanded the first cover of Life magazine), my senses were thrown off guard not by immensity, durability or 185,000 kilowatts of power, but by Callie's fashion.

We inspected the usual fare of a power plant — clickety turbine runners, galloping generators, posters preaching mantras of safety and immaculate machine shop floors. When we shuffled through a dank cable tunnel, I asked Callie to recall stories from days of dam building.

"There were eighteen towns around here during construction," she started. "Boom towns. Shanty towns. Some people lived in tents. One guy who came on this tour said his family lived under an overturned wagon box. The biggest, most notorious town was Wheeler, 'last of the Wild West.' Had workers getting drunk and driving seventy miles an hour down the road center. Had sixteen fires one year. Because you bring ten thousand men with money to an isolated place and suddenly you have a red light district and twenty-four hour saloons. There was no law here until a few deputies arrived from nearby Glasgow."

I later learned how Wheeler's more than four thousand workers lived in cheap wooden tenements. One resident said you could bulldoze the town and do no more than three thousand dollars of damage. Customers drank nickel beer or carted it off in pails from the town's half dozen all night taverns. In this hotbed of whiskers and whoring, holdups were as common as venereal disease. A local doctor named C.C. Lull fussed over ailments as varied as employees who tromped into his clinic — spider bites, gunshot wounds, frostbite, even smallpox.

"You could see hope the dam brought," Callie continued. "Roosevelt visited when he was president. Some towns were named New Deal and Delano Heights. But once the dam was constructed, towns blew away. They were made of nothing. Only one remains down the road — Park Grove. There's not much there."

I asked Callie what differentiated this oldest, westernmost mainstem dam from others along the Missouri River.

"Hold on," she said, and scampered upstairs to the engineer's office. Two minutes later she returned, her eyes blazing with success.

"This was the world's largest 'hydraulic fill' dam," she said.

"Great," I said. "What's that mean?"

She gave a blank stare. We both laughed.

I later learned how during construction a group of boats nicknamed the 'Fort Peck Navy' dredged the Missouri River. They pumped this slurry into miles of massive pipelines that poured it over the dam centerline, forming its core — the 'hydraulic fill.' Seven years after work began, 125 million cubic yards of earth bloated the dam and blocked the Missouri's flow, changing the squibbling river to a landlocked fjord.

Callie mentioned how the dam brought hope. I considered the past. During an age when food was relatively abundant, electric power widespread and employment plentiful, working construction on the dam was considered a gift. Regardless of how the Missouri River changes in the future and whether mainstem dams will stand

222

for another century, just looking at this structure gave me an appreciation for what it meant to the people of its day.

I thanked Callie and drove west — toward the most desolate stretch of the Missouri River shoreline.

Chapter 33

WHEN THE LAND BELONGED TO GOD

West of Fort Peck, no roads parallel the Missouri River but angle in from afar, like capillaries nourishing an engorged vein. Along this cranberry colored stretch of roadside I half expected to see gypsies trundle by in oxcarts. Yet to keep it from development, this desolate land had been lavished with protection.

It had been over three months since leaving St. Louis. I drove twenty-six miles along a dirt road to a site called The Pines along Fort Peck Lake. An oily wind blew in from the north. Hills looked as unshaven as a chin before breakfast until I rounded a hump and saw a string of evergreens scattered by the water. I aimed toward this confluence of buttes and pines in terrain as worn as the gloves on a nomad, a narrow life zone where rough winters once whittled the courage of pioneers thin.

I parked on a dirt incline. Water that normally lapped only feet away now sat a quarter mile distant. The campground was abandoned. I paced through moonbeams to the cracked shoreline where a dry wind licked drier skin. The fizz of nearby insects sounded like a cigar dunked in liquid.

A wildlife refuge bristling with more than a million protected acres surrounds Fort Peck Lake, stretching 120 miles from the east to the west. Longtail voles, silver-haired bats and yellow belly marmots thrive in this refuge, as do rarer whimbrel, cinnamon teal, and orange-crowned warblers.

This Fort Peck Game Range Refuge was granted status in 1936, thanks to the efforts of a jaunty optimist named Olaus Murie, a man who later wrote: "There is glamour of early explorations over it all, the romance of historic events..."

In the late nineteenth century the U.S. public grew intrigued by life in the western states, inciting magazines like Harpers and Century to crave images of Montana. A painter named Charles Russell, born in 1864, helped satisfy their appetite by delivering them with feisty scenes of a local crossbred culture, one where cowboys, Indians, ranchers and wildlife shared dust smoldered trails. After Russell's popularity soared, the Fort Peck Game refuge was renamed after him. Inside Montana's Historical Society two of his paintings show the importance of the Missouri River to his life. In the self portrait *Charles M. Russell and His Friends* the saddled painter waves his left hand toward an onrush of Indian warriors and scraggly cowboys scurrying up a cleft before the Missouri River. Another canvas titled *When the Land Belonged to God* shows a stampede of buffalo swerving before the Missouri.

After a night at the Pines, I woke and repaired a flat tire, then moved south of the refuge and west across Musselshell River to enter Petroleum County. Here drivers wore cowboy hats; trucks wore canoes.

During annual migrations, buffalo once crossed waters at the confluence of the Missouri and Musselshell rivers. They were so plentiful that Crow and Gros Ventre Indians came to Fort Musselshell to trade buffalo robes for a mere ten cups of flour (or six cups of sugar) apiece. This was before trains chugged over the land and the Missouri River formed the principal passageway into and out of Montana, a time when whisky traders and woodchoppers and the likes of Kid Curry skulked about the Missouri River bottoms (during times when the Kid wasn't running with Black Jack Ketchum or Butch Cassidy and the Sundance Kid).

Rustlers who raided Montana and Wyoming ranches wrangled cattle away at gunpoint and led these to their base at the Musselshell / Missouri River confluence. There they altered brand marks, then herded the cattle north to sell in Canada. In 1884, Granville Stuart led a group of cattlemen in a bout of vigilante justice; he hung four thieves and then killed another five in a gun battle. When the shootout ended soldiers apprehended five more fleeing rustlers and handed them over to 'Stuart's Stranglers' to be lynched. This homegrown justice ended cattle rustling in the region.

I considered a cadre of near mythical explorers who had vanished in the past: Earhart over the Pacific, Saint Exupery over the Mediterranean, Haliburton on a Chinese junk and Wegener (father of the theory of Continental Drift) along a Greenland ice cap. If I vanished, who cared? I have had no fame or following or family, no wife or tots awaiting postcards or chatty emails. Even astronauts, regardless their distance from earth, have dozens of ears and eyes to hear their musings, plot their trajectories and measure heart rates. In contrast no one knew my location or timetable, much less in which geographical or mental state I was. Few could identify what type of truck I manhandled over wavy bucolic roads. This freedom embodied a desultory sort of bliss. It could also turn lonely. On a whim, east of Winnett, I phoned a brother in Denver and told him my license plate number, in case I vanished and Six Pac was found abandoned near some remote cow pasture.

I turned north and passed Box Elder Creek. To the west lay a chain of peaks. I soon pulled into the James Kipp Recreation Area to spend the night. Chilled air that evening felt like a wool shawl over bare flesh — scratchy, uncomfortable — perfect weather for chickpea soup and lemon tea.

In the morning I followed the Missouri River's beveled banks westward along Knox Ridge Road. A sign warned 'impassable when wet.' The vista from shore looked supreme and inviting. I pulled over and parked Six Pac and hiked down a slope to one edge of the Missouri River. There I peeled off clothes, paced through muddy goo and plunged in. The water was cool as dew and knocked air from my lungs. I bobbed for more than a quarter mile downriver. While floating through the water I considered the history of this land.

On October 2, 1968, President Lyndon Johnson signed The Wild and Scenic Rivers Act into law. Its goal was to preserve free flowing stretches of great rivers 'before growth and development make the beauty of the unspoiled waterway a memory.' To gain eligibility for wild and scenic designation a stretch of river must contain at least 'outstandingly remarkable' value — whether scenic, geologic, historic, cultural, or related to fish or recreation.

Four years later President Ford applied this designation to the segment of Missouri River between Fred Robinson bridge and Fort Benton, Montana. More than two decades after that, in 1999, Secretary of Interior Bruce Babbit floated along this river section with authors and Lewis and Clark aficionados Stephen Ambrose and Dayton Duncan, as well as Montana's Senator Baucus. Impressed by the river's quality, Babbit wanted to afford more protection to this corridor of water. He decided to issue a 'segregation order' for much of this stretch of the Missouri River. This order would halt new mining claims and leave scant room for new riverside activities outside the land's current use.

When they learned of this move, ranchers holding grazing rights along these 'Missouri breaks' howled in anger. Montana's congressional delegation then aligned with these ranchers, inciting Babbit to withdraw his notion. He asked instead for a Resource Advisory Council to recommend how to manage these breaks in the future. Meanwhile locals opposed to protecting this part of the river created the 'Take Back Montana' organization. To counter these 'take backers,' a group of wildlife and hunting organization banded together to form the 'Wild Missouri Campaign.' Listening to these diverse viewpoints, the Bureau of Land Management council held public meetings in the towns of Lewistown, Great Falls, and Havre where they won — by a narrow margin — needed support to add protection to these breaks.

This council then forwarded to Babbit their recommendations for managing this portion of the Missouri River. When he heard a virtual fifty/fifty split in opinion about whether or not to protect the breaks, Babbit pushed Montana's legislature to resolve the deadlock.

When the state failed to foster consensus on time, Babbit let the federal government take action.

In the same White House room where Thomas Jefferson and Meriwether Lewis once rustled maps before launching their expedition westward, President Bill Clinton signed a law designating the Upper Missouri Breaks as a national monument, a region withdrawn from mining, oil and gas field development. Today the breaks span 149 miles of the Wild and Scenic Missouri River and include more than 370,000 acres of land. This territory includes part of the route traveled on by Lewis and Clark, as well as a portion of the trail Chief Joseph took on his epic flight toward the Canadian border.

While still bobbing through the river water at Knox Ridge, I snatched glimpses of bony outcrops and brown earth. Dried grass poked through rock fissures. The heat of summer had toasted the land. I soon walked out of the Missouri's flow.

During recent weeks I had heard complaints that this wild segment of the Missouri River would soon be overcrowded — congested with families squeezed onto rafts. One man warned me about the future. He told how campgrounds would fill up with bickering multitudes littering comic strips and empty potato chip bags along its sandy shores.

Someday, perhaps. But on a Saturday midmorning in August, beneath a clear sky and generous sun, I spent hours dawdling along the Missouri River without seeing another boat or human. So much for rumors.

Chapter 34

BIRTHPLACE OF MONTANA

View of Missouri River outside Fort Benton, Montana

I pulled into Fort Benton, Montana, with bloodshot eyes and dusty nostrils. The heat was raw. A scrawny doe the color of bone walked into a vacant lot, picking a path without regard for nearby traffic. Along the main street a family stepped out of their truck with red and white canoes lashed to its top. The vehicle was a Mazda, the first foreign vehicle I'd seen in months. The car was a sign of things to come. From St. Louis, Missouri, until Montana's Fort Peck, the mindset of the Midwest had prevailed. Fort Benton formed a gateway to a more western set of attitudes.

The Missouri River wound past the town center, flanked by mowed grass banks and dotted with signposts that explained local history. Fetid grass blooms made the river look like broccoli soup, but its slender flow was still the town center's highlight. Fort Benton's respect for the river reflected a collective memory of how this water brought the town life.

During the nineteenth century steamboating era, Fort Benton was a river terminus and a den for wayfarers in transit. The town was a fur trading center and an outfitting post for miners, trappers and sharp toothed explorers. Freight, stage and mail routes poked out from town like spokes on a wagon wheel and the 642 mile long Mullan Wagon Road — linking the Missouri and Columbia rivers — touched Fort Benton at one end. After slogging more than two thousand miles upriver from St. Louis the locale was a welcome sight to steamboat passengers. Hoards of miners with dark beards, blonde curls and an eerie stamina trudged off each incoming transit, eager to traipse south and seek their golden windfalls at Bannack, Virginia City and Last Chance Gulch.

Fort Benton now calls itself 'Birthplace of Montana,' although it was once described as 'a straggling hamlet of rude log cabins interlaced with deeply rutted wagon tracks.' Five hundred people lived there in the mid 1800s. Farmers fresh from the east coast, California miners, fur traders, trappers and 'the soft spoken southerner, flotsam of the wrecked Confederacy' mingled together with scoundrels lying about false bonanzas. The Fort Benton Vigilance Committee were responsible for so many hangings that miners were able to throw their saddlebags filled with gold dust on the floor of the local I.G. Baker and Company store, then wander off for a week. When they returned they found their goods untouched.

"Mountain steamboating was the greatest steamboating this country ever knew. The Missouri River was the greatest highway that the world has ever known," boasted Fort Benton's *River Press* in June, 1937. The article described an era that ended in the 1880s.

From the time the steamboat *Independence* entered the Missouri River in 1819 until the *Chippewa* pulled beside Fort Benton in 1859, the ascent of steamers further up the Missouri leaped ahead in small gulps — a hundred or two hundred miles at a time.

The risks of fighting local tribes, ramming into snags, freezing in ice or exploding boilers formed principal perils of steamboat travel. In the state of Missouri in 1854 the steamboat *Timour's* boiler detonated three miles below Jefferson City, erupting like a huge powder keg in a confetti of splinters and strafing nails. The blast killed thirty passengers and it threw the boat's safe to the top of a nearby bluff. At Fort Benton in 1861 a deck hand snuck into the bowels of the *Chippewa* clenching a candle in one fist. He intended to steal a draught of smuggled liquor, but his flame detonated twenty-five kegs of gunpowder and demolished the boat. Merchandise was later recovered three miles downstream.

Seven years after the first steamboat *Chippewa* reached Fort Benton the gold rush was in full swing; during one season thirty-nine boats docked in town, including steamers big enough to carry four hundred passengers. These boats hauled eighty percent of precious metals downriver. The richest cargo taken on one steamboat journey was supposedly $1.25 million in gold dust ('and 230 hard-bitten, well-armed miners') that descended the Missouri River in September of 1866.

The journey began smoothly. But hundreds of miles downstream the crew was forced to dislodge the grounded steamer near the mouth of Milk River. When the boat squirmed like a prodded slug, it threw a passenger named McClellan overboard. Though the water was only two feet deep, McClellan's leather belt bulging with gold dust weighed his body down, drowning him. The current then carried away this victim of his own hoarded riches.

The truck radiator boiled over south of Fort Benton, and I pulled into a rest stop near a cluster of hay bales. There I stood at the edge of a semicircular rimrock wall hundreds of feet above river and plains. Below, the Missouri River curved like a rope, carving a path parallel to this cliff. It seemed as much a presence as a river. I envied the farmer who lived below and woke each dawn to this vista of cliffs ringed by muscular water.

The vista below reminded me of Alan Watts' words from his book *The Wisdom of Insecurity*. He told how life is a state of flux and that wanting fixed security — stasis — is to desire that which is not a part of life. When we try to stake ourselves and our egos to a secure shore, we often find that the river of life drifts away, inflicting us with a sense of unease that makes us yearn for even more security.

"It must be obvious, from the start, that there is a contradiction in wanting to be perfectly secure in the universe whose very nature is momentariness and fluidity," he wrote. "If I want to be secure, that is, protected from the flux of life, I am wanting to be separate from life. Yet it is this very sense of separateness in which we feel insecure."

His words were inspiring. I believed that by maintaining optimism and flexibility, the future would unfold in a way both benign and prosperous.

The day felt suddenly easy. I moved away from the cliff and breathed deep beneath a mackerel sky. Uncertain of what lay ahead I was willing to roam and learn. For a rare moment in life both hands stayed loose of certainty while the hours swelled with the rich bliss of knowing that nothing stays secure. There is no predicting where the river of life will carry us.

Chapter 35

GREAT FALLS

Each year the Missouri River Natural Resources Conference opens at different riverside cities. I decided to attend this three-day gathering at Great Falls, Montana. Once there I sat in the hotel's sizable meeting room with several dozen people. On the first morning a cluster of Assiniboine and Blackfeet Indians gathered before us to sing and knock on drums and tell how the river influenced their tribal heritage. This emphasized the conference theme: how people, culture and history related to the Missouri River.

Keynote speaker Daniel Kemmis then stood before a pine podium. This ex-mayor of Missoula, Harvard graduate lawyer and author of the book *This Sovereign Land* pointed to a map of the Missouri River watershed.

"This place," he told the audience, "is now becoming a very important community, one that has to learn how to take care of herself."

He then posed a pivotal question about managing riverside land. "Is there any way of inhabiting these watersheds of the West sustainably unless we come up with something totally new?"

The concept of a watershed is pivotal to Western land management. Basically, moisture running over a watershed drains to a common destination — usually a river aimed toward an ocean. Watersheds can be immense or puny. Like a state is composed of separate counties, big watersheds are comprised of smaller watersheds. While water in the Missouri River watershed meanders to the Atlantic in time, water within the Columbia watershed flows toward the Pacific Ocean. Both of these watersheds are comprised of thousands of smaller similar units.

To emphasize the importance of watersheds, Kemmis told the conference how he considered the explorer John Wesley Powell to have been a prophet for the West. A one-armed civil war veteran, Powell first rafted through the Grand Canyon along the Colorado River in 1869. Based on his exploration of arid western states, Powell considered how to divide and manage land in the western U.S. He criticized dividing land with square grids and warned of tragedy if homestead laws and survey methodologies from the east coast were transferred to the rugged, western landscape. He suggested that watersheds, rather than arbitrary rectangles, be considered as practical units for dividing Western terrain. Powell believed that political jurisdictions should be based not on how compass arrows swing through a magnetic field, but on how water flows across earth. In this way, the landscape itself forms a guide as to how it should be divided.

"It's as if landscape is dictating to stupid humans how to govern the land," Kemmis explained. One of his hands gripped an edge of the podium before him and he described how Powell believed "that homesteads should not be drawn according to the grid, but according to topography. Powell said draw political jurisdictions according to the way water flows, and people will govern themselves more efficiently and more cooperatively."

Instead, politicians applied the Federal Township and Range system to the West, a sort of third grade level attempt to impose order on landscape by dividing it into topographical squares. Subdivided land in this system is laid out in blocks called townships and sections. Each square mile 'section' can be divided into half and quarter sections (or even quarter of quarter sections) and farms are often laid out according to these squares.

Powell's desire to divide land using watersheds never took root. Instead the government divided territory based on straight line surveys adopted from cozy little glens and humble mountain ranges of the eastern U.S., ignoring the larger western watersheds. This last truth rankled Daniel Kemmis.

"The idea that people in New Jersey have as much to say as to what goes on in the Bitterroot mountains as people in the Bitterroots is just wrong," he stated. He then lightened his tone and mentioned how he had noticed a change of late, a paradigm shift toward the way natural resources were being managed out west. He described how communications had improved between professionals and lay people along the Missouri River and throughout its watershed; he spoke of how a 'confluence of ideas of watershed and collaboration' was beginning to turn powerful, swung into place by some invisible impetus independent of government.

Listening to Kemmis re-emphasized for me the value of gathering local knowledge before making decisions as to how to manage landscape and rivers. Dividing land in the West, including the creation of allotments on Indian reservations, was decided on by those who spent too little time assessing local conditions. This truth formed the most strategic lesson I learned during my journey — that to effectively manage our great rivers in the future, we must listen to those who live along their banks. Hearing Kemmis speak made me recall my past months of moving upstream. I had plotted no course, but chose to stop based on suggestions given along the route or from newspaper clippings gathered in libraries. When I realized that observations Kemmis made aligned with identical insights I gleaned from conversations along the river, this mode of travel was suddenly vindicated.

Kemmis spoke in clean, wise paragraphs, exhorting the role of visionaries rather than technical specialists to map out a future for the Missouri River — one that intertwined communities with geography. He emphasized that what really mattered was the way personal lives wove themselves into the communities they belonged to. Kemmis advised those in the audience involved with managing the Missouri River to "Consider yourselves not to be managers of a resource, but managers of a community."

He then asked "Where is history headed? Where is the river of history flowing?" His own answer was that "At a number of different scales — from global to local — we are coming to inhabit 'real' places again. Within the context of globalism, we are becoming aware that we are a part of continents."

These words were inspirational — an insinuation that despite our past neglect of watershed awareness, people were starting to appreciate real environments of prairie, mountain, sagebrush and natural rivers once more over artificial domains that include mega malls and drive through taco outlets.

Author Wallace Stegner wrote about this when he described the psyche of the Western landscape: "This is the native home of hope. When it fully learns that cooperation, not rugged individualism, is the quality that most characterizes and preserves it, then it will have achieved itself and outlived its origins."

To thrive economically, Montana's vision of its future will have to integrate into a larger vision of how the state interacts with both the rest of the country and with the world. Its ranch exports feed international markets while the Missouri River and its tributaries draw tourists from other countries who canoe, fly fish and raft.

The keynote address was inspiring. To manage land and rivers, Kemmis advised that we first take care of securing a vision for both.

After the tribes stepped away I listened to another speaker — John LaRandeau from the U.S. Army Corps of Engineers. With a few well selected facts, John erased a romantic misconception about the historic Missouri River — the myth that Lewis and Clark ascended a river that was generally a 'braided stream' with multiple meandering channels.

"How do you want the Missouri River to look in the future?" he asked the audience, like a waiter wanting to know how they wanted a T-bone steak cooked.

He pointed to a map of the river.

"Side channels here? Shallows? Think about it," he said, referring to the Corp's ability to adjust the river's course. "But the 1890 maps are probably not a vision of the future river."

John appeared compact and orderly, a professional attuned to the pitfalls of distorted history. In 1979, just before the Corps of Engineers completed their stabilization work along the Missouri River, the Iowa Geological Society published a special report for the Iowa Conservation Commission titled "Changes in the Channel Area of the Missouri River in Iowa, 1879 - 1976."

The report's executive summary states that: "Between 1804 and the late 1800s the regime of the Missouri River, particularly north of the Platte River, changed radically from a meandering stream, with a single sinuous channel, to a semi-braided stream with numerous multi-channel reaches."

In other words when Lewis and Clark poled, rowed, sailed and cordelled up the Missouri River in 1804 and 1805, the expedition, in general, moved up a river with an appreciable main channel, a 'sinuous ditch.' But the *later* river of steamboat days changed to a braided stream — a series of shallow meanders that flicked all over the floodplain. The earlier river was hardly stiff and often sloppy. But it allowed the expedition to move upstream through a vaguely coherent stream of water, not a beef jerky pattern of woven currents that existed by the end of the nineteenth century. Why did the river change? Floods, most likely. A series of frequent deluges (perhaps related to the changing climate of the time, LaRandeau remarked) pummeled the Missouri Basin during the nineteenth century. Changes to weather patterns, climate and riverbank stability caused the Missouri to adjust its flow.

Like other conference speakers (including author Stephen Ambrose and paleontologist Jack Horner) LaRandeau's words highlighted the truth that a sound vision for managing the river must respect its historical context.

Chapter 36

STRAW BALES

Dan Ryan outside his straw bale house near Eagle Rock, Montana

Roads running between Great Falls and Helena, Montana, weave back and forth across the Missouri River. Along one of these I learned how both respect for the history of Lewis and Clark and for community consensus help define how pockets of riverside land are managed.

At Hardy Creek I parked outside Osterman's Missouri Inn. I sat inside the bar beside a man with three holes in his straw hat, as though he'd ducked during a shootout. His oval glasses magnified bright eyes.

"How are you today?" he asked, sipping ginger ale from a can.

"Weary."

"Traveling?"

When I mentioned my route along the Missouri River, he rocked his head in slow motion.

"Should come to a meeting at Dearborn Lodge tonight. Highway Department wants to transfer a piece of land to county control that includes Tower Rock. They were using it as a quarry for years, chopping blocks off. That all stopped quick when someone realized that Lewis once climbed it.

"Name's Dan," he added. "Dan Ryan. Live nearby. Eagle Rock One is my address. Not much of a place but it's got a million dollar view."

Dan reminded me of a brooding lawyer from a spaghetti western. I even snuck a low glance to check whether a watch chain looped out of his hip pocket. He was Montana minus cowboy and a man who adored open minds as much as open space.

"I, eh, live in a straw bale house," he said with a mixture of pride and bashfulness. "Built it myself. Took three years and one hundred straw bales. Bound them in chicken wire."

My eyes kept contact, not knowing that this invited his quick sermon on construction techniques.

"It's fifteen by twenty four feet. I coated it with cement. Used pallets for the floor and cut and barked lodge pole for rafters. Then I put Styrofoam between the perlins and the tin roof. Can you guess the cost?"

"Fifteen grand."

"Twelve hundred bucks," he continued. "My grandkids call it the Flintstone home, and let's not hear any three little pig stories," he added.

"Come to the meeting at seven tonight," he insisted. "Tower Rock should be protected for its historical value. This Lewis and Clark Bicentennial is just the opening. The flood of people will start coming after that. It's up to us to protect this land and river."

That evening I stopped at the inn in Dearborn and sat inside a huge dining hall beneath hefty timber beams. Faces from the Highway Department, the County Commissioners office and the Bureau of Land Management reclined at a narrow table before the audience. Thirty of us listened to them prattle about a land swap.

By directive the Highway Department had to sell surplus land not used for roads or maintenance. It was preparing to cut loose a 136 acre parcel where Tower Rock sprouted. A map at the front of the room delineated this site. If not sold or traded to another government entity the land would go to public auction — with potentially dangerous effects on the future sanctity of the rock.

Dan raised his hand. He then stood in clean jeans to speak. He was eager to out-maneuver any adversaries who hoped to entrust this land to private development. He spoke slowly, flavoring his arguments against this prospect with common sense rather than acrimony. He appealed to reason rather than to fine print.

"If the federal government wanted to turn Yellowstone Park over to the state of Montana, they'd want us to have a plan for how to maintain it," he stated. "As stewards, you need to develop a land-use-plan before getting rid of Tower Rock. We're just trying to preserve another monument, like Pompey's Pillar. I don't think anyone can put a dollar value on historical significance."

One commissioner spoke. She offered to write the Governor, asking her advice about handling this sensitive land transfer. A wiser, wrinkled bureaucrat from the highway department advised her against that move, certain the governor would just pass the letter her way.

"And all you'll do is create a circle," she sighed.

A hoop yes, but a circle of power for an aspiring commissioner who wanted to flaunt her name before the Governor. Her personal agenda sent creeps up my spine, making me admit that this show was getting good. I wished then that I had upped the emotional value of my root beer by adding a dabble of Scotch before the meeting began.

A sneering bulldog scurried across the floor, hacking its claws against the polished pine. The bartender whistled and clicked his fingers and tried to shoo 'Alfie' back, a scene that caused a few laughs and deflated tensions in the room. A BLM representative named Richard Hopkins next stood. He surprised us by revealing that his agency was interested in acquiring the Tower Rock site. This revelation opened up an avenue for the federal government to maintain the property, a proposition that put dimples into Dan's cheeks. Within an hour the BLM and county agreed to try to protect Tower Rock and Dan and I agreed to charbroil burgers at his house.

Lewis would be astounded by all the fuss.

"We can use places like Tower Rock to educate kids," Dan said when we stepped outside the building into a luscious purple evening. "It's not all about selling land and making money. I mean two minutes after he dies, Ted Turner is no different than me."

Dan's frugality and protectiveness toward open land reminded me of Marlin the Nebraskan canoe outfitter, or Wolf River Bob.

These three men shared a value system that elevated land stewardship to a plateau of simple sanity. History recalls how the artist George Catlin scrapped his career as a lawyer to follow his heart song as a painter, then lived and died poor. Financially, perhaps. Men like Dan, Marlin and Bob were similar to Catlin in that although their bank accounts hardly bulged they never considered themselves poor. They had food, shelter, health, open space and freedom to live as they chose.

I followed Dan. He drove his '93 pickup with a beaten tailgate to his straw bale bungalow, a simple brown box that sat on two acres of sloping hillside (his neighbors called it "Little House on the Prairie").

Cosy interior of Dan Ryan's straw bale house –
impervious to Montana's temperature swings

"My Camelot," Dan said and waved me toward his porch. "Better than a three bedroom home on a corner lot with too many things to pick up."

I walked up the wooden porch steps and stepped inside. There was a distorted balance inside his hacienda, an inadvertent feng-shui arrangement of imperfect angles and non-linear joints. Mortar met wood and tile touched rock in an organic construction that broadcast a sense of inner comfort. Plaster coating the walls was unfinished; glossy timbers were unplaned. This gave Dan's nook a look of wild durability. It reminded me of the effect seen from standing above unchanneled and undammed stretches of the Missouri River where willows, croaking cottonwoods and haphazard sandbars emanated a sense of harmony.

Two gold plated musical saws, four silver Charlie Russell plates and a bottle of Willie's Hemp Soda stood on a shelf above the front door. I inspected titles on the bookshelf to one side: *The Straw Bale House, Flea Markets, Old Fishing Lures, Concise Atlas.*

Dan set two glasses of milk and a bowl of homemade oatmeal cookies on the patterned tablecloth. We sat to talk.

"Cut, hauled and split each log myself," he said. "Splittin' took most time. A day apiece for each log. I drove five miles upriver to get clean sand and hauled more loads in that half ton Toyota than I can count. Moved twenty-nine tons of earth with a pick and shovel.

"It's worth it though. This place has an insulating value of R-50. In winter when it's thirty degrees below I light up that stove," he said and pointed toward a black box no bigger than a twenty-inch television set. "Gets so hot in here that I have to open the windows and sit in my under shorts."

He then stood and pulled a painting off one wall, revealing a glass pane behind it. This looked not to the outside world but to the wall's interior — showing a grid of straw.

"Truth Window," he explained.

Without this window there was no way to tell that a hundred straw bales weighing eighty pounds each formed the enclosure around us that warded off the nip of winter and the pinch of summer's heat.

The next morning we sat on Dan's porch. Together we stared out toward Eagle Rock and its adjacent valley.

"I planned on being a millionaire by the time I was thirty-one," Dan said. He thrust his Swiss army knife into a hunk of Colby cheese and handed me a cut square.

"When that didn't pan out I realized that what mattered was raising my kids. My grandkids love this home and land. Out here they can pee anywhere."

With my health restored and appetite quelled, I was ready to ramble on and hunt fresh tales and information. Meeting Dan and witnessing how a riverside community resolved its problems shook away feelings of loneliness born from crossing eastern Montana. It also reminded me of what Montana author Norman MacLean wrote: "I did not know that stories of life are often more like rivers than books."

Dan walked to my truck window before I drove off. He handed me a single strand of straw.

"This is a starter kit," he said. "For when you build your own house."

The further west I moved, the quicker my intrigue with trailside characters transformed to genuine fondness.

Chapter 37

THREE FORKS

Lewis and Clark named the river tributaries meeting at Three Forks, Montana as the Jefferson, Gallatin and Madison — and considered their confluence an 'essential point' in the continent's geography. Yet *exactly* where the Missouri River begins is still disputed.

Before it reaches Fort Benton the Missouri River changes course from its thousands of previous miles. The flow still clicks back and forth like jagged lightning, but aims south instead of north or west. This course passed Dan's straw bale home, slithered east of Helena and transformed to the hooked teardrop of Canyon Ferry Lake. South of this lake I drove to where the Missouri River lay in a valley, infantile and blue. Summer's heat had taken away most of the water and the river looked not big or muddy, but medium and mossy. Its low flow exposed rounded rocks the size of papayas. From there I drove to Three Forks, source of the Missouri River and veritable end to my inquisitive half-continent long slog. Legend tells how at this river confluence the Blackfeet Indians, ravaged by drought, consulted a moose for advice. He counseled them to mend their ways by working together to solve problems. When they did as instructed it rained for twelve days, teaching the tribe to respect Mother Earth for what she bestowed.

Wearing shorts and a t-shirt, I stepped outside the truck at Three Forks and heard a voice.

"That's not the Missouri River," a man with a gray beard and grungy jeans said, pointing at ruffled water. He clutched a fishing pole and stood on a dirt bank.

According to a sign thrust into the earth by the U.S. Geological Survey near his feet, the Missouri River originates where two — not three — of its tributaries meet.

Not true, this man declared. His name was Larry Clark.

Larry Clark, fishing guide at Three Forks, Montana

"Now this is the Madison right here. And that's the Jefferson over there," he said and pointed at two slinking strands of river that wove before us.

"A lot of people argue with me ever' day that is the Missouri. That's *not* the Missouri River. The Missouri is over there!"

He pointed toward water two miles distant. There the Gallatin River thrust itself, like a copulating tiger, into the combined flow of the Madison and Jefferson rivers.

"The sign here says Missouri River Headwaters. It's *not!*" Larry grunted. "I argue with people ever' day. Guy who works with the Fish and Game Department had some people here from Germany — dozen of them. I'm sittin' and arguin' with this guy. I say, 'what do you do sir?' He says 'well I work for Fish and Game and I put up the signs,' and I say 'well you better take 'em down 'cause they're not right!' In my world it takes three rivers to make the Missouri. They don't call it Two Forks, they call it Three!"

Larry shook his head that gave the impression: *government idiots.*

"Madison, Jefferson, Gallatin rivers. Which was President? Which was Secretary of State? Which was Secretary of Defense? Some argue they were all presidents. Weren't. Jefferson was president at that time, Madison was Secretary of Defense and the guy with the big money, the guy who wrote checks, was Gallatin."

The sky looked squeegee clean and the landscape was profuse with growth. Life around Three Forks appeared to be an uncomplicated affair.

"Rivers change every year," Larry added. "The Jefferson used to come right into the Madison here. Five years ago it changed. Now the channel goes thataway," he said and pawed toward some vague space downriver.

"Madison changed this year. Clear up to the beginning of where the dam is. We had big ice jams. Made new channels. Cut through farmers' fields. Goes where it wants to go!"

Larry grabbed his hooks and bent toward me. For him the river was a prankster, a friend to play with each morning.

"They moved town," he continued. "In 1909, they had a big flood over at Old Town Three Forks. Moved bigger buildings. The river just said it's gonna flood. Did flood. It took out a lot of old homesteads so they moved it outta the floodplain. We were eight hundred, now we're eighteen hundred people in Three Forks. People work in Bozeman and live here. Commute down the highway ever' day."

Larry snapped his eyelids closed and turned upward toward a sapphire sky. He then opened an eye to inspect the notebook in my hand.

"You some sort of government agent?"

"What?"

"You know. Agent. Government. Washington, DC."

"Try Albuquerque, Larry."

He rolled his eyes and let loose a *humph,* then looked past the water.

"See any houses there? I don't. It's what I love about this place. I've been here since 1942. This is my home, my love, my beloved Montana. I meet so many people every day here on this river. I'm part owner in a rock shop, candy store, motel type thing in Three Forks. We get people from all over the world. They love Montana! There was a big group from Norway here Thursday. They floated the Jefferson and said it was a lot warmer than Norway. They were tickled to death to be here. It's a beautiful place, just peaceful and quiet. There'll be a deer or elk over on that far bank. I've seen mulies with white tails right there. The rivers, I've floated every one of them — the Madison, Gallatin, Jefferson.

"She'll freeze over all winter long. December we had twenty-seven degrees below here in this valley. But not enough snow. Last year they closed my beloved Jefferson 'cause there wasn't enough water. Usually by Saint Patrick's day, middle of March, I'm out here fishin' this hole. There's all kinds of bald eagles. Seven of them last week. Jest followin' each other and drawin' on wind."

After thousands of miles of tracing a river I had reached its nominal source. There, Larry's voice rooted me to the earth.

"I'm related to William Clark," he said, disrupting my fantasy.

"I have a certificate that says so on my wall. Came through the Mormon Church out of Salt Lake. They keep track of everything that happened in England clear back to 1653. We're *way* back.

"Three Forks is home. Don't care if it's twenty seven below in the middle of December. I'm not movin.' You get acclimated, like anything else. My body's took it for sixty years. I love Montana. It's sort of hereditary."

Larry's intrigue with rivers marked not affinity, but obsession.

"Through them trees there's a big mountain range called the Tobacco Roots. One road in, one road out. Piece of heaven. Everybody has their own preference. Mine is the Tobacco Roots where the Jefferson River comes out. Fish you wouldn't believe, and I've fished every crik around here. I was there at the end of June last year and seen four people. And I was one of 'em! If that ain't a piece of heaven I don't know what is."

The location of Three Forks was no dramatic symphony of merging tributaries roiling into some mighty river but a collage of flat land peppered by reeds, grass, the odd bald trunk and what appeared to be irrelevant flows. But their characters were pronounced to Larry.

"I'd say the Gallatin changes most of all three rivers. Gallatin is for kayakers and people who like fast water. Jefferson is the neatest float of all. The Madison, blue ribbon trout fishin.' Big logs too. Dunks a lot of canoers. We have cold water leeches in the Madison. This old boy, see them feet? They're dry. I ain't goin' in there. We had a kid that had seven of them big leeches out here six weeks ago.

Took a needle and heated that sucker up and made 'em back out. He was screamin.' Eighteen years old and he was pissed. No warning signs you know. I see everybody playin' in the water. Well, ain't gonna be me.

"River'll change. Invariable," he added. "Everything changes."

He eyed the lazy water before us.

"See that fish jump there? Fishin's always good, it's the catchin' that's tough sometimes," he said with a guffaw.

Larry stumbled toward his car and motioned me to follow. He opened the door and held back a wave of blankets and pop bottles and blocks of stained wood, then pushed a gift into my hand.

"Piece of blue agate stone," he explained. "From the Madison River."

I thanked Larry. His rough exterior housed an apple pie soul, a man textured by deep winters and fortified by the land's beauty. I appreciated his souvenir and his generosity with time. I then pushed one bare foot against the truck's accelerator and moved south, eager to inspect that 'beautiful piece of heaven' Larry spoke of — his beloved Tobacco Root mountains.

Chapter 38

TOBACCO ROOTS

Close to four months after leaving St. Louis I was about to leave the Missouri River watershed. But I first wanted to learn more about how time and glaciers shaped the river's course. South of Three Forks I stopped at a roadside phone booth and phoned professor Johnny Moore at the University in Missoula, Montana.

"There's an extremely small amount of Pleistocene geology studied in Montana," he told me. "Nobody here works on that stuff. Material is really old. It's a big place, there's not many people to cover it, and there's no interest in it economically."

He suggested I visit the town of Butte. There, at Montana Tech, I could search out a relevant paper published by the U.S. Geological Survey in the 1930s.

I drove to Butte. The texture of the town looked ancient and inviting. I moved up wide, steep streets with the names Platinum and Mercury and passed run down buildings with worn names across decaying brick facades — *Milwaukee Tavern, Copper King Saloon* and *Opera House*. Butte was no cashmere reality for tourists but the remnants of guts, gore and bruises that built Montana — huffing, grinding, steaming bodies that mined the bowels of earth. When Dan sat on the porch of his straw bale house he told me how the town of Butte — after Bombay — once sported the world's second largest red light district ("There were three cathouses within three blocks of Butte High School," he said. "My friends saved their lunch money all month so they could go").

I parked at the end of Park Street and walked into the library at Montana Tech. The librarian was a tall woman with peach colored hair. She led me to the second floor. Paintings on liver colored walls displayed the lure and danger of Butte's mining culture. Images were titled "Ore Drilling," "Zinc Smelter," "La Prieta Mine," and "Ore Body of Santa Barbara." In one titled "The Flood" seven bodies floated in an inundated mine shaft while a survivor (still wearing his straw hat) swam for safety. In "Premature Detonation" boulders bigger than tractor tires coughed out of a yellow fireball toward three squealing boys. These anguished images in the dark hallway reminded me of scenes from a Robert Louis Stevenson novel.

The librarian moved to a row labeled 'I' for Department of the Interior, then stood before a bookshelf holding Professional Papers published by the U.S. Geological Society. I pulled out Volume 74 by William C. Alden — *Physiography and Glacial Geology of Eastern Montana and Adjacent Areas.* This green hardback book cost only a dollar when it was published in 1932.

Black and white photographs inside showed Alden and his accomplices in 1911 and 1913. They wore wool caps and neat jackets and poised beside reposed blocks of Paleozoic limestone on the "bouldery top of terminal moraine." In Montana and Saskatchewan they cranked over what look like bomb-scarred earthen plateaus in their Model-T, crossing rocky fields near the Sun River and fields of rocks at the moraine of Clark Fork Glacier.

Alden's report mentioned the Beartooth, Big Horn, Castle and Crazy mountains and described the Flaxville Plain, Pliocene fossils and Keewatin ice sheet. My eyes skimmed over his mention of gravel-capped terraces and igneous laccolithic buttes and learned that the history of the Missouri River in Montana was simply that an ice sheet once interfolded into drainages as far south as Great Falls. This altered the course of the old Missouri River which ran northeast to Hudson Bay (along the route where the Milk River and Sandy Creek flow today). After ice thawed, the Missouri River maintained the same general western route from its headwaters — as far as what is now Williston, North Dakota. But from there it changed course and slipped southeast toward where St. Louis lies today.

Rural road in Montana at dusk

Wiser about the Missouri River's general history, I next drove to a region southwest of Three Forks. Wind punched Six Pac over the roads like flotsam on a train of waves. Between the Jefferson and

Madison rivers I veered away from the towns of Harrison and Pony and crept into Potosi Campground below the Tobacco Root Mountains.

I parked beneath a spruce tree and stepped onto spongy cones. A nearby camper was spray painted with lilac and burgundy handprints. Children's names were speckled below these. A man by the creek side held a ruffled towel and smiled at me with sleek ease. He wore a single earring and radiated a calm grace, as though he'd shaken awake from some deep, pleasant meditation. He walked over and introduced himself. Craig was a bald headed, soft spoken and radiant carpenter from Michigan who was spending a year traveling with his wife and eleven- and thirteen-year-old children.

"Sold our house and possessions," Craig told me, explaining how his family began their surge over the continent. They spent their first winter in Baja, jogged north to British Columbia and were now crawling south toward western Mexico.

"Tough part about traveling with kids is home schooling," he admitted.

That was only partially true. I suspected that for his kids, just ogling at novelty each day on the road sowed seeds in their minds that might lay quiet for decades until watered by desire. When that future day came, Craig's kin would be ready to hit the road again without hesitation.

I asked where his incentive for travel originated.

"I'm the same age as when my father and grandfather died. I also make caskets as a carpenter, so I was faced with questions of mortality. What's it all about? Took this sort of trip once before, alone. Didn't notice much change in myself, but when I got home friends hardly recognized me."

"Where to next?" he asked me.

"Canada. Columbia River."

"Go to Canal Flats," he suggested. "Where the Columbia and Kootenai Rivers almost touch. There's only one café in town. Ask about the guy who dug the canal."

The next morning I left the campground and entered the town of Pony to buy stamps. A woman with garish eyelashes asked my destination. I told her.

"Leaves are changing in Canada now," she said. "It's a little cold, but beautiful there."

Combined with Craig's encouragement her words solidified my tentative travel plan. I would first move up the Yellowstone River, then head north into Canada. From there I could explore the Columbia River from its origin. I appreciated her optimism and Craig's advice. The fortune of road and river smiled again: when I needed encouragement, incentive arrived.

Chapter 39

YELLOWSTONE

The headwaters of the Yellowstone River slough out of the Absaroka Range in Wyoming, bubble north to Montana and cut east across the state like half a pincer before they join the Missouri River. This largest tributary of the Missouri forms no even keeled flow. The day that I left Great Falls, Montana, the local tribune told how a seventeen-year-old boy from Sidney jumped in the river's fringe at Seven Sisters Wildlife Refuge and vanished. Searchers hunted for his body for two days without success. A woman I met at the conference in Great Falls also told how she and a friend once canoed four miles down the Yellowstone River. Toward the end of the trip a snag twirled their boat and dumped both paddlers. Pinned by a half submerged log they finally struggled free. The ordeal left the narrator draped hip to ankle with what she called the 'hematoma from hell.'

To follow the Yellowstone River I had to cross southern Montana from east to west. Along the route I eyed its dark course oozing like motor oil through a funnel of grainy banks. Four miles before the border that separates Montana from North Dakota the Yellowstone and Missouri rivers meet. I parked upstream from this confluence and walked along a river bank. A man wearing crusty white tube socks and sandals nodded at me.

"Plenty of fishin' here," he said. "Catfish, carp, shiners, walleye, saugers 'n paddlefish. They go as far as the dam."

Dam?

How could this be? All I had read about the Yellowstone called it the longest free-flowing river in the United States, undammed and unspoilt, a pristine gooseneck of everclear water where families paddled their squeaky rubber canoes and sang praises about its unhindered flow. Dam?

"Diversion dam's what they call it," he said. "See those lines ahead, metal cable things? They run between two 'A' frames on each shore. Sometimes a car runs on a pulley between them and dumps rocks in the river. That makes a diversion — pushes some water in a canal running clear up to Sidney and Fairview. Have a look from up there on the hill."

I paced up the hillside bank to a sign that read Lower Yellowstone Project. There an archaic timber structure resembling a medieval siege tower rose higher than a two- story condominium. A thick cable ran hundreds of feet away to an identical tower on the opposite shore. Beneath this cable the river's current ran ripped and jagged over a string of boulders that altered the flow's direction and pushed part of it sideways through holes at the base of a shoreline dam. From there water cruised through a diversion canal and moved north to irrigate sugar beets.

I later learned how similar dams line other sites along the Yellowstone River. Most are puny affairs that each filch small quantities of irrigation water. Despite these dams the smoldering Yellowstone is still considered one of the most 'natural' big rivers in the continental U.S., chock full of sediment. Rare fish still breed inside its unclubbed environment — shovelnose sturgeon, sicklefin chub, blue suckers.

When I returned to the shore the same man approached again.

"People catch paddlefish here. Not me," he said. "Think it's cruel."

Paddlefish weighing ninety pounds live for over three decades along this section of water between dams. These roaming phantasmal shapes move upstream from Lake Sakakawea toward the Yellowstone River, spawning each spring in an agreeable concoction of temperature and environment. The biggest ever caught near the turn of the century weighed 198 pounds. Because the fish eat microscopic plants and animals and don't bite baited hooks, inventive fisherman have mastered other tactics to haul them in. Using hardware that includes saltwater rods, reels and large treble hooks, fishers cast and jerk their lines, hoping to gaff a paddlefish along its gelatinous body. The fish are not speared or hooked or shot or scooped, but snagged and dragged along the rocky riverbed. A sign on the bank announced caveats on how to play this 'sport' during the prime fishing months of May and June: 'snagging paddlefish from a boat is illegal; the release of paddlefish after snagging is illegal.' These rules did little to downplay the barbarity of the method. One magazine even described how 'landing a whopper (seventy or more pounds) can be a real challenge.'

Some challenge.

Still, the feisty Yellowstone River refuses to release its jewels of life without a fight. A photograph behind plexiglas on the bank showed a smiling, bony boy wearing basketball clothes. The text described how his "beautiful life was taken by the Yellowstone River…while paddling for paddlefish."

Six Pac parked along the Yellowstone River in Montana

Chapter 40

JOE MEDICINE CROW

While driving parallel to the Yellowstone River, I took a wrong turn and headed south instead of west. This inadvertent error led to a trove of wisdom.

Miles after making the turn I suspected the route was unsound, pulled off the highway and confirmed the deviation on a map. The thought crossed my mind that there might be a reason for this wrong turn. I scanned the territory ahead and regarded the map again. The Crow Indian Reservation lay to the south. The Bighorn River, a tributary of the Yellowstone, ran inside of it. This river was blocked by Yellowtail Dam. I decided to continue south to see both river and dam.

South of Hardin I passed windblown rows of lettuce and compact tractors with skewed wheels. Hand-dug irrigation canals wove through a polygon of small farms. The Bighorn River here looked deep and turbid, though the shoreline was rank with cow dung and broken beer bottles.

Yellowtail Dam is wedged tight in a narrow rock canyon. An elevator inside of it took a minute and a half to take a group of us to its base.

"Where are the workers?" I asked our guide, a young Crow woman.

"Aren't any. Today's vacation. It's all operated by remote from computers in Casper, Wyoming."

"What if something goes wrong?"

"Like what?"

"Like it busts."

"Dam was built to last two hundred years," she said. "Concrete won't even have cured for another fifty years."

"Say there's an earthquake. Boom — dam crumbles. What then?"

"In that case," she revealed, "the town of Hardin will be under sixty-one feet of water in half an hour."

"I'd want to be in Casper too," I admitted.

A Crow man from Billings herded his granddaughter and grandson toward the generator room.

"Dam is a hundred forty-five feet wide at the base, twenty-two at the top," our guide Jessie told us.

"I'm this old," the granddaughter said, flashing four fingers.

"Provides electricity for seven states, enough for the needs of 124,000 households," she added.

"And last year I was this old," granddaughter added, winking three fingers.

"Five hundred and twenty-five foot high wall," the guide Jessie continued. "Built of concrete blocks, eight tons each."

We stood in daylight at the base of the dam, bending our necks and gaping at a slick gray wall that curved slightly like a fluted column in an outrageously tall cathedral. Just eyeing the wall gave me vertigo. The young granddaughter just shook her head.

Minutes later we rode the elevator upward again to the visitor's center, where we watched an ancient video. It showed power lines, swaggering cattle and semi-blurred water skiers wearing skin-tight Speedo swimsuits. A bass voice deified the glories of dam building:

264

"The river runs though Crow land — more benignly now, more beneficially," it said, then told how "the rambunctious river was put to work."

Put to work. In an era when dam building was as American as barnstorming, constructing these Pick-Sloan projects ricocheted with a familiar battle cry: that idle hands — in this case idle rivers — were the devil's playground.

When the tour ended and other visitors dispersed, I walked with our guide Jessie along the curving top of the narrow dam.

"Our people once hunted bighorn sheep, buffalo and elk where the reservoir is now. Crow people didn't want the dam," she told me. "We went to court and lost."

"What do they think of it now?"

"They can see the good part of it. Me, I prefer the lake to the river. Canyon walls all the way up. Beautiful. You should talk to Joe Medicine Crow," she added. " He knows a lot of history. You can find him at Lodge Grass, further east."

I phoned Joe. The next day we met at a picnic table outside the Little Bighorn campsite. His wife parked their gray Ford Crown Victoria and Joe stepped out to inspect my camper. He hunched low and shook his head. He held an *Applause Coffeehouse* mug in one hand and ran his leathery palm over one curved edge of Six Pac.

"This is really good!" he said, then sat at a picnic table in the shadow of a birch tree.

Though he verged on eighty-eight, Joe looked seventy-five years old. He drummed one hand on the table, then lifted it to inspect his missing half pinky fingernail. The tube of a hearing aid curled over his left ear and magenta stripes on his unbuttoned Royal

Robbins shirt blew in a scruffy wind. Joe's hair ran in dual streaks of gray and black. Lead colored stubble coated his chin. He lay his wicker cowboy hat on the table; a neat band of brown feathers coated its rim.

Joe was born in Lodge Grass, Montana and later got his Ph.D. in anthropology from the University of Southern California. This combination gave him both internal and external perspectives on his people's customs.

I asked Joe what the Crow thought when the government decided to build Yellowtail Dam. Traditionally rivers have served as dividers of nations and tribes. But on the Crow Reservation a dam, not a river, divided people.

"That was in the early 1950s the idea come up," he said, selecting his words with measured care.

"Bureau of Reclamation 'n Corps of Engineers were in a dam building frenzy at the time. Built several down in the Dakotas. They were interested in the big canyon."

"Let's back up a little bit," he said, teasing me with the hint of a story.

"The ancestral Crow tribe arrived in this part of the west by 1700. They had come from east. To them it was the kind of a promised land they were looking for. On their way west one of their chiefs had a vision. He was given some sacred seeds by the Great Spirit and was to come to the big mountains of the west and plant the seeds. So long as they did that, his people would become rich, grow in population, be strong people. The Great Spirit would give them a good place to live. Good land.

"They would look for this good place for one hundred years. They started out there about 1600, goin' all over Canada, Salt Lake, Oklahoma. Finally got here. About 1700 they looked around, said 'this is it.'

"Bighorn River was to them perhaps the most sacred of rivers. There's a lot of rivers — Yellowstone, Musselshell, Tongue River, Little Bighorn, all named by the Crow. They were the first tribe that got here, so they named all these mountains, rivers, and other landmarks."

Joe's words embodied a collage of tribal wit and college research. He spoke with not only well-fathomed deliberation, but obvious reverence for the lore he passed on.

"One time a teenage boy had fallen off a cliff — high up the mountains there. Real high cliff — matter of fact his stepfather pushed him off. He was caught on a ledge down the side. Couldn't get out either way. Miraculously he was rescued by mountain sheep. Bighorn sheep. Seven of them. They told him after they rescued him: 'Now this is our mountain. Call it Bighorn Mountain. And the river down there, call it Bighorn Sheep River. Never change the name. If you do, you'll lose us.'

"This man's name was Baked Metal. He turned out to be quite a chief and Medicine Man. I would say this happened sometime after 1735, because the Crows acquired horses by then, and horses were mentioned in that story. So that's the naming of the river. It's always been regarded as bloodline of the Crow country.

"About 1953 the Bureau of Reclamation wanted that for a dam site. The Crow tribe said: 'No. Can't do that. That's sacred river there.' But the politicians really put pressure on, so tribal people were — more or less — bought."

Joe laughed at the past.

"It went over. The tribe was splittin' up. Some wanted it, some said no. Bureau of Reclamation, Corps of Engineers said either you sell it to us or we'll condemn it and take it. We didn't have a chance. It got to be a showdown. Finally our leaders said: "we're going to

267

lose it, at least let's sell it." So they sold it. First it was five million dollars, and later sued for five more million."

Joe balled one fist. With a smooth and focused drop he hammered an ant heaving over the picnic table.

"The dam was built quickly. They did a good job. Fast job. With all the political controversy they were in a hurry to put it up. They were three years ahead of schedule. It's one of five highest dams in the country. They called it after Robert Yellowtail, hoping they'd win his support. But that made him fight them all the more.

"After the dam was built they called the impounded water Yellowtail Lake. The tribal elders said, 'that's wrong, we're not supposed to change the name of that river. We're losing our rights.' Blamed all their tribal problems on that dam. So they went to Washington, DC and the Bureau of Geographic Names or some department. It almost took an Act of Congress to change it to Bighorn Canyon Reservoir. So the Bighorn has come back, at least the reservoir part of it.

"The people who objected to it, including Bob Yellowtail, they're all gone now. Young people have forgotten about that. It's pretty well accepted. It's okay. Eventually healed over. Old people died. So there's no bad feelings about the dam now."

No bad feelings. Joe could have launched into a seat-shaking diatribe about interfering engineers and the repercussions of how erecting a dam affected tribal integrity. He did none of that. He held no grudges against a wrenching episode from his people's past. His demeanor was that of a wise mentor, not an agitated warrior.

I asked if he thought the future harbored more conflicts.

"The Indian is always concerned about the environment, mainly land, air, water, heat, or fire — Grandfather Sun. Those four basic things that constitute life are pretty important to Indian people. Our young ones, we keep telling them 'be careful with these things.' We tell 'em the more you respect and preserve these four things, how they interact, the more power you will have. Use it right. Most rivers come off the mountain and mountains are sacred."

Joe also knew that trash laced some river shores within the reservation.

"We try to keep our country clean as possible, but can't do it," he said, giggling at the strange twists of speeding development. "Economics goin' too fast."

His weathered finger drew a circle on the picnic table and divided it into segments like a pie.

"We're losing language. When the language goes, the rest of the cultural elements go too."

He pointed to the center of this imaginary thin crust.

"Cuts represent economics, religion, social and other elements of tribal ways. In the middle is language, 'cause that's the network of communication to all these segments. When the language goes, lack of communication sets in. Lot of tribes are losing languages. There are only two left who speak it at Fort Peck. The Northern Cheyenne — only a few still speak the language. We're losing ours here too. My grandson there," he nodded at where his car engine groaned under a cirrus sky, "he can't speak it."

Joe's wife waved at him from the car. He raised his eyebrows, indicating it was time to return to his family. We shook hands, then parted.

I took Joe's advice and drove to the town of Garryowen. While standing outside the Little Big Horn Museum I considered Joe's cultural insight and understanding. But who was Joe Medicine Crow?

A new memorial erected a week earlier stood outside the museum. A bust of Chief Sitting Bull and another of Lt. Col. George Armstrong Custer flanked a slab of polished black marble — eight feet by three feet in size. The slab's quote read:

"When we stand side by side in the circle of no beginning and no ending, the first maker, creator of all things, is in the center.
He hears the words of supplication and blesses us with his infinite love which is 'peace' itself."

> Joe Medicine Crow, Ph.D.
> "High Bird" – Dagak Bako
> Crow Tribal Historian
> Grandson of Custer's last scout – Whiteman Run Him

Joe! So Joe was the Tribal Historian for the Crow people. By not knowing that when we sat together, our anonymous exchange was unfogged by titles and credentials. We just talked. To me Joe was a man who inspected my camper and nodded approval, a man who sat on a picnic table sharing stories in the sun. Good stories. Stories I discovered by taking a wrong turn in the right direction along a highway.

Once again, listening to intuition had paid off.

SECTION SIX:

BRITISH COLUMBIA, WASHINGTON, OREGON

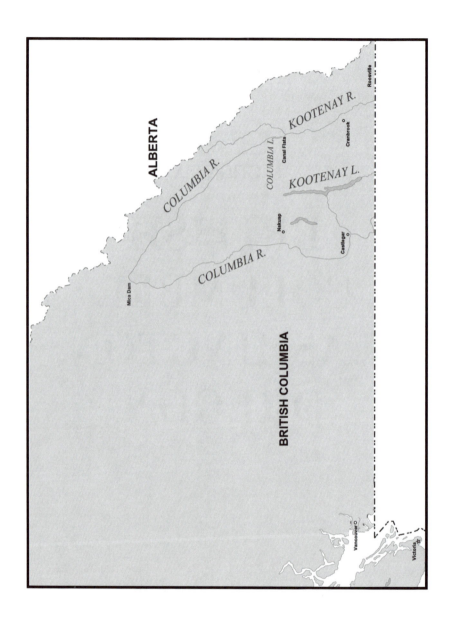

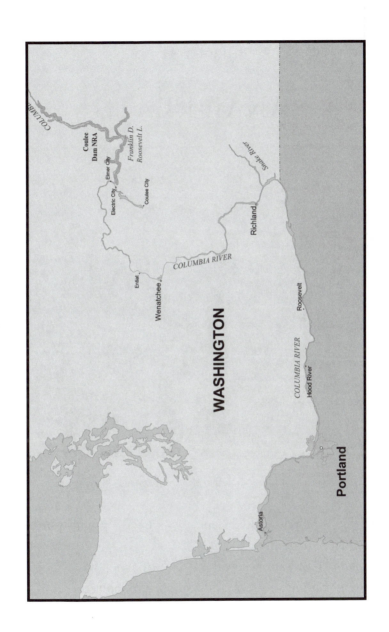

Chapter 41

CANAL FLATS

British Columbia highlands, Canada

I left the Yellowstone River and meandered through northwest Montana, passing the

Flathead Indian Reservation and trucking past peaks and billowing forest fires. In Kalispell I stopped to replace a set of worn tires, then veered west of the Whitefish Mountains toward a different topography, country and river.

At the Canadian border post at Roosville, I declared three plums and half bottle of vodka to a border guard. She waved me through toward a sign that read *Think Metric*. Crossing into Canada felt like entering Narnia: same language, dissimilar attitudes, stunning landscape. The Canadian Rocky Mountains looked perkier than their southern brethren and aroused a steep and swirling geography of imagination, a place where recollections of Great Auks and mastodons came to mind.

While heading north toward the source of the Columbia River, I stopped in the town of Cranbrook and passed Granny Cottle's British Café, the Baker Street Pub and an Esso station. A teenage girl with Asian features honked her convertible Porsche outside the Bank of Hong Kong.

Cranbrook formed a microcosm of U.S./Canadian comparisons: the town had no fire station but a 'fire hall'; newspapers referred to the United States as 'America,' and despite fall weather, women dressed in lacey sweaters and slit skirts — revealing European style in a town that was already a meld of Swiss landscape, British commerce and French haute couteur. Americanisms also seeped in — bank tellers told customers to 'have a great day' and children pulled their parents' coat tails in the direction of Arby's for lunch. Politeness was definitely in décor. When I pulled over on a roadside to let a semi truck pass, the driver honked his thanks, then rolled down a window and waved.

I moved north toward the source of the Columbia River. This third longest river in North America begins its 1,240 mile voyage at Lake Columbia, located over ninety miles north of the Canadian/U.S. border. From there the river angles northwest into British Columbia province, then wrenches south into Washington State to suck up water from its thousand-mile long tributary — the Snake. The river then bee-lines west, whittling out the boundary line that separates Washington and Oregon. It finally dumps into the Pacific Ocean via a river mouth gaping six miles wide. This river that once boiled over topography like acid across sandpaper today plods through a staircase of fourteen sizable dams.

Wrapped around this flow, the Columbia River watershed is shaped like a teardrop with fractal edges. Its 259,000 square mile area is about the size of Vancouver Island, or just a hair smaller than Texas. It envelopes portions of British Columbia and seven U.S. states: Washington, Oregon, Wyoming, Montana, Idaho, Nevada and Utah.

Lake Columbia, Canada

From its shoreline, the Columbia River appeared different from the Missouri. It looked as aloof as a cat on the prowl — exuding a mighty and quiet grace. Whereas the Missouri hauled a crude soup of mud, the Columbia ferried microscopic rock particles that gave the water its turquoise luster.

Another mighty river named the Kootenai (spelled Kootenay in Canada) runs parallel, then south of the Columbia — creating a 'V.' It flushes out of British Columbia to Montana's dammed up Lake Koocanusa, then turns north to Canada again. The Kootenai extracts more water from Montana than even the Missouri River, eventually delivering this gush to its intersection with the Columbia River at the Canadian town of Castlegar. These two mighty rivers *almost* join at another location near Columbia Lake. This 'almost' was temporarily breached when the waters did mix, and therein lies the bizarre story of a sanguine adventurer with too much time on his hands. Had it not been for the influence of Canadian rail builders at the turn of the twentieth century, a segment of the Columbia River might flow today with even more water than it does.

In 1882, William Adolph Baillie-Grohman moved from Europe to British Columbia. Grohman's mother was an Irish cousin of the Duke of Wellington, his father was English and his grandfather part Austrian. Grohman grew up in both a rain-pelted house in Tipperary and an Austrian castle. He spent his youth as a noble adventurer, became a lawyer, and published his first big game hunting book at the age of twenty-four. Between evenings of sipping vintage port in a paneled library and days of making forays to bag mountain goats near his British Columbia home, Grohman decided to build a canal less than two miles long that linked the Columbia Lake (source of the Columbia River) to the Kootenay River. By draining the Kootenay ten feet lower into Columbia Lake, Grohman reasoned he could halt the Kootenay's annual flooding near Creston. One of the project's understated effects was that it could triple the Columbia River's flow.

Grohman was an aspiring businessman. He knew that if he succeeded in building his canal without flooding Kootenay Flats, he would gain a land concession of 47,500 acres. He moved ahead with his plans and formed the Kootenay Syndicate Limited in 1886.

The Canadian government was then hip deep in constructing the Canadian Pacific Railway. Word of Grohman's venture was as welcome to CPR executives as a basket of fleas in a rest house. They feared the canal might alter lake levels and impact the operation of steamboats, hence their profits. Heeding concerns from the railway, the Ottawa government told Grohman to exercise care with his venture. Yes, they decreed, he could build his canal. No, it could not be free flowing. He also had to control its course by fitting locks to each end and had to maintain a waterway at least thirty feet wide. The news flustered Grohman. Dispirited, he was left with two

Six Pac at Lake Columbia in Canada, source of Columbia River

options: abandon the project and lose the land or heed the caveats but storm ahead. Not one to simmer in ambiguity, he shucked his pride and decided to build. In 1887, government engineers approved Grohman's plans and he sent a steam-powered sawmill to prepare for excavation at Canal Flats. The effort turned Herculean. It took more than twenty days to move this sawmill the final one hundred miles to its destination. Once accomplished, Grohman built a town and became both postmaster and Justice of the Peace.

Using side-tipping wheelbarrows, sweating Chinese laborers soon hauled away earth excavated from Grohman's canal. Removing soil was straightforward; draining the ditch with steam pumps proved difficult. Embittered at having to build locks but consumed by his goal, Grohman declared that the construction task was one he would "honestly recommend to those desirous of committing suicide in a decent, gentlemanly manner." When he completed the ten thousand dollar canal on schedule in July, 1889, it was forty-five feet wide and ran more than a mile long.

North of Cranbrook I drove past fanged mountains and the turquoise sheen of the Kootenay River, then pulled into Canal Flats. This town (*"Home of the Mighty Columbia"*) was a sparse collection of buildings between Lake Columbia's southeast shore and the Kootenay River. I drove past acres of debarked timber and a steaming green warehouse at the nearby Tembrec Sawmill, then parked and entered a simple café with plain formica tables. Photographs on a wall showed turn of the century scenes — a Leyland tractor hauling barked timber and lumberjacks bundled up in wool scarves and thick caps.

A waitress brought hot chocolate and lemon pie, then talked about the canal. She handed me a clipping that described Grohman's adventure and nodded toward a bulky man nearby. He wore two shirts unbuttoned to his mid chest and his black cowboy boots were slit along each side. This outfit made him look ready for a quick getaway from his clothing.

"Want to visit the canal?" he asked. "Take you if you're rarin' to go, kid. You can see old timbers at the crossing."

"Whenever you're ready," I told him.

"Roy McGee," he said, and dropped fingers from his mug to shake hands.

Minutes later our vehicles sloshed over a dirt road with the consistency of mulch and the color of tapioca. We passed the Canal Flats Curling Club and a den of quirky mobile homes resting on cement blocks. Roy revved down Thunderhill Road and I clattered behind him in Six Pac. He parked his green Ford Escort near the abandoned canal and we stepped out to hear a squabble of duck calls beside a pool of stagnant water. Roy pointed to the puddle at the old lock, then said 'farewell lad,' and parted.

I ignored the 'private' sign and trudged through muck. In sections of the abandoned canal, rainwater pooled two feet deep. The shore was lined by deer tracks dappled in fungus. Soggy planks prodded into the air. This foggy tableau was straight from a Conan Doyle novel, a displaced Dartmoor beneath a gloomy sky. Past an abandoned beaver dam lay one old canal gate, its semicircular metal plates still pegged to rotting timbers.

I looked to where sawn stumps, folded metal strips and planks with nails pounded halfway through lay inside this water. I imagined finding some trace of Grohman here, a lost medallion or watch hasp, some artifact to bind the past to present. Instead there were only flecks of birch bark and a discarded Glacier Berry Cider carton.

Only two boats ever passed through the gates of Grohman's canal — the *Gwendoline* in 1894, and later the *North Star*. The government then decided to close Grohman's monument. They were concerned that the lock gates were not sturdy enough to hold back a flood. They also worried that altered lake levels might affect river traffic linking segments of the Trans Canada railway.

Building the canal and changing the river's flow won Grohman a chunk of dank realty. It also blasted his name throughout the province — the man who clasped two mighty rivers together. Considering that Grohman worked soon after Ferdinand De Lessepe built the Suez Canal (linking the Red and Mediterranean seas) he seemed to me to have been a bit of a visionary man in copycat mode. His story was of a lone man who wanted to change a river's course against odds, an individual who wanted his venture, ultimately, to win his name a place in history. But regardless of Grohman's motives, he built a town, paid his workers and completed a decent canal. Anyone had to respect that.

Chapter 42

MICA DAM

Ferry carries Six Pac across Arrow Lakes (Columbia River) in B.C., Canada

From Canal Flats I drove north to Columbia Lake, where reeds poked through the shoreline and a brisk wind stung earlobes.

Glacial valleys to both sides formed a poster image for tourism in British Columbia — vistas of buttercups and moraine.

Upstream from this lake, source of the mighty Columbia, the river looked like a sloppy tidal pool spattered by chunks of land in the shape of dog biscuits and snails. I chugged north of there to the town of Revelstoke, where between the Selkirk and Monaghee ranges, traders once foraged for beaver pelts while Indians landed

282

scads of salmon. Today hotels named Mountain View, Swiss Chalet and Alpine Inn poked out near the Snow White Laundry and Alpine Village Shopping Centre. Even the architecture of 7-11 melded in with this Tyrolean theme. Gruff mountain bikers wearing hand-stitched backpacks pedaled to a grocery store called a 'Groceria' in a town that advertised itself as a gateway to bear country. Banners on street lamps read *Year of the Great Bear*, while bruin images pointed toward the town center. A carved bear and cub guarded the entrance to Makenzie Street's pedestrian market.

I stopped in Revelstoke to drink burnt coffee with sweet cream before motoring on toward Mica, tallest earth-filled dam in North America and northernmost dam along the Columbia River. This point was also the most northern tip of my journey.

Six Pac huffed uphill in low gear and passed clearcuts running across mountain inclines. The only other vehicles in sight that morning were logging trucks — snorting behemoths snarling through mist. This was a land of cold storms and soul cleansing grandeur, a place where mountain air held the tangy scent of cold pine at altitude. A lone moose heaved out of a swamp and lumbered past fetid logs, then shook its body like a wet kitten. Snow clouds and golden maples covered U-shaped valleys.

I parked on a gravel pullout beside the dam. Its deep form mirrored the steep peaks to both sides. At the end of an inclined dirt ramp lay Kinbasket Lake — 135 miles long. The silence was bare, the day gray. Mist raced up pine trunks. I splashed lake water onto cheeks and rolled up sweater sleeves.

A pickup truck pulled up with two mountain bikes in its bed. A couple who appeared to be fit and in their sixties stepped out. When the stout blonde woman plodded off to walk with a heavy dog her radiant husband approached me. He had thin white hair and a wizened nose above a lean, taut body. He introduced himself as Tony Csaky and spoke with a smoldering accent from another continent. Tony told me he was born in Hungary and moved to Argentina when he was young.

"Difficult farming there," he explained, scuffing one of his boot soles against the gravel.

"My father did not do so well. When I was offered a job with a consulting company in South Africa I decided it was a better opportunity, so took it."

Tony later moved to Canada. He had been settled there for two decades.

"I've worked all over Saskatchewan, Montana and in the Uinta mountains in Wyoming. Retired. Done my travel," he declared.

He adjusted a limp collar on his wool workshirt, then dug hands deep in a pair of blue mechanic's trousers. He spoke about his days of working near Angola's oil rich Cabinda province and described years living in mountainous Bolivia. He told of his own sheep and cattle farm across mountains to the west. With his European accent, South American wife and relaxed Canadian attitude, Tony was proud of the decisions he made in life. He described how he had fit his skills, education and talents into a global community of technical specialists.

Meeting Tony aligned with thoughts that day. The man was both practical and inspirational, a person whose days of travel — despite what he said — were far from over. His skills, like the Columbia River's water, knew no national boundaries. He freed himself of borders and any single national identity to offer his services. Speaking with Tony was a reminder that to benefit from the gifts of civilization, we need to interact with societies we belong to. During this journey part of me toyed with the notion of eventually settling in some remote, gorgeous mountain outpost, far from society and hectic communities. But while standing within a niche of slouching peaks, I realized that our endeavors, solo or not, must be accomplished with the ultimate intention of aiding others. Lindbergh's solo flight asserted that simplicity in craft and spirit can prevail where complex engineering and arrogant attitudes fail; Thor Heyerdahl's float on a balsa wood raft across the Pacific westward from Peru was born of his desire to free minds of rigid preconceptions. Lewis and Clark's foray opened a continent to settlers. Speaking with Tony about his work that day was a reminder of how working toward the collective betterment of others was not only admirable, but essential to humans' integrity. Our purpose on this planet is to serve others. When we stop doing that, we lose our sense of balance.

Tony and his wife pulled away. Meeting them at the northernmost point of the journey was a reminder that there was a huge world to interact with out there, filled with lively communities and increasingly irrelevant borders.

Chapter 43

GRAND COULEE

Near the town of Grand Coulee in Washington came a lesson that time and disparate economies can wedge cultures apart with greater force than any dam.

After traveling for almost five months. I crossed the border back into the U.S. near Castlegar, then drove south beside Franklin Roosevelt Lake, impounded behind Grand Coulee Dam in 1942. This biggest hydroelectric complex in the U.S. churns out enough megawatts to power the cities of Portland and Seattle, holds back three trillion gallons of water and spits an average of more than a million gallons of liquid downstream each second and a half.

The arid land around Grand Coulee had constantly challenged settlers. During the era before the dam was raised, cattle rustling was a sport, gunfights were legion and brewing moonshine was considered a countryside pastime. One local schoolteacher used to stash a pint of whiskey and a razor blade in her classroom drawer, ready to aid students bitten by a rattlesnake. Red dust storms ransacked this rimrock valley: when residents spied rogue squalls barreling up the coulee from miles away, they shut their windows (even in 110 degree heat) and waited hours until the storm swirled past.

I drove into town past rugged scrubland, buttes and gorges, and entered the visitor's center. Black and white photos on a wall showed ravages of past droughts: a plow wheel abandoned in sand, a wobbly two story home shored up in dust. Before the dam was built farmers needed a significant outlay of cash to buy irrigation pumps. Few had the money. The result: farming was a difficult prospect.

President Roosevelt's Public Works Administration created the Grand Coulee Dam during Depression years. Just shy of a mile wide, today the mammoth dam is poised as crown jewel of the Columbia River Irrigation Project, a choreographed assembly of dams, reservoirs, pumps and pipes supplying water for crops and power.

Construction began in December of 1943 when Governor Martin dumped the first 'official' bucket of concrete in dam block 16G. A year after work began a cold snap froze the Columbia River bank to bank, plummeting temperatures so low that work was paralyzed until spring. Yet despite the weather, seven thousand workers lunged at the job of creating this behemoth. As at Fort Peck, a round-the-clock work schedule kept 'redlight houses' busy and wives and mothers earned tips as 'taxi dancers' by serving drinks and gyrating hips at bars.

The need to irrigate acres in the Columbia River Basin formed an ostensible reason to build the dam. But the real value of Grand Coulee came from churning out the hydro watts needed to fabricate aircraft aluminum that was used to combat enemy forces during World War II. Not until seven years after the war ended did Grand Coulee's irrigation water start moistening crops. A complex tangle of tunnels, siphons, reservoirs, feeder canals, pumping plants, and discharge tubes now irrigate over a half million acres of the region's land. Sweet corn, alfalfa, sugar beets, potatoes and grain all slurp up the Columbia's water to buoy up an agricultural economy.

I crossed a wide street in town, then stepped into an antique store and café that sold hand dipped French vanilla ice cream bars. Inside I perused a 1943 *Life* magazine and ordered an oversized glass of frozen tea topped with whipped cream. A man in his early thirties, groomed to a fault, stood ready to pour grenadine, angelica or aniseed liqueurs over ice cream concoctions. He wore navy blue ankle socks and smelt of after shave.

"Visiting?" he asked.

"Just stopped at the visitor's center at Grand Coulee."

"You mean the town of Coulee Dam," he countered. "Gets a little confusing. This is Grand Coulee. Down the hill is Coulee Dam. Twenty-eight miles down the road is Coulee City."

"There's about three hundred people in both Coulees," he continued. "Put that together with Electric City and Elmers City — like the glue — and the population is almost five thousand. During dam construction there were nine thousand workers plus their families. This was a shanty town. People lived in the boxes that pianos were sold in. When the project was finished they'd get up and just move on to another site."

I sat on an antique pink sofa and picked at pages of *From Pioneers to Power,* a book about history of the dam. It told how before the dam rose and the lake appeared, whites and Indians gathered to watch wild horse races at the annual Pow Wow in Nespelem. These stories highlighted the constant interaction between Indian and settler communities. Tribal pride then surged and Indians often frequented Grand Coulee town.

Habits and attitudes had changed over the decades.

"What about the nearby reservation?" I asked. "Worth visiting?"

The employee folded a towel into a perfect rectangle and draped it on an immaculate counter.

"Why? You, eh, know someone there?" he asked. His voice turned tense.

"Just curious."

"It's like a lot of reservations," he said with a hushed voice. "Cars are laying around abandoned. Trash is uncollected."

Disdain with a capital D was written across his face. My interest in the local reservation irked him, as though its existence might taint his image of Grand Coulee. His attitude was that the reservation was a vacant lot for car wrecks while Grand Coulee formed a hip, thriving retail boutique selling gourmet ice cream. His attitude was puzzling, disappointing, and also enlightening: in a country that prides itself as a melting pot, there are still huge rifts between some of our communities and cultures.

Chapter 44

SPRING CHINOOK

I descended the Cascade Highway south of Chelan, passing the Central Washington Holiness Camp and groves of apples along the Entiat Valley. This valley was once a tapestry of Chinese miners, sheep herders, lumberjacks, and fruit farmers who worshipped, as deities, hard work and persistence. A roadside poster advertised this as John Muir country, telling how the land is where "winds will blow their own freshness onto you, and the storms their energy, while cares will drop off like autumn leaves."

Close to Roaring Creek I parked outside the Entiat Fish Hatchery, wanting to learn more, first hand, about the plight of salmon in the Columbia River and its tributaries.

In seventeenth century Europe, maps of the New World showed a voluptuous "River of the West" flowing toward the Pacific Ocean. This was the Columbia. When Lewis and Clark forayed up the Missouri River corridor they extended a route that traders and trappers had already explored. Crossing west into the Columbia watershed, however, marked their transition into alien terrain — not only cultural, but dietary.

Before the Corps of Discovery moved down the Columbia River, few Europeans ever glimpsed at where this river sluiced toward the coast. Most who did had peered from ship decks in the

Pacific Ocean. The Columbia was then a zesty river that plunged past rainforest, desert and mountains and passed land lined with riverbank tribes including Yakama, Umatilla, Warm Springs and Nez Perce. When Lewis and his team veered down the Columbia they noticed how fish formed the gastronomic, cultural and economic core of these tribes. The fish provided Indians with totemic identity as well as protein. Before the expedition passed by, tribes had subsisted on salmon for ten centuries; the mid portion of the Columbia then formed a fish trading network hub between the soaring Rockies and the Pacific Ocean. This most salmon-laden river system in the world yielded fifteen million pounds of fish annually (*"This river is remarkably clear and crouded with salmon in maney places,"* William Clark wrote about the river during the fall of 1805). Every year sixteen million salmon ascended hundreds of miles up the Columbia and Snake rivers, completing a migratory loop began years earlier.

In January of 1806, Lewis estimated that the Indians *"annually prepare about 30,000 lbs. of pounded sammon for market."* Hillsides and gullies were as speckled as a quail's egg with collections of smoked fish. William Clark once counted more than a hundred stacks of these dried, pounded salmon by the riverbank, *"which must,"* he described *"have contained 10,000 lb. of neet fish."*

Expedition members enjoyed the taste of salmon (*"I think the finest fish I ever tasted,"* Clark wrote), but were so accustomed to red meat from east of the Rockies that they also consumed dogs by the dozen (*"We got several dogs from these Indians, which we find strong wholesome diet,"* wrote expedition member Patrick Gass).

Once the Corps of Discovery cracked open a westward path for Europeans, demographic changes came swift to the Columbia's water and watershed. Four decades after Lewis first tasted salmon in an Indian bower near Lemhi Pass, wagons of immigrants flowed over the Oregon Trail and spread out to crowd along riverbanks. A decade later a series of treaties ceded the bulk of the region's Indian land to the U.S. in exchange for limited fishing rights. If fishing is compared to rubber tapping, salmon was the latex, a mind-boggling food prize available for relatively scant effort. Six decades after the Corps forayed to the Pacific, the first salmon cannery was cobbled together along the Columbia's banks; by 1883 forty canneries along the river squished thirty-five million pounds of Chinook between tin sheets each year. While profits soared, the river's salmon quantities plummeted.

A salmon's life cycle forms a tribute to the intricacies of migration. Between April and August, silver 'smolts' the length of fingers are washed hundreds of miles and thousands of feet in elevation downriver to the Pacific Ocean. Once there, internal changes transform their resilient bodies into salt water fish. Within two to five years these youths complete a grand, self-guided tour northward past icebergs and whales toward the Gulf of Alaska. Plump and eager, many return and swim up the Columbia to the same 'natal stream' where their lives began.

Although the quantity of salmon moving up the Columbia River has surged and dipped in cycles over time, the first wave of modern decline began when canneries were raised along the riverbanks in the late nineteenth century. The second wave rolled along when twentieth century dams transformed the Columbia into the most developed river system in the world.

Soon after the Grand Coulee Dam was constructed another half dozen dams were stacked along the channels of the Lower Snake and Columbia rivers. Together these formed the earth's largest coordinated hydroelectric system. Fourteen major dams and more than two hundred lesser dams now plug up the Columbia and its tributaries. Where tribes once dwelled, industries now flourish.

What was once sagebrush desert now blooms as well watered farmland.

This piecemeal division of the river was not only incongruous, but spectacular: it turned Lewiston, Idaho, into an ocean port 465 miles away from the Pacific.

To allow salmon and steelhead to leap upstream through a series of pools, many dams included fish ladders. But for years there was no provision to let young fish migrate downriver toward the Pacific with ease. The assumption was that they could slip unharmed through dam turbines. This was mistaken: more than a quarter of those that did so were killed. Others that rolled over dam spillways perished from nitrogen saturation in the froth below — a form of the 'bends.' Today nine tenths of all juvenile salmon along the Columbia avoid this long slog of contending with turbines and concrete. Instead they are sucked into pipes, pumped into special barges and 'bussed' downriver to the ocean, care of the U.S. Army Corps of Engineers.

Though admirable in intent, transporting these smolts hardly cured the problem of migration. After spending years in the ocean, many of these 'bussed' fish never return toward their upriver homes, which is one reason why the Snake River Coho went extinct in the 1980s.

Dams along the Columbia River yielded electric power, crop water and navigation routes and percolated into the Northwest's economy in the form of jobs and industry. Yet delivering these assets incurred future liability. Magnificent benefits came at the expense of calamitous sacrifices: grassy canyons were flooded, scribbling falls were lost, fish numbers declined and elegant species disappeared. This constitutes a list of facts, not blame. One benefit of history is that it can incite our desire to improve future outcomes.

The Entiat Fish Hatchery was a brown structure that set next to a canal. This held sloshing water diverted from the local creek. I roamed inside the building, eager to speak to anyone who chose managing fish as a career. A crew cut man with a goatee rocked his hips to the blaring lyrics of the Smashing Pumpkins. He looked agitated, as though he had spiked his mug of Nescafe with a shot of epinephrine.

Near the Entiat Fishery, Washington

"What type of fish?" I asked, inspecting soggy pink marbles steeped in shallow water trays.

"What?"

"Type of fish?!"

"Spring Chinook Salmon."

"How many?"

"What?"

"How many?!"

He reduced the volume on his portable CD player and smiled, then introduced himself as Rod.

"Eggs? About a half million here. Four hundred thousand when they're all ready. See the little eyes? A month old now. Pretty resilient."

Rod pulled a tray of pink salmon eggs from an elevated bank of shelves. He dumped these in a bucket of water and then poured the mix in a second pail, like a hyperactive bartender concocting a hefty drink.

"Shocking them," he explained. "Fertilized eggs have a broken membrane. Other membranes break when I pour them between buckets. Turns 'em white. That's how we separate out infertile eggs.

"3500 to 7000 eggs from each fish. Fifty days to spawn at fifty degrees. But we'll set the temperature lower, to thirty-seven degrees. That way instead of hatching in December they'll be ready in March or April, like in the natural world. We lose about five percent of them at each stage of the process, so about eighty-five percent live."

"I've worked here eight years. Live in a government house up the hill. 'S okay. But you're surrounded by work. Other neighbors who couldn't handle it moved out. But I don't want to get into buying a home and getting a mortgage. They want you to though. 'S all part of the system. Prices are adjusted so it takes two people, married couple, to pay for one house. Part of the system. Bad news if you get a divorce."

I nodded at eggs, silently wondering who 'they' were who ran this mysterious 'system.'

Rod pulled out shelves from his damp organic filing cabinet, each replete with watery pink eggs.

"You can't fish this nearby tributary now," he said. "Low water. Fish are listed as endangered anyhow. Lot of salmon around here are listed."

"You spawn listed species?" I asked.

"No way! They don't want us messin' with them. They think fisheries fish are domesticated like cattle. But I don't know any cows that can migrate hundreds of miles for three years, then find their way home again."

I wondered: was the same mysterious 'they' who bumped up mortgages? Perhaps 'they' were simply all voices of authority Rod questioned.

"We let fish right out of here into the Entiat River. They go down to the Pacific, come back in one, two, three years. How many come back? Well, not so good. We only get point one percent here. About four hundred fish. That's what we should get, but this year we got three thousand. So we took four hundred. Gave the rest to the Indians."

I wondered how Rod felt when four hundred of his adoptees returned home after years on the move. Meanwhile, an affectionate and butter colored Labrador sidled beneath my hand.

"That's Alex," Rod said. Both man and his best friend then regarded me with rural smiles that seemed to read — 'what's your rush?'

Dams and canneries had created Rod's career, one he loved. He was an odd blend of puritanical work ethic and Bohemian thought, a man enamored by damp salmon eggs and wired up on gnashing tunes. He was unpretentious, unambiguous and unimpressed by most models of existence offered by the mainstream society he chose to live on the fringe of. Rod's community was his family, work mates and fish. Like one of the few determined salmon to brave odds and leap past high dams through fish ladders in order to return home again, Rod was determined to live as he chose, regardless of what structures and customs society raised around him.

I walked outside and sat on a split rail fence above the Entiat River. The thought of smolts riding barges and salmon kicking past the Kenai fjords of Alaska made me smile. A cone of sunlight washed senses. The day, the week, the months ahead bifurcated and jammed together in a long internal rock and roll paean, one Smashing Pumpkins tune at full volume.

Chapter 45

TOUCHED BY GOD

A cluster of nine nuclear facilities along the Columbia River have turned, unexpectedly, into guardians of wild salmon genes. But unless the land where they stand is cleaned, the waste from these plants may eventually damage human genes.

The threat of a determined foe provided plenty of incentive to build the atomic bomb during World War II. Part of this effort took place at the Hanford Nuclear Reservation in the state of Washington, at a 560 square mile block of land that today is home to earth's densest concentration of nuclear reactors.

In the 1940s, 50,000 employees converged at Hanford to create a plutonium core for Fat Man, the atomic bomb ejected over the city of Nagasaki in Japan to end World War II. Part of this focused community working on the Manhattan Project banded together near the Columbia River.

The Columbia River sits deep in a green valley north of the Hanford Nuclear Reservation. I drove past a vineyard, shredded windsock and a sign far from any ocean that read 'entering Port of Mattawa.' Graffiti at the gas station read *Jesucristo Vive! Yo soy la verdad y la vida.* ('Jesus Christ lives! I am the truth and the life').

The Hanford reservation sits on an expanse of rusty terrain, thin on soil and frugal with precipitation — six inches a year on average. Bluebunch wheat grass spreads over a yawning mesa where — according to native Yakama nation lore — north winds once battled southern gales.

Before beginning this riverside venture, I lived in Panama in Central America. One evening a group of scientists from the Smithsonian Tropical Research Institute invited me to dinner. We sat down to dinner alongside the Panama Canal in a house tucked inside the chirping rainforest. We dug our forks into grilled corvina fish and fried plantains. When I described my upcoming trip, biologist Dr. Allen Herre, a fifteen year veteran of foraying through tropical rainforests, dictated the name and phone number of his mother who lived in Richland, Washington. She had worked on the Manhattan Project. I folded the number up and decided to call her when in Washington.

Along the road next to Hanford I unwadded this piece of paper and phoned Allen's mother at her home in South Carolina. Just the mention of Hanford unmoored a raft of memories for Rebecca Wesbster. She recalled trips she and her husband took down the Snake and Columbia rivers.

"We went down the Snake twice," she recalled. "First time in 1945 and second in 1967. It was wild, exciting, beautiful. First trip we slept on the beach. Wild horses came down in the middle of the night. Second time it was dammed. A lot tamer. That 1967 ride wasn't quite as wild and wooly, not as impressive as the first. Scenery was not as spectacular. The Columbia wasn't nearly as pretty. When we were out at Richland, my husband Ed and I used to bicycle down to the river and go fishin,' or fill a bucket with giant sour cherries.

"We were all working on the Manhattan Project," Rebecca recalled. "Sort of nuclear pioneers. We thought we were pretty spectacular. Felt vindicated. We lived in the little town of Richland. Plant was far away. I had to be cleared — top secret. Never met so many brilliant people in my life."

(Rebecca also worked on the project at Oak Ridge, Tennessee. She recalled when a leading scientist, Enrico Fermi, visited: "One day when Fermi was visiting Oak Ridge all the big shots had cars. He insisted he'd ride the bus and got on with his hulking bodyguards. He was a sweet, humble man. Ate at the cafeteria too. Bumped his arm into me once there, then apologized profusely. I thought I'd been touched by God!")

"Most of the University of Chicago people would refer to the Hanford site rather contemptuously as that 'DuPont factory in the West,'" Rebecca added. "That was where the large scale production was going on. To get to the plant, workers went by bus. Long ways. About forty miles I remember.

"One day a fellow who lived next door came over. He had a newspaper published in the west and was talking about a big explosion. That was it. Shortly after that Truman announced it. The place went wild. They knew it worked. Dropped two bombs. Wanted to be sure both worked. One was made of plutonium and the other enriched uranium. We'd been working on the plutonium project.

"Now the land is thoroughly contaminated with nuclear waste. They did a good job of inventin' the bomb but didn't do a good job cleaning up afterward. I've heard from people who say the Richland site is an unbelievable mess. It's scary with these crazy terrorists loose now."

Until the plant's focus changed in the late 1980s, weapons grade plutonium was manufactured at Hanford. Today, according to the Department of Energy's Office of Environmental Management: "The primary mission at Hanford is the cleanup of the site."

There is plenty to do. Two thirds of the country's nuclear wastes lay at Hanford. More than 170 steel tanks are buried on site, brimming with radioactive waste, a substance Meriwether Lewis would fathom even less than the sight of power lines that now click across the country. More than fifty million gallons of radioactive slurry are stored at the site. According to a report prepared by the government's General Accounting Office, hundreds of thousands of gallons have already seeped away from their tanks. Cesium 137, strontium 90 and trace amounts of plutonium (with a half life of eighty million years) now migrate below leaking drums, percolating through subsurface soils and eking a slow but perhaps inexorable path toward the Columbia River.

State and federal governments signed an agreement to pump out more than six millions gallons of liquid nuclear wastes buried at Hanford — one of a multitude of cleanup operations on site. I shook my head and whistled at the breadth of this problem. Nuclear engineering embodies the premise that human ingenuity can tame nature's most powerful force. Hanford's contamination reveals a misbegotten downside to this attitude, the truth that some natural resources must be negotiated with on a daily basis, like a restless government on the throes of dictatorship.

An unexpected consequence of building Hanford was that plant administrators opposed constructing more river impoundments nearby. They feared dams would raise local water tables and possibly impact buried wastes. The result: a fifty-one mile long dam-free corridor, the Hanford Reach, is now the only site where salmon spawn naturally along the Columbia River.

I looked out again toward the Hanford reservoir. Under the soil, a hidden estuary of neutrinos made their subterranean journey toward the Columbia River. This reality was alarming. If we're clever enough to carve atoms into electricity and mushroom clouds, are we wise enough to put the skids on contamination plumes that now strike toward the Columbia River?

Rebecca spoke again, expressing fresh ambivalence on the project's outcome. Her previous sense of pride now mixed with a tone of horror.

"We didn't know what we were starting," she added. "Didn't realize we were doing the work of the devil."

Chapter 46

CATACLYSM

North of the Columbia River and south of Yakima Indian Reservation in the state of Washington, I stopped at a campsite near the town of Roosevelt. A sign outside this half ghost of a community coughed up statistics:

Roosevelt, Washington, 99356

Elevation — 367 feet

Population — Yes

From there I chugged to a riverside park before the Columbia River. Preparing to take a siesta on the grass, I sat beside an angled boulder half as big as a Volkswagen Beetle. A sign before it told how this rock was no ordinary boulder but an 'erratic,' displaced from its origin. Reading this made me wonder why the rock was there. This query sent me scurrying into Six Pac to jostle through an orange crate and haul out papers and books. A story they told delayed the desire for a snooze.

According to what are now accepted geological theories, this 'erratic' rock piggybacked on top of a rather sizable chunk of ice that coursed down the Columbia Gorge during one whopper of a flood. It was not alone. Other erratics weighing up to two hundred tons and as tall as bungalows lay splattered not only throughout the Columbia Gorge, but from Lake Pend Oreille in Idaho south to Eugene,

Oregon. The downriver dance of water that placed these erratics revealed how a series of biblical grade floods helped scour out the Columbia River Gorge.

Fifteen thousand years ago the Cordilleran ice sheet slithered south into Montana's Clark Fork River valley. It created an ice dam there almost a half mile high. This obstruction blocked water east of Lake Pend Oreille and created the ancient and Herculean 'Lake Missoula,' one half mile deep and thousands of square miles in area. Each time the lake burst through its confines, it hurled a cannonball of a flood down the Columbia River drainage. How big? The volume was ten times the combined flow of all rivers on earth, enough to inundate sixteen thousand square miles in silt-fogged water hundreds of feet deep. It wrenched fifty cubic miles of sediment out of its path and carved chunks of Washington and Oregon into fluted channels. Not one, but several dozen of these floods flowed over millennia.

Learning about this series of floods was as intriguing as reading about the man who unraveled how they ran, a scientist who was once ridiculed, excoriated, criticized, mocked, ribbed, jeered and discredited all the way from western geological societies to eastern Ivy League halls. In 1932, this doctorate in geology, J. Harlen Bretz, published a paper that described how a massive flood swept erratic boulders throughout the Columbia gorge. Bretz was not only a rock hound who revered field work, but an analyst able to discern patterns in nature, regardless of how ludicrously large they appeared. When Bretz aligned physical evidence with what others considered to be wild conjecture, he formulated a conclusion that astonished his scoffing peers. For decades several of these academics heckled Bretz about this theory. They even invited him to seminars so they could ridicule him in public.

Photographs of Bretz in the field show him wearing oval spectacles and a hardhat. He stoked Edgeworth tobacco in a pipe using his tanned forearm. What these pictures can never show is the man's patient and unwavering conviction in what he believed. It took him fifty years (and a few field trips for critics to inspect reality for themselves) before geologists stopped criticizing Bretz's logic and accepted his theory of how cataclysmic floods once wracked the Columbia River gorge. His trump card of vindication came two years before Bretz died at age 98; the Geological Society of America awarded him the Penrose Medal, the country's highest award in geology. The satisfaction from biding time and adhering to beliefs must have been enormous. Reading about Bretz's life was inspiring because of a simple, powerful lesson it embodied: never disregard the validity of common sense just because it is common.

After taking a geologically enlightened siesta I woke up to blue skies and fickle warmth and marched to the Columbia's flattened edge. There, deep walls of the gorge ran ahead and behind. Twilight soon misted in and a Chinook wind blew across deep grass. I dunked into the Columbia River, plunging shoulders and scalp inside the moonlit sheen, swirling nostrils below its viscous glass. Wet and energized and bobbing like an apple in a vat, I imagined the scene from the past: castoff ice blocks carrying spindrift, toppled boulders on their journey downstream.

I dried, dressed and watched a Westfalia van pull into the empty parking lot. A couple wearing shorts and polypropylene tops walked to the shore with what appeared to be their four year old towhead daughter. They sat together before the moon, resting heads to shoulders and cheeks to temples, a repertoire of felicity oblivious to my presence.

Minutes later the family returned to their blue van and drove off, content, rejuvenated and happily unaware of the niceties of how floodwaters and rodeoing ice clods had helped shape the river valley surrounding us.

Seeing the family was a reminder that I had been on the road for too long alone. I missed friends and having a base to work from. Just as rivers change with time, this trip had changed me. It quenched, at least temporarily, an inner wanderlust. I was ready to wrap up the traveling and find a community to call home.

Chapter 47

HOOD RIVER

"We used to be considered blatant radicals. Completely off the scale. Off the charts, absurd. Fifteen years ago when we stared working here we were lone rangers, stuck out like sore thumbs," Jerry Bryan told me, pacing in mountaineering sandals around his desk.

"That's not so true anymore," he added.

Jerry pulled one hand from a pocket of his creased khakis and stroked his gray-black beard. His t-shirt showed a purple wolf on a hilltop baying a full moon. Behind him a photograph of Mother Theresa hung on a wall next to the poem *The Last Salmon*. Beneath this, another picture of a crooked stream sat above the quote: "In Wilderness is the Preservation of the World."

The building Jerry worked in was nestled between trees and farmland along the Country Club Road in Hood River, Oregon. His office echoed his own eclectic meld of professional and personal fascinations — engineering and holistic land stewardship: two calculators lay on his desktop next to texts on calculus and turbulent flow.

After tantalizing me with these opening remarks Jerry dove into a description of the management philosophy for the Farmer's Irrigation District in Hood River, Oregon.

"We try to show that properly oriented resource stewardship is good ecology, good economy and good in the realm of social equity," he said. "Those are our three big time platforms. The more we demonstrate the economic benefits of this cleaner, ecological way of doing things, the more people embrace that."

Adhering to this vision helped Jerry run his projects throughout the local watershed. Yet it had taken years to align local opinions with this progressive attitude.

"I hated working here for eight years until we started getting somewhere. We submitted the first of the state's water conservation management plans to the Oregon Water Resources Department. Gave an outline of how we were going to do things. Started feeling pretty gawdang exciting. Then we came on a book written by William Ashworth, *The Economy of Nature*. He was prophetic, writing before sustainability became a buzzword. His whole notion is that ecology is good economy and good economy is good ecology and if one argues to the contrary, we're all missing the boat."

Jerry stood before three shelves. Books stacked on these had titles relating to the mechanics and economics of controlling water: *Handbook of Hydraulics, Natural Capitalism, Cadillac Desert.* He then handed me a six page paper titled: 'Farmers Irrigation District Sustainability Plan.'

This small epistle was his own Master Manual, a framework for action on how irrigation water was to be used, a launching point for a man who spoke not of battles fought but of compromises tweaked. Jerry's goal was to maximize irrigation water taken from tributaries of the Columbia River by cutting down on leaks and waste, a process that involved changing mindsets as much as adopting new technologies. His focus was not on wrestling control, but on incrementally changing attitudes toward conservation. The opening page of his plan included a scolding quote from Wendell Berry's *Recollected Essays*.

"We have lived by the assumption that what was good for us would be good for the world. We have been wrong. We must change our lives, so that it will be possible to live by the contrary assumption that what was good for the world will be good for us…For it is only on the condition of humility and reverence before the world that our species will be able to remain in it."

Following this came a dedication to Tashi Tsering, of Tibetan heritage, who taught the Irrigation District that "we should never make too much of ourselves."

I flipped to the segment titled *Vision*. It stated only: "The District strives to promote economically sustainable agriculture and natural resource use for the good of all creation."

The booklet's philosophy was backed up by a list of accomplishments: 'reduced 34 unscreened diversions to 16 fully screened diversions;' 'converted 35 percent of our residential users to microsprinkler technology;' 'planted 6600 trees in the riparian areas of Green Point Creek.'

"This is our philosophy as to how we ought to conduct ourselves within the context of community," Jerry explained.

By sponsoring classes, substituting plastic pipes for open canals and instructing farmers how to read soil moisture sensors, Jerry's band of 'blatant radicals' had pushed water conservation along local tributaries of the Columbia River. When simple convincing failed, they patrolled as meter readers.

"If a farmer is really overusing water, we shut them down," Jerry explained. "Then that behavior goes away."

He emphasized how that action was a last resort.

"We try to work in the realm of carrots versus sticks," he added.

"Irrigation district is relatively small. Six thousand acres in Hood River Valley. High value growth — pears, apples, cherries. This year was an unprecedented drought for the life of all of us, even our fathers and their fathers. If our conservation projects hadn't been in place, we would have dried up every stream in the basin trying to get as much water as we could."

Jerry glowed at the success of what he and his 'lone rangers' had accomplished over a decade, delivering water to virtually the entire irrigation district — despite droughts. In Jerry's ideal world, the irrigation district he tended would be a microcosm of social bonhomie. The man was neither an institutionalized lug or a cranky scholar but a practical, modest fellow graced with flights of visionary taste. Hearing his sermon after months of listening to conservative opinions was no less surprising than if a stranger invited me to dinner and served up turtle soup and kangaroo meat. Hearing his progressive attitude was refreshing. Part of Jerry was grounded in stark economic realities; another part of his psyche fluttered in a cloud of the abstract. The result was idealism that lacked enigma. He was able to back his talk of lofty goals with the nitty gritty statistics of accomplishment. The attitude he adopted toward managing smaller river tributaries — *good ecology is good economy* — also applied to the Columbia River, a far larger and more complex water resource.

I stepped outside and considered Jerry's efforts as both a battle and a mantra — an onslaught of education against entrenched attitudes and an attempt to realign short sighted mindsets. Tasks, deadlines and paycheck propelled Jerry no more than his adherence to beliefs about improving the community he was a part of. In this regard he reminded me of the geologist Bretz, a man who wielded unflagging patience as a tool to attain outcomes reflecting integrity.

Hearing Jerry reminded me of listening to Steve Gough five months earlier in St. Louis. The geomorphologist then told me that managing rivers was really "all about diversity." The memory of these men's voices reemphasized a truth: managing rivers requires soliciting local input.

I left Jerry and entered downtown Hood River. Arriving there ended a lonely stretch of time on the road. For the first time in months I visited friends — a couple not seen in a decade — Andrew, Caroline and their son Sage. Their home lay behind a white picket fence draped with curling pink roses. Andrew led us to his back porch where he uncapped two bottles of Corona. We sat before a panorama of Mount Adams. Our connection during this visit was a mutual fascination with the Columbia River, the visible force that propelled Hood River's economy and vitality.

Andrew's simple hospitality reminded me of another quote from Jerry's booklet. A member of the irrigation district said: "More isn't always better. Sometimes it's just more."

During the ten years since we last saw each other, the lives of Andrew and his family had jogged ahead in geometrical rather than linear blimps. Same business — expanded; same home — refurbished; same union — now with a child; same afternoons spent bicycle riding for Andrew — though more focused. Considering how their lives had altered made me realize how personal and domestic growth often take place in invisible ways; the straight line of change we observe is just the radius of the circle of transformation expanding around us.

I grew to like Oregon and Washington. People were receptive to influx and change and the climate juggled mindsets as well as air masses. Both east and west winds blew up the gorge, keeping residents used to constant deflections of the norm, mirroring threads of adaptation they wove into patterns of daily life. Attitudes in Hood River were both progressive and practical.

I wanted to stay. But the smell of ocean air blew up the gorge, a reminder that the journey was not yet over.

Chapter 48

ASTORIA

West of Portland the Columbia River spreads like a fat schoolboy sprawled out on grass. I stopped at Wolf Bay, a merger of muddled wetlands, snags and dark forest where seals grunted and Canada geese honked. A wood fence beneath a parasol of trees looked over these shallows. Boats puttered a half mile distant, past grass flats and islands. Two men wearing camouflage suspenders hobbled over to this viewing point. One trained his pair of tapered binoculars at the river, as though aiming a harpoon toward a whale. He talked about mud flats and mallards, prompting me to ask about hunting.

"Puddle ducks," he said. "Pintail, widgin, teal. Got to be careful here. This swamp loses two to five people a year. Drownin.' Hypothermia. A few months ago three of 'em, including a little boy, got in a dinky boat with a mound of gear and a dog. Water blew in. Filled the boat. When that happens you're too cold to even steer or start the engine. They didn't wear flotation devices. Dead, all of 'em."

"I'm gittin' cold," blubbered his bald friend. "Nothin' here to hunt anyway. It's all out on the islands. So let's get in the boat."

The two wedged themselves in an SUV that towed a camouflaged boat with camouflaged seats, then vanished.

I listened to pops, rattles and booms in the marsh. These were gunshots — the music of slaughter. Above me the Pacific Flyway formed a corridor for migrating birds. The Corps of Discovery entered these marshes in November, 1805. Nasty weather made them hug the banks and they subsisted on the chilly provender of fish and fowl.

Astoria, Oregon, is a shoreline town. It reminded me of a flattened version of England's Dover. A clammy wind blew the scent of vinegar and greasy burgers through the streets; decaying architecture tried looking buoyant in a gray world. From here coke, potash and lumber shipped westward in the Pacific Ocean. This town was once a whaler's launching point. Sinewy captains then nuzzled their eyes against brass telescopes while butcher crews readied blubber forks, cutting spades, flensing knives, harpoon toggles and two-flued irons to dissect incoming catches. Scrimshaw artists carved roses and flags and images of well-formed maidens onto strips of baleen; they fashioned cribbage boards from walrus tusks.

Astoria was once a ghetto of salmon canneries and rattletrap shanties that swarmed with vermin. Thousands of Asian immigrants in town then toiled over deep sinks in cold, manky canneries. In 1889, Rudyard Kipling wrote in a letter: "the crazy building was quivering with the machinery on its floors, and a glittering bank of tin scraps twenty feet high showed where the waste was thrown after the cans had been punched."

Every year, between April and August, fishermen used nets and traps to capture Chinook salmon ascending the Columbia River (one old photo shows a fisherman holding an eighty-two pound salmon, its length half that of his body).

Inside Astoria's Maritime Museum a sepia brown photograph shows Celilo Falls in 1899, located upriver on the Columbia. There was no scaffold, dam, steel cables or fishermen in view. Instead three Indians stood before the falls, two of them wrapped in blankets. Each wore a brimmed hat. One sat with his fist against his cheek, gazing at a gush of aerated water. Nothing in the men's stance indicated their disposition for accomplishment. They appeared not to be visiting, resting, or waiting, but quietly attentive to a moment, engulfed in the power of the vista before them. It was as though they were soaking the view in as nourishment, as an ancient form of entertainment requiring no rifle or camouflage suspenders. Of all past images of Celilo Falls, I found this the most charismatic. It captured a realization that crystallized during my months spent moving upstream — that rivers and falls court us with inspiration and soak us with the understanding that life, like their flow, is a constantly changing musical score. Another lesson they teach, perhaps even bigger, is that to try to grasp hold of unchanging security is folly.

A later image of the falls, taken in 1915, showed the river from a different angle. A bridge then crossed to a shore pocked with homes and creased by railway lines. By then the region had turned to prime fishing terrain. Its scene had transformed from inspiration to production.

The exhilaration from nearing the trail's end made rolling through Astoria's Maritime Museum powerful. Photographs of the coast and falls gave me a feeling as though a lost soul inside me found eyesight for viewing reality. Inspired, I later considered what I saw while pacing along a sidewalk outside the museum. I realized then that exploring these western rivers meant slipping through their communities in the same way a migrating salmon darts through current. This transience of the journey had worn on me. Just as the Columbia turned to a wide ocean near Astoria, my wanderlust was transforming to a larger desire for home and community.

Standing before the stretching estuary I considered lessons learned during past months. It became clear that the significance of rivers varies from person to person. For some, rivers mean food. For others, power. For many, the Columbia, Yellowstone and Missouri rivers had once formed some type of utility, appliance or service. These included potty, faucet, food source, graveyard, and dishwasher. One reason these rivers changed is because they could change, because those who live on their banks found other services to take care of these household needs — outhouses, public service companies, supermarkets, undertakers. For other people these rivers embodied a route for transport. But railroads, the Wright Brothers and Henry Ford obliterated any need to rely on rivers for shifting troops or pioneers between towns such as Boonville and Oswego on the Missouri River, Big Timber and Sheffield on the Yellowstone, and Blalock and Washougal on the Columbia.

Time, ingenuity and invention had stripped away most day-to-day utilities these rivers once provided. Yet their flow and shores still form essential homes for wildlife. Nature may be a dazzling web of complexity, but some of her tenets are obvious: tread lightly before hacking away species that constitute any of her interconnected strands. In tweaking these waterways in the future — perhaps a bit more deftly — it will behoove us to solicit input from local voices along their banks. Lewis and Clark's success in exploring these waters, after all, hinged on their reliance of local knowledge. The time has come for river managers to relearn that lesson.

I also learned that rivers exist for function, not form. They are sewers of landscape, conduits to flush erosion's wastes out to oceans — the planet's ultimate septic tanks. We can deify, glorify and beautify rivers, but there's still no taking the mud out of Muddy Moe, or sifting glacial rock flour out of the Columbia.

Ultimately, rivers mirror our own values and culture. To mistreat their flow is to abuse our collective integrity. When cities and communities turn their backs on rivers, residents turn away from topology, wild grass, pelicans and battling eddies that formed reasons why they built cities along the water in the first place. When a group of youths floated their homemade timber and barrel raft named *Eulenspiegel* down the Missouri River, one raft builder named Rick Rottman said: "We're seeing a lot of what used to be river towns that have just turned their backs on the river. They have forgotten what they used to be."

Ignoring our waterways can circle back and haunt us in unpredictable ways. These include pollution. Yet we have to be wary how we manage their flow. Fixing a river to one course is like asking Pegasus to file a flight plan. A channeled river is like a mythical horse stripped of magic, a society that never deviates from status quo, or a person who believes they have reached a state of perennial security. For me, the trip's most alluring revelation was realizing that such intransigence is illusory: how a river changes is not as riveting as how humans and wildlife adapt to that change.

The trip also taught me an attitude. To improve the overall quality of rivers for the future we have to get creative, not frantic. What matters is today. We waste time and energy if we consider the past as a source of material for complaining about. The value of regarding history is that it can enable us to forge stronger, brighter attitudes for future actions.

A cold breeze blew off the Columbia River and I pulled on a worn beige oxford shirt. Compared to months earlier, my life seemed more sensible, yet less practical. It formed a hinterland of fresh insights and only one probable truth — that what matters is not where any river carries us, but why we choose to journey along its course. Rivers, after all, can remind us that security is an illusion.

I laughed and sniffed a brilliant dose of ocean air. It was time to head south, and find a home.

NOTES

Chapter 1. Flood

1. "This most significant flood…": Lee W. Larson, *The Great USA Flood of 1993,* Presented at IAHS Conference: Destructive Water: Water-Caused Natural Disasters — Their Abatement and Control. Anaheim, California: June 24 – 28,1996.
2. "By mid summer soils…": Ibid.
3. "Engineers drilled holes…": Ibid.
4. "Their cans read…": Michael D. Sorkin, "Mistake Spells Arrest," *St. Louis Post Dispatch*, July 20, 1993.
5. "As though to emphasize…": *St. Louis Post Dispatch*, August 1, 1993, Section A, p. 1.
6. "They'd take off in all different…": Ibid., p. 12.
7. "At its peak, the '93 floodwaters…": *Today's Farmer Magazine*, October, 1993.
8. "For many, the cost to remove…": *St. Louis Post Dispatch*, October 31, 1993.

Chapter 3. Gateway

9. "Sponsored by a beer manufacturer…": *St. Louis Post Dispatch*, October 4, 1980, Section A, p.1.
10. " I've been skiing for myself until now…":   '381 Mile Trip Set On Skis to St. Louis,' *St. Louis Post Dispatch*, August14, 1984, Section A, p.5.
11. "She told how she had found his bottle…": 'Ulster Girl Finds Bottle From Midwest,' *St Louis Post Dispatch*, November 11, 1986, Section B, p.12.

Chapter 5. Glasgow

12. "There the flood of '93 barreled into the…": *The Glasgow Missourian*, July 15, 1993.
13. "The economy was rescued fifteen years later…": Interpretive Information — Arrow Rock State Historic Site — Visitor's Center, MO.

14.   "A copy of the *Glasgow Missourian*…": *The Glasgow Missourian*, July 15, 1993.

15.   "Photographs showed Army Company C 158th Aviation Unit helicopters…": *St. Louis Post Dispatch*, July 20, 1993.

16.   "Three years before the flood of '93…": *St. Louis Post Dispatch*, July 20, 1993.

Chapter 6. Snags and Sprinkling Pots

17.   "In the Murkey water below…": Greg Hawley, *Treasure in a Cornfield: The Discovery and Excavation of the Steamboat Arabia,* Paddle Wheel Publishing, Kansas City, Missouri, 1998.

18.   " 'At the age of 27, I found myself…' ": Greg Hawley, *Treasure in a Cornfield: The Discovery and Excavation of the Steamboat Arabia,* Paddle Wheel Publishing, Kansas City, Missouri, 1998, p.18.

19.   "Sample cores drilled in the *Twilight*": Greg Hawley, *Treasure in a Cornfield: The Discovery and Excavation of the Steamboat Arabia,* Paddle Wheel Publishing, Kansas City, Missouri, 1998, pp. 28-32.

20.   "The tons of cargo include 700 window panes…": Tim Janicke, "Last days on the water,' *The Kansas City Star, Star Magazine,* February 18, 2001.

21.   " 'Since nothing is more inspirational than a challenge,' ": Greg Hawley, *Treasure in a Cornfield: The Discovery and Excavation of the Steamboat Arabia,* Paddle Wheel Publishing, Kansas City, Missouri, 1998.

22.   "Their average life span was estimated…": Greg Hawley, *Treasure in a Cornfield: The Discovery and Excavation of the Steamboat Arabia,* Paddle Wheel Publishing, Kansas City, Missouri, 1998, p.22.

23.   "Cargo insurance cost up to ten percent…": Robert Kelley Schneiders, *Unruly River: Two Centuries of Change Along the Missouri,* University Press of Kansas, 1999, p. 57.

24. "when author Mark Twain rode…": Michael Gillespie, *Wild River, Wooden Boats*, Heritage Press, Stoddard, WI, 2000, p. 50.

Chapter 7. Engineering a Waterway

25. "A year later the *Independence* thrust up the Missouri River…": Michael Gillespie, *Wild River, Wooden Boats*, Heritage Press, Stoddard, WI, 2000, p. 16.
26. "Calhoun thought the river was more…": *Heartland Engineers: A History*, U.S. Army Corps of Engineers, 1992, p. 7.
27. "In 1838 two of these sidewheelers…": Michael Gillespie, *Wild River, Wooden Boats*, Heritage Press, Stoddard, WI, 2000, p. 46.
28. "…started yanking more than thirty snags…": Hermann Museum interpretive display, May, 2001.
29. "Suter had no doubt…": *Heartland Engineers: A History*, U.S. Army Corps of Engineers, 1992, p.28.
30. "The buffalo, the Indian, the steamboat…": *The Bismarck Tribune*, February 5, 1980, p. 10E.
31. "Five years later the Missouri River Navigation Congress…": John Ferrell, *Soundings: 100 Years of the Missouri River Navigation Project*; U.S. Army Corps of Engineers, 1996, p. 33.
32. "He suggested that the Corps…": Robert Kelley Schneiders, *Unruly River: Two Centuries of Change Along the Missouri*, University Press of Kansas, 1999, pp. 98 – 99.
33. "Because rail had then triumphed as…": John Ferrell, *Soundings: 100 Years of the Missouri River Navigation Project*, John Ferrell; U.S. Army Corps of Engineers, 1996, p.135.
34. "By 1932, more than $60 million…": John Ferrell, *Soundings: 100 Years of the Missouri River Navigation Project*, John Ferrell; U.S. Army Corps of Engineers, 1996, p.72.
35. "Speaking in hindsight…": John Ferrell, *Soundings: 100 Years of the Missouri River Navigation Project*, John Ferrell; U.S. Army Corps of Engineers, 1996, p.133.

36. "It also states that since the Corps adopted...": John Ferrell, *Soundings: 100 Years of the Missouri River Navigation Project*; U.S. Army Corps of Engineers, 1996, p.133.

37. "In 1916 this group's rebuttal of Deakyne...": Robert Kelley Schneiders, *Unruly River: Two Centuries of Change Along the Missouri*, University Press of Kansas, 1999, p. 100.

38. "The Missouri River Navigation Association...": Ibid.

39. " While several hundred persons looked on...": "Flood Wall Work Begun on Missouri," *New York Times*, March 22, 1946.

40. "It was supposed to quell 'interecine congressional...": *New York Times*, November 19, 1946.

41. "This shotgun matrimony between landscape and engineering...": *Soundings: 100 Years of the Missouri River Navigation Project*, John Ferrell; U.S. Army Corps of Engineers, 1996, p. 138.

42. "Channelization lopped off 127 river miles...": American Rivers. #1 Missouri River, 1997 (online edition).

43. "This helped to eradicate a third of a million...": U.S. Fish and Wildlife Service. Lower Missouri River Ecosystem (online).

Chapter 8. Variety

44. "This, they complained, could lower flow levels...": 'River Water Shortage by 2000 is Foreseen,' *St. Louis Post Dispatch*, February 17, 1978.

45. "A court ruled that Watt lacked...": William C. Lhotka, 'Ruling Blocks Diversion of Missouri River Water,' *St. Louis Post Dispatch*, March 14, 1986.

46. "Studies showed that toxins in the water included chlordane...": *St. Louis Post Dispatch*, May 21, 1985, Section B, p.2.

47. "Days later, this marble tinted sheen...": Robert Manor, 'Oil Slick Leaves Mark On 150 Miles Of Rivers,' *St. Louis Post Dispatch*, December 30, 1988.

48. "A St. Louis beer manufacturer...": *St. Louis Post Dispatch*, January 4, 1989.

49. "When the Corps of Engineers narrowed and confined the river…":Valerie Rapp, *What the River Reveals," The Mountaineers*, 1997, page 115.

50. "The decision to clamp the river down and confine it to a barge channel…": 'Don't Fight the Missouri,' *St. Louis Post Dispatch*, October 9, 1996.

51. "Colonel Lewis Pick of the U.S. Army…": *St. Louis Post Dispatch*, September 6, 1993.

Chapter 10. Weston

52. "This building that houses the winery…": Weston Historical Museum — Interpretive Display.

53. "Just a year later…": *St. Louis Post – Dispatch*, December 12, 1999, Travel Section.

Chapter 11. The Love of Farming

54: "Their project could, therefore, be viewed as…": John Ferrell, *Soundings: 100 Years of the Missouri River Navigation Project*; U.S. Army Corps of Engineers, 1996, p. 141.

55. "In the town of Hermann, Missouri…": Norm Stucky, 'A Look Back at the Great Flood of 1993,' *Missouri Conservationist*, August 1995, p. 9.

56. "The evidence 'indicates that levee construction…' ": R.E. Criss & E.L. Shock, 'Flood enhancement through flood control.' *Geology*, 29, 2001, Pp. 875 – 878.

57. " 'When people are determined to avoid…' ": Jeffrey Rothfeder, *Every Drop for Sale*, Penguin Putnam, New York, 2001, p.41.

Chapter 12. Sitting Tight

58. "In 45 minutes five inches of rain…": John C. Petterson, 'Two Formidable Floods Washed Atchison into the 20th Century,' *The Plainsman,* September – October, 1965, p. 39.

59. "This flood derailed three freight cars…": 'Devastating Flood Hits Atchison,' *Atchison Daily Globe*, July 11, 1958, p. 1.

60. "It rummages its fist down a basement...": 'Devastating Flood Hits Atchison,' *Atchison Daily Globe*, July 11, 1958, p. 1.

61. "Together with his 50-year-old wife...": 'Devastating Flood Hits Atchison,' *Atchison Daily Globe*, July 11, 1958, p. 1.

62. "The paper then boasted that...": 'Devastating Flood Hits Atchison,' *Atchison Daily Globe*, July 11, 1958, p. 1.

63 " 'caught one alive, by pouring...' ": *Journals of Lewis and Clark*, Edited by John Bakeless, Penguin, 1964.

Chapter 13. Doniphan

64. "Two warehouses, stocked with cargo...": Daniel Fitzgerald, *Ghost Towns of Kansas — A Travelers Guide*, University Press of Kansas, 1988.

65. "...ominously struck by a blizzard...:" Daniel Fitzgerald, *Ghost Towns of Kansas — A Travelers Guide*, University Press of Kansas, 1988.

66. Omitted

Chapter 16. Restaurante Mamasitas

67. One 19th century steamboat pilot named Joe Oldham...": Michael Gillespie, *Wild River, Wooden Boats: True Stories of Steamboating and the Missouri River*, Heritage Press, Wisconsin, 2000, p. 72.

Chapter 17. Images from Vanished Culture

68. "Clark convinced Maximilian that...": Mildred Goosman, John Lepley, Mark Brown, 'The Missouri: Timeless Wilderness,' *Montana Magazine of Western History*, Number 3, July 1970, Montana Historical Society, Helena.

69. "In Pennsylania in 1763...": Russel Thornton, *American Indian Holocaust and Survival: A Population History Since 1492*, University of Oklahoma Press, 1987, pp 78 – 79.

70. "In three months the disease killed...": R.G. Robertson, 'Rotting Face: Smallpox kills 20,000 Americans,' *True West*, February/ March 2002, p. 63.

71. "He grew up in a log cabin...": 'Indian Blood Runs Deep,' *Bellevue Leader*, March 17, 1982.

72. "One was to enforce the concept of private property...": *The Upstream People: An Annotated Research Bibliography of the Omaha Tribe*, reference No. 607.

73. "Fine print within the lofty 1854 treaty...": *The Upstream People: An Annotated Research Bibliography of the Omaha Tribe*, reference No. 762.

74. "Based on this provision, the 1882...": *The Upstream People: An Annotated Research Bibliography of the Omaha Tribe*, reference No. 934.

75. "Sixteen years after the law was enacted...": *The Upstream People: An Annotated Research Bibliography of the Omaha Tribe*, reference No. 969.

76. "He suggested that non-Indians be evicted...": *The Upstream People: An Annotated Research Bibliography of the Omaha Tribe*, reference No. 962.

77. "...the Dawes Severalty Act...": *The Upstream People: An Annotated Research Bibliography of the Omaha Tribe*, reference No. 934.

78. "Ironically, those lawmakers who created...": *The Upstream People: An Annotated Research Bibliography of the Omaha Tribe*, reference No. 936.

79. " 'In 1910, a bill was introduced to tax...' ": *The Upstream People: An Annotated Research Bibliography of the Omaha Tribe*, reference No. 902.

80. "By 1976, 82 percent of land on the Omaha...": *Omaha World Herald*, July 26, 1976.

81. "Others would be brought to a federal court...": *Omaha World Herald*, November 1, 1970, p. 16-B.

82. "But the Omaha were adamant...": *Omaha World Herald*, February 11, 1966.

83. "They set up a teepee and tents..." *Lincoln Evening Journal*, April 6, 1973.

84. "This time the same legal tactic could no...": *The Lincoln Star*, April 5, 1975, p. 7.

85. "Judge Andrew Bogue sympathized...": *Omaha World Herald*, May 5, 1977, p. 1.

86 " 'We certainly say from the attitude of the Judge...": *Lincoln Journal*, May 5, 1977, p. 36.

87. "The group ignored this, supported by...": *Lincoln Journal*, May 24, 1977, p. 21.

88. "After 14 years of effort...": *Lincoln Star*, January 16, 1980, p. 17.

Chapter 24. Joe Day Bay

89. "When winter tosses bald eagles out of Canada...": Interpretive Sign — Fort Randall Dam.

90. "This ritual that once thrived along the Missouri...": Jodi Rave Lee, 'Yankton Reservation bringing back Coming of Age ceremony,' *Dakota Bismarck Tribune*, July 11, 2001, p.1B.

91. "Young female initiates camped...": Jodi Rave Lee, 'Yankton Reservation bringing back Coming of Age ceremony,' *Dakota Bismarck Tribune*, July 11, 2001, p.1B.

92. Omitted

Chapter 27. Inundation

93. "This region around this Missouri River tributary...": Interpretive Sign, Knife River Indian Villages National Historic Site, North Dakota.

94. "The combination of smallpox...": George Catlin, *Letters and Notes on the Manners, Customs, and Conditions of North American Indians,* Letter No. 11, Dover Publications, 1973.

95. "About this incident Lewis only wrote that...": *Journals of Lewis and Clark* – DeVoto (12th October, 1804).

96. "A recipient of the Silver Star...":*The Bismarck Tribune*, July 3, 1945.

97. "He just called the dam construction...": *The Bismarck Tribune*, July 3, 1945.

98. "Though sympathetic to her grievances...": *Fargo Forum*, Jan 31, 1946, p.2.

99. "...a housewife from Granville won $24...": *Granville Herald*, February 28, 1946, p. 1.

100. "He died before any deputies showed up...": His concern about unmarked graves was real: when I camped in the area the radio told how a group campers discovered shards of three individuals' skulls on Gull Island.

101. "Nine Indian villages were flooded...": *Sioux City Journal*, September 17, 1991, p. A-10.

102. "...how electricity it generated was to illuminate homes...": *Minot Daily News*, January 21, 1956.

103. "Before Garrison and Oahe dams rose...": *North Dakota Outdoors*, March 200, 'Cross the Wide Missouri,' by Greg Power, p. 7.

104. "The total flow of the Red River at Fargo...": *North Dakota Outdoors*, April – May, 1995, 'A River of Perspective,' Greg Power, p. 21.

105. "Ecosystems for cells, tissues and organs...": James Lovelock, *Gaia, a New Look at Life on Earth*, 1979.

Chapter 32. Boom Town

106. "When you went to lunch, the grasshoppers...": Sid Moody, 'Fort Peck Dam Stemmed The Flood Of Despair,' *St. Louis Post Dispatch*, August 12, 1983.

107. "Fort Peck's earthern dam was drawn...": Kevin R. Quinn, 'Fort Peck — a half-century and holding,' *District News*, Volume 11, No. 2, Summer 1987, p. 2.

108. "One resident said you could bulldoze...": Sid Moody, 'Fort Peck Dam Stemmed The Flood Of Despair,' *St. Louis Post Dispatch*, August 12, 1983.

109. "Customers drank nickel beer...": Sid Moody, 'Fort Peck Dam Stemmed The Flood Of Despair,' *St. Louis Post Dispatch*, August 12, 1983.

110. "A local doctor named C.C. Lull fussed...": Kevin R. Quinn, 'Fort Peck — a half-century and holding,' *District News*, Volume 11, No. 2, Summer 1987, p. 16-18.

Chapter 33. When the Land Belonged to God

111. "They were so plentiful that Crow and Gros Ventre Indians...": Interpretive road sign between Jordan and Mosby, Montana.
112. "Listening to these diverse viewpoints...": *Wild Montana: Newsletter of the Montana Wilderness Association*, Winter 2001, pp 1-2.

Chapter 34. Birthplace of Montana

113. "Farmers fresh from the east coast...": Dan R. Conway, *The Grass Range Review*, article in vertical file of Montana Historical Society.
114. "When they returned they found their goods...": Dan R. Conway, *The Grass Range Review*, Article in vertical file of Montana Historical Society.
115. "...boasted Fort Benton's *River Press*...": 'Fort Benton — Head of Navigation,' *The River Press*, Fort Benton, Montana. June 16, 1937, p.6.
116. "From the time the steamboat *Independence*...": 'Fort Benton — Head of Navigation,' *The River Press*, Fort Benton, Montana. June 16, 1937, p.6.
117. "The blast killed thirty passengers...": Robert P. Crawford, 'Romantic Days on the Missouri,' *The Country Gentleman*, March 1928, p.4.
118. "Merchandise was later recovered...": Robert P. Crawford, 'Romantic Days on the Missouri,' *The Country Gentleman*, March 1928, p.4.
119. "These boats hauled eighty percent...": Robert P. Crawford, 'Romantic Days on the Missouri,' *The Country Gentleman*, March 1928, p.4.
120. " 'and 230 hard-bitten, well-armed miners' ": 'Fort Benton — Head of Navigation,' *The River Press*, Fort Benton, Montana. June 16, 1937, p.6.

121. " 'If I want to be secure...' ": *The Wisdom of Insecurity: A Message for an Age of Anxiety,'* Alan Wilson Watts, Random House, September 1968.

Chapter 35. Great Falls

122. "...changed radically from a meandering stream...": 'Changes in the Channel Area of the Missouri River in Iowa, 1879 – 1976,' Iowa Geological Survey Special Report Series Number 1, 1979.

Chapter 38. Tobacco Roots

123. "But from there it changed course...": William C. Alden, 'Physiography and Glacial Geology of Eastern Montana and Adjacent Areas,' Professional Paper 174, US Department of the Interior Geological Survey, 1932.

Chapter 39. Yellowstone

124. "Four miles before the border that separates Montana...": Greg Power, "A River of Perspective," *North Dakota Outdoors*, April – May, 1995, p. 23.

Chapter 41. Canal Flats

125. "By draining the Kootenay ten feet...": William Dietrich, *Northwest Passage: The Great Columbia River*, University of Washington Press, 1997.

126. "He moved ahead with his plans...": Display — Windermere Valley Museum, Windermere, British Columbia.

127. "No, it could not be free flowing": Fergus Cronin, 'Canal Flats,' *Western People*, May 3, 1984.

128. "It took more than 20 days to move this sawmill...": William Dietrich, *Northwest Passage: The Great Columbia River*, University of Washington Press, 1997.

129. "Embittered at having to build locks...": Fergus Cronin, 'Canal Flats,' *Western People*, May 3, 1984.

Chapter 44. Spring Chinook

130. "The Columbia was then a zesty river…": Roberta Ulrich, *Empty Nets: Indians, Dams, and the Columbia River*, Oregon State University Press, 1999.

Chapter 46. Cataclysm

131. "His trump card of vindication came…": John Eliot Allen and Marjorie Burns, *Cataclysms on the Columbia,* Timber Press, Portland, Oregon, 1986.

Chapter 47. Hood River

132. " 'For it is only on the condition of humility…' ": Wendell Berry, *Recollected Essays 1965 – 1980*, North Point Press, September, 1987.

Chapter 48. Astoria

133. "They have forgotten what they used to be…": Monte Plott, 'Floating Our Their Fantasy,' *St. Louis Post Dispatch*, July 21, 1981, Section D, p.3.

Index

333

Want to buy another copy of
Rivers of Change?

Here's how:

Internet: www.riversofchange.com – click on the 'Order' tab.
(or email: roundwoodpress@riversofchange.com)

Phone: Phone 800-247-6553 and speak to Bookmasters.

Mail: Send this page to:
Bookmasters
30 Amber Wood Parkway
Ashland, Ohio 44805

Fill out your information:

Name:_____

Address:_____

City:_____

State:_____Zip Code: _____

Country:_____

Payment: Each book is $25.95. Add $3.95 for shipping for first book and $1.95 for additional books. Add 7.5% tax for products shipped to California and Ohio addresses.

Make checks or credit card payable to: **Bookmasters**

Credit Card:_____

Card Number:_____

Expiration Date:_____

Name on Card:_____

Signature:_____

Want to buy another copy of *Rivers of Change?*

Here's how:

Internet: www.riversofchange.com – click on the 'Order' tab.
(or email: roundwoodpress@riversofchange.com)

Phone: Phone 800-247-6553 and speak to Bookmasters.

Mail: Send this page to:
Bookmasters
30 Amber Wood Parkway
Ashland, Ohio 44805

Fill out your information:

Name:_____

Address:_____

City:_____

State:_____Zip Code: _____

Country:_____

Payment: Each book is $25.95. Add $3.95 for shipping for first book and $1.95 for additional books. Add 7.5% tax for products shipped to California and Ohio addresses.

Make checks or credit card payable to: **Bookmasters**

Credit Card:_____

Card Number:_____

Expiration Date:_____

Name on Card:_____

Signature:_____